AUSTRIA: A STUDY IN MODERN ACHIEVEMENT

Der Österreicher hat ein Vaterland,
Und liebts, und hat auch Ursach es zu lieben.

(The Austrian has a Fatherland,
And loves it, and has good cause to love it).

Schiller: *Wallensteins Tod*, 1,5

Austria: A Study in Modern Achievement

Jim Sweeney and Josef Weidenholzer

Translating Editor: Jeremy Leaman
Translations by John Manton and Susanne Sweeney-Novak

Avebury
Aldershot · Brookfield USA · Hong Kong · Singapore · Sydney

Published by
Avebury
Gower Publishing Company Limited
Gower House
Croft Road
Aldershot
Hants GU11 3HR
England

Gower Publishing Company
Old Post Road
Brookfield
Vermont 05036
USA

British Library Cataloguing in Publication Data
Sweeney, Jim
Austria : a study in modern achievement.
1. Austria — History — 20th century
I. Title II. Weidenholzer, Josef
943.6'05 DB96

Library of Congress Cataloguing-in-Publication Data
Austria : a study in modern achievement / [edited] by Jim Sweeney and Josef Weidenholzer : translating editor, Jeremy Leaman: translations by John Manton and Susanne Sweeney-Novak.
p. cm.
Includes bibliographies and index.
ISBN 0-566-05252-0 :
1. Austria—History—20th century. I. Sweeney, Jim, 1933- .
II. Weidenholzer, Josef, 1950- . III. Leaman, Jeremy, 1947- .
DB99.2.A825 1988 943.6'05—dc19 87-33254 CIP

ISBN 0-566-05252-0

Typeset by Guildford Graphics Limited, West Sussex
Printed and bound in Great Britain by
Biddles Limited, Guildford and King's Lynn

Contents

PART IV SOCIAL AND CULTURAL ISSUES

PART V EPILOGUE

PART VI APPENDICES

List of contributors

Gerhard Botz is Professor of Austrian History in the University of Salzburg.

Alfred Dallinger was Chairman of the Union of Private Employees in Austria (until his recent retirement). Since the early 1980s he has continuously held the position of the Minister of Social Affairs in the Austrian Federal Government.

Dr Hans Dvorak is Head of the Adult Education Division in the Austrian Ministry for Education and Art.

Dr Irene Dyk is a member of the Provincial Parliament of Upper Austria and Lecturer for Social Policy in the University of Linz.

Klaus Eitzinger is a white-collar employee at present completing his doctoral thesis on the Freedom Party of Austria.

Heinz Fabris is Professor and Head of the Department of Journalism and Communication Science in the University of Salzburg.

Willi Filla is the General Secretary of the Austrian Association of Adult Education.

Heinz Fischer is at present Leader (Chief Whip) of the Socialist Party in the Austrian Parliament. Between 1983 and 1986 he was Minister of Science and Research in the Austrian Federal Government.

Felix Kreissler was prominent in the Resistance Movement in Austria against Fascism and after arrest by the Gestapo was interned in Buchenwald. He is Professor and Head of the Centre for Austrian Studies and Research in the University of Rouen in France.

Dr Herbert Krejci is the General Secretary of the Federation of Austrian Industrialists.

Dr Franz Lettner is the Director of the Chamber of Labour for Upper Austria.

Adolf H. Malinsky is Professor for Agricultural Policy, Land Development and Environmental Protection in the Department of Social Policy in the University of Linz.

Eduard März, before his recent death, had been Head of the Department of Economic Science of the Vienna Chamber of Labour and later Professor of Economic History in the University of Salzburg.

Herbert Moritz is the Vice-Governor of the province of Salzburg and Minister of Culture of the Provincial Government.

Ewald Nowotny is Professor and Head of the Ludwig Bolzmann Institute for Research in Economic Growth in the University of Vienna as well as a member of the Austrian Federal Parliament.

Anton Pelinka is Professor and Head of the Department of Political Science in the University of Innsbruck.

Dr Anton E. Rauter is the Chief Executive of the General Association of Austrian Cooperatives.

Dr Herbert Reiger is Deputy General Secretary of the Austrian Chamber of the Economy.

Walter Schwarzenbrunner is employed as an economist in the Chamber of Labour for Upper Austria.

Gerhard Steger is a Civil Servant in the Austrian Ministry of Finance and Chairman of the Austrian Work Group for Christianity and Socialism.

Alfred Ströer was the First Secretary responsible for Finance and International Affairs of the Austrian Federation of Trade Unions until his recent retirement. He is currently chairman of the Bank for Work and Economy (BAWAG).

Dr Melanie E. Sully is Senior Lecturer in History at the North Staffordshire Polytechnic.

Jim Sweeney is Lecturer in Industrial Relations at University of

Loughborough and has for some years been Adviser to the Austrian Federation of Trade Unions.

Josef Weidenholzer is Professor of Social Policy and Head of the Institute of Social Planning in the University of Linz.

Preface

The contributions to this Reader are written by those with knowledge and experience of the many facets of Austria and who can offer individual and personal perspectives of that small republic. By utilizing this knowlege and experience in this collected form it is hoped that some degree of understanding of what 'modern' Austria is can be arrived at. 'Modern Austria' in this work is concerned with the period from 1918 and the establishment of the First Republic to that of the present Second Republic. As will be made apparent however, it is in the nature of the theme that the analysis and explanation of the events and processes of Austria's evolution cannot be solely confined by a strait-jacket of rigid time limits. On the other hand despite the flexible treatment in these pages, the specialist reader, particularly the historian, may not be wholly satisfied: certain specific historical landmarks, regarded as fundamental to historiography, may find no place here. Thus the Battle of the Lech, near Augsburg in 955 AD and the defeat of the Magyars, the accession of the Babenburg counts to the suzerainty of the province of Ostmark in 976 AD, or even the later extension of territory and power under the Habsburg Dynasty, by which the processes of state- and nation-building of modern Austria were set in train, are not included. Interesting and important though such historical phenomena may be, we shall stress those features which distinguish Austria from other countries in more recent times and which highlight its national attributes.

The articles which compose this work are primarily intended to arouse the curiosity of the serious reader; they are of varying length and this has nothing to do with the importance of the topic under review, but rather more with the freedom of each contributor to treat the material as he or she thinks best or appropriate to explain a new field of knowledge or enquiry. It matters little whether or not the reader has a previous acquaintance with those characteristics which constitute a quite different national community to his or her own. This it is hoped should be no obstacle to an appreciation of the subject-matter. For the college or university student the disregard for the genre of the narrow academic discipline to be found here may be considered refreshing. A much more diversified approach is called for today as well as adding a sense of realism.

In addition we hope that this publication will also be of use for individuals who see it as an accompanying guide or as a preliminary *aperçu* in connection with a visit to Austria for the purposes of business, general interest or pleasure; the representatives of organizations too may find it an appropriate backcloth for the serious intentions of international gatherings.

There will inevitably be 'gaps'. Even though the 'overlap' of the subject-matter should enhance the unity of the book's content, there will perforce be particular areas of knowledge which are not catered for, either for reasons of space or those which a limited introductory work such as this does not make possible. No reference for example is made to the development of the natural sciences, philosophy, music, art and literature in modern Austria; nor have the country's legal system or its military preoccupations and traditions been expounded upon. This is not to say that the universal, unique or creative contributions of Freud, Bolzmann, Schrödinger, Schönberg, Berg, Klimpt, Otto Wagner, Musil, Kraus, Handke, Wittgenstein, Popper or Max Adler, to name but a few of the country's most famous sons, are not important. Nor should the fact that no space is given to some of the country's great women of vision — Bertha von Suttner or Adelheid Popp for example — be construed as a slight on the cause of women or a deprecation of the role of women in Austrian society. We would only point out that this work has to be seen as a starting point for the reader who wishes to pursue other, specialist, topics of this nature.

To atone for these omissions and to aid further enquiry the reader is directed to the sections entitled 'Further Reading' pertaining to each chapter and the complementary 'Selected Bibliography' which appear at the end of the book. These may act as a starting point for any subsequent endeavour, discovery or research, although the sources we cite are in book form only. Our one regret in this regard is the relatively few references which appear in English and we hope that this pioneering work will lead to the promotion of 'Austrian Studies' in the English language.

Even though we aim at an integrated text from the efforts of 25 individuals, the structure of this work is such that it should be worthwhile for the reader who requires to 'dip into' the text for specific purposes or to accommodate those with special interests. For those with a penchant or eye for graphic, statistical or quantitative data, the Tables and Appendices at the end should in themselves provide interest, even though many of these relate to references in the main text.

Most of the selections collated here are translated from German. Some concepts and terms may not render precise meanings in translation or may even be a matter of linguistic dispute. Whether or not this appears to be the case, the editors, on advice from the translation team in such cases, have exercised a degree of discretion and judgement; in the main however, they have followed the usages of Austrian and German writers or organizations as far as possible, and some explanation of this is given in the Glossary of Terms at the end. We hope that the discretion so exercised does not detract from the meaning or enjoyment of the work and for any errors or discrepancies which occur we as editors are solely responsible and unreservedly apologize.

This book consists of voluntary contributions of people who lead busy and active lives and for these contributions we cannot begin to express our gratitude. Particular thanks go to the translating editor, Dr Jeremy Leaman of Loughborough University who, in addition to ensuring consistency in language throughout, has arranged the Glossary of Terms, the statistical and other data and has also compiled the index. For the actual spadework of translation, the main burden has fallen on another Loughborough colleague, Mr John Manton. This task has been executed with skill, precision, dedication, patience and great care, given the difficulties associated with German language usage, particularly those terms which are specifically Austrian. To him we are deeply indebted. His work has been supplemented by that of Mrs Susanne Sweeney-Novak of the University of Vienna to whom we are also grateful. For the typing of the manuscript we are indebted to Mrs Patricia Swift and Miss Felicity Nash of Loughborough University.

Taken as a whole this venture is one of Anglo-Austrian co-operation, and one in particular which arises from the close association between the University of Linz in Austria and Loughborough University of Technology in England. It represents the first work of its kind undertaken in Britain to meet the current and growing demands of academic and comparative studies. To have made this possible our sponsors are owed our final expression of gratitude. These include Dr Ernst Menhofer of the Austrian Institute in London and Dr Bernhard Stillfried of the Austrian Foreign Ministry in Vienna and the support of their institutions; the Federal Economic Chambers, particularly their Banking section in association with the Creditanstalt Bank; the Austrian Trade Union Federation and the Upper Austrian Chamber of Labour, and the other agencies who have backed our endeavours to disseminate information and knowledge of things Austrian to other countries. Such help and co-operation are deeply appreciated. In conclusion, we hope that their confidence in us is not misplaced and that this publication will stimulate an interest in, and present a profile of, a country small in territory but large in influence, which though no longer at the centre of the world's stage as in the past, represents a power for good in a troubled world.

Jim Sweeney
Josef Weidenholzer
November 1987

PART I
HISTORICAL FOUNDATIONS

1 The making of an Austrian nation

Felix Kreissler

The question of the existence or non-existence of an Austrian nation is the focal point of much contemporary debate both inside and outside Austria. What follows therefore is a brief and succinct summary of the making of Austria, written so that foreign readers may understand how this nation, which has been the subject of so much dispute, came into being.

First, a word of explanation: we shall not be speaking of some historical/political entity whose origins lie in the dim and distant past and whose champions therefore have to rely on myths about dynasties, languages and religions of one kind or another — myths which serve no useful purpose today. We shall be speaking rather of the modern Austrian nation which did not fully materialize until the twentieth century — much later than other nations such as England and France — with the twofold founding of the Austrian Republic under the very diverse conditions of 1918 and 1945. However, since this nation, like any other, had its antecedents and did not arise in a vacuum, a brief historical survey must first be given.

Over several centuries of political activity the Habsburgs had succeeded in creating a multi-racial empire in Central Europe — they were renowned for their marriage policies — and by the mid-eighteenth century had been able to consolidate its various feudally constituted territories into a state. In this state, where Hungarians, Germans, Italians, Czechs, Slovaks, Poles, Serbs, Croats, Jews, Romanians, Ruthenians and others managed to live together — or side by side — more or less peaceably, there were no national or nationalistic problems since allegiance to one's particular territorial prince was based entirely on the feudal relationship of fealty and obedience and was in no sense dependent upon cultural or linguistic ties. There was also a further factor which was of overriding importance within the Habsburg territories: the Habsburg princes were at the same time the rulers of the 'Holy Roman Empire of the German Nation', which was neither holy nor Roman and was most certainly not of the German nation since as yet there *was* no nation, the empire being a conglomeration of innumerable peoples and ethnic groups.

Certainly from 1648 onwards, when the Peace of Westphalia put an end to the Thirty Years' War, the empire began to disintegrate into its component parts or at any rate to become a patchwork of increasingly independent states whose official head, the Emperor, could exercise very little power within the individual member states since such power had been expropriated by their ruling princes.

On the other hand, from the reign of Maria Theresa (1740–80) there arose within the Habsburg territories an awareness of Austrian statehood, which can probably be regarded as a precursor of things to come even though it did not amount to an awareness of distinctive nationhood. At any rate the idea of an Austria came to the fore at that time, and when the fiction of the Holy Roman Empire of the German nation finally collapsed under the hammer blows of Napoleon's armies, Emperor Franz II took the next logical step: having already proclaimed himself Emperor of Austria in 1804, he now, in 1806, laid down the German imperial crown once and for all and so became Emperor Franz I of Austria.

Although Napoleon had succeeded in utterly crushing the first German Empire, the ensuing wars waged by Austria and her temporary allies against the Emperor of the French revealed for the first time the existence of an Austrian patriotism, albeit heavily overlaid with dynastic allegiance.

What can be stated with certainty is that the process whereby Austria was to become a nation began in 1804 with the proclamation of the Austrian Empire. The process could not have commenced any earlier since the economic, social, political and cultural development which was to lead to the establishment of modern nations did not set in until the beginning of the nineteenth century. In other words, Austria like other countries was seeing the start of the process which would end in the replacement of feudalism by modern capitalism.

Even at that period, numerous elements of the future Austrian nation were present, though its evolution was greatly complicated by the belated development of capitalism in Austria, and this in turn led to those problems of identity which persist to this day.

It should be explained that at the beginning of the nineteenth century there was the possibility of a national development along other lines, namely that the various Austrian peoples might coalesce into a large supra-lingual, multi-ethnic nation in the heart of Europe, with a decidedly 'cosmopolitan' culture, by reason of the unified territorial area (both politically and economically speaking) which appeared to be emerging. Nothing came of this, however, for many reasons, chiefly the inability of the Habsburg dynasty and the ruling aristocracy to secure the peaceful co-existence of the various nationalities under the monarchy.

The ruling classes were unwilling to renounce their privileges and kept the different national groups in a condition of political, economic and cultural backwardness which these groups were less and less willing to tolerate.

Shattered hopes

The revolution of 1848 raised great hopes among all the peoples of Europe but in particular among those living under the Habsburg monarchy: they wanted freedom, i.e. a constitution and the end of the Metternich regime. The overthrow of the revolution, however, brought precisely the opposite: neo-absolutism and stronger centralism.

Within the Habsburg empire this resulted in various conflicting problems. The awakening of the national groups and their struggle for freedom brought about a sense of nationalism hitherto unknown, which was particularly marked in the case of the German-speaking population. This group, however, manoeuvred itself into an almost hopeless situation: on the one hand it was unwilling to give up its dominant role under the monarchy, but on the other hand it dreamed of a united Second '*Reich*'. This schizophrenic attitude arose from a superiority complex *vis-à-vis* the non-German races under the monarchy, and an inferiority complex *vis-à-vis* the Germans in the *Reich*, which incidentally no longer existed or did not yet exist. Then there was the intensifying rivalry between Austria and Prussia for the leadership of the German Confederation (a federation of 35 'sovereign princes' and 4 'free cities', founded in 1820 and under Austrian presidency). This rivalry ultimately led to the war of 1866, Austria's defeat at Königgrätz and her total separation from Germany — a process which culminated in the formation of the German *Reich* in 1871.

With the 'Compromise' (*Ausgleich*) of 1867 the 'Dual Monarchy' came into being, whereby the Emperor of Austria also became King of Hungary. It was merely a kind of provisional state, for which Robert Musil invented the name '*Kakanien*' (from k.u.k. = '*kaiserlich-königlich*').

Pan-German ideology took hold among the establishment (the intelligentsia, the bureaucracy, industrialists, etc.), but also among the German-speaking masses within the Empire. Under the leadership of Georg von Schönerer the pan-German movement (*alldeutsche Bewegung*) came into being, which with its racial antisemitism and its demand for the union (*Anschluss*) of the German-speaking areas with Germany and for the dissolution of the Habsburg monarchy created an irredentism which was hostile to the state and which ruined every attempt at solving the nationalities' problem. At a later date, Hitler was to make use of Schönerer's doctrines in order to justify his annexation of Austria.

Thus the Austrians were to be hindered from gaining an awareness of their own distinctive personality. The process leading to Austrian nationhood was faced with constant opposition from pan-Germanist ideology, which disputed (and still disputes today) Austria's right to national identity, appealing essentially to the fact of a common language with the Germans, if not to common 'blood' and 'race' (wholly untenable criteria scientifically), or to a so-called 'millennium of common history', which is a total illusion since there has never been any such thing.

It was just at this time that a number of the best writers developed a fresh awareness of Austria and expressed this in their works: Hugo von Hofmannsthal, Leopold von Andrian, Hermann Bahr and Arthur Schnitzler, who stood consciously in the tradition of their poetic forebears Stifter, Grillparzer, Raimund and Nestroy. Their voices were to be drowned, however, in the chauvinistic tumult of the First World War.

1918 — the establishment of the Austrian nation

The disintegration of the Habsburg empire into its component parts in November 1918, a prime cause of which was the inability of its rulers to solve the above-mentioned problems, gave the Austrians the opportunity of establishing their own nation state. They took the first step towards this by proclaiming the Republic on 12 November 1918. But the process of founding such a state (an important step towards the goal of nationhood) was hampered from the outset by various conflicts of a schizophrenic nature. It was not the great majority of Austrians, but the political leaders whose ideology had been moulded by the Pan-Germanism of the second half of the nineteenth century who continued to ask the nonsensical question whether the Austrians were Austrians or Germans. The causes of this schizophrenia also lay in the traumas of having lost the war and of seeing Austria shrink from a great power to a small state, and furthermore in the severe social disruptions of the post-war period. As long as there was a prospect in Germany of progressive social development, the Austrian Social Democrats thought that Austria might benefit, then later when National Socialism raised its head, it was the pro-German nationalists who saw their salvation in union (*Anschluss*). One of the much-quoted arguments was that of the alleged non-viability of Austria, that small country where industry and the banks sought to strengthen their position through 'trimming down' and consequent mass unemployment.

The myth of Austria's non-viability was refuted as early as 1925 by two experts who were sent to the country by the League of Nations: the Englishman Layton and the Frenchman Rist. In a detailed report they drew attention to Austria's natural resources which were sufficient to bring the country out of poverty. After the Second World War their statements received spectacular confirmation in the upswing of the Austrian economy.

But there was a further phenomenon which similarly bore testimony to the viability of Austria and created a new self-image, so encouraging a positive attitude to the Austrian nation. This was the programme of social development undertaken in 'Red Vienna', i.e. by the capital's Social Democratic municipal authority, which injected new blood into every area of community life: there was the authority's house-building programme which provided workers' families with hygienic, modern accommodation; the school reform introduced by Glöckel which aimed to give children of all social classes equal educational opportunities; health care and a welfare scheme for young people and the elderly which sought to help particularly those who were deprived; a modern health service; and innumerable societies and associations, each of which had its own particular mission to fulfil. All this produced a new Austrian vitality, giving to those involved a sense of optimism for the future. Unfortunately, however, this phenomenon was limited to Vienna, the result being that the capital came to be out of step, both politically and socially, with the other provinces where the backward-looking spirit of provincialism was both unable and unwilling to free itself from a nostalgia for the one-time monarchy of Greater Austria.

The fatal flaw in the Vienna development programme, as seen by Christian Social or Pan-German Nationalist politicians, was that it was being carried out by the Social Democrats in a spirit which they dismissed as 'Austro-Bolshevism'. In reality, however, Austro-Marxism went far beyond politics and was a cultural movement on a grand scale, which sought to educate men of all social classes and make them into 'new men'.

Austro–Marxism gave rise to numerous cultural achievements whose creativity was a source of universal astonishment and at the same time bore testimony to the viability of the new Austria in more than a purely material sense. The world of the intellect was represented in the Austria of that period by such diverse writers as Karl Kraus, Robert Musil, Alfred Polgar, Franz Werfel and Hermann Broch; composers such as Webern and Wellesz; painters and sculptors such as Hanak, Merkel and Kokoschka; and scholars such as Bühler, Freud, Kelsen, A. Adler and Otto Neurath — all of them world-famous names. And the list could be considerably extended.

Soon there came the counter-attack from the anti-Marxists, whether Christian Socialists, supporters of the *Heimwehr* (a para-military local defence corps), pan-German nationalists or National Socialists. To these latter groups Austria's democratic tendencies were seen as a weakness, and they had no time for the concept of an independent, viable nation. This nation did in fact already exist but was not yet aware of the fact mainly because its leaders, in their nationalist schizophrenia, misguidedly regarded Austria as a 'second German state' — so the nation was already under sentence of death when it began to decline. One milestone in this decline was the destruction of democracy by armed force in February 1934, the end-point of a development which had begun on 15 July 1927 with 100 people being shot dead in the streets of Vienna and whose penultimate stage had been reached with the suppression of Parliament in March 1933.

February 1934 saw not only the end of democracy but also the beginning of the Austro-Fascist corporate state whose leaders (Dollfuss, Schuschnigg, Starhemberg etc.), giving themselves up as ever to nostalgia for the past glories of the monarchy, suddenly 'discovered' Austrian patriotism and 'the Austrian man'.

However, since at the same time they were also pursuing their pan-Germanist dreams, they simply presented Hitler with the weapon he would eventually use to impose *Anschluss* by force. On 12 February 1938 Schuschnigg, who in 1936 had proclaimed the virtues of what he called 'the German way', was summoned to Berchtesgaden where Hitler presented him with an ultimatum which he did not have the courage to reject. Despite the fact that the clauses providing for Nazification and *Anschluss* were meant to be kept secret, the truth leaked out and caused panic among the people of Austria. In the face of imminent invasion by the armed forces of the Third Reich, there arose in the final weeks of Austria's existence (February–March 1938) a great patriotic movement in which all the country's political groups participated apart from the Nazis who, though relatively numerous, were nonetheless in a minority. The climax of this movement was to be the referendum on the independence of Austria set for 13 March. Hitler, however, precisely because he feared the outcome of the referendum, sent his troops in on 11 March. Schuschnigg, still in his pan-Germanist dream world, capitulated, and on 15 March 1938 the annexation was officially announced.

Resistance, exile, liberation — milestones on the road to nationhood

Goebbels' propaganda persuaded the world — and it is a lie which is still widely believed today — that the Austrians welcomed the invasion of Hitler's troops with enthusiasm. In fact this was true only of the Nazis, still a minority in March 1938 albeit well organized and noisy. And so the referendum of 10 April, ordered by Hitler and Himmler and held in an atmosphere of terror and force, was presented to the world as a genuine expression of the popular will, a claim from which political capital is still being made today.

The reality was very different: the extinction of Austria accelerated the formation of national awareness among the Austrian people. There were several reasons for this: the realities of life after the *Anschluss* came as a shock even to those Austrians who had hoped for great things from 'reunification with the Reich'. The occupation of all command posts by 'Germans from the Old Reich', the deterioration in living standards experienced by workers and white-collar employees, the economic exploitation of the country, the militarization of both public and private life, plus all the accompanying brutality and terror — these things produced a cruel disillusionment which was merely intensified by the outbreak of war, once temporary illusions of a speedy victory had passed away. But there were real difficulties in the way of organized resistance: all known party officials were arrested (70,000 had already been detained in March, the first batch being transported to Dachau on 1 April, 10 days before Hitler's 'popular referendum'); all Austrian organizations were destroyed, and the labour movement, which even before this had been forced into illegality, was totally smashed. These moves exacerbated the problems faced by the Resistance — problems which had already been created by the public declarations of the Austrian bishops and of the ex-Chancellor Karl Renner. So at first organized resistance was only on a small scale, but as the situation developed the problems it faced were largely overcome.

One of the most significant features of the Austrian Resistance was its diversity: Catholic Conservatives, Legitimists, Communists, Socialists and Liberals repeatedly met together to uphold the idea of Austria's rebirth despite the terror and repression from the Gestapo. Historical justice demands acknowledgement of the part played by the Austrian Communists in these costly struggles. Although the Resistance did not assume the same popular proportions as in many other lands, it did tie up a considerable part of the Nazis' apparatus of repression particularly during the final phase of the war.

After the great turning points of the war such as Stalingrad and

Tunisia, and in particular after the Moscow Declaration by the Great Powers (1 November 1943) concerning the restoration of an independent Austria, the Austrian Resistance took on an increasingly national character. There were acts of sabotage, and in the mountains (especially those of Carinthia and Styria) small groups of partisans were formed, receiving support from those of Tito. It is therefore fair to say that the Austrian Resistance played an important part in the growth of national awareness among the people of Austria.

A major factor in this process was the part played by Austrian exiles from 1938 to 1945. Their groups, highly diverse in terms of ideological and political orientation, all helped in their own way to keep the name of Austria alive throughout the world. The 150,000 or so Austrian exiles founded groups in 89 different countries, and in such groups an important part was played by representatives of cultural life, writers, composers, scientists, etc. The 'Free Austria Movement' in Britain made a pre-eminent contribution: it succeeded in bringing together all the groups throughout the world to form the 'Free Austrian World Movement', not only opening up the prospect — despite all their political differences — of restoring an independent and democratic Austria but also actively working towards a new national self-awareness. Even if it were possible, there is no need here to go into the differences which undoubtedly existed between the various groups, since such differences have tended to counteract Austria's progress towards nationhood.

Those world-renowned Austrian writers who were forced to emigrate made a considerable contribution through their publications in exiles' journals such as *Österreichische Post* and *Nouvelles d'Autriche* in France, *Zeitspiegel* in Britain and *Austro-American Tribune* in the USA. Not only did they demonstrate the originality of Austrian literature but they also made public opinion in the free world aware of the Austrian people's desire to live in a nation of their own.

Thousands of Austrian volunteers joined the ranks of the allied armies and saw active war service while thousands of others joined the European underground Resistance movement in France, Belgium, Italy, Yugoslavia and other countries, where the Austrian freedom fighters were held in especially high regard.

As mentioned above, national unity was also fostered by the Moscow Declaration which gave fresh hope both to the Resistance within Austria and to Austrians in exile. In the final phase of the war all the Austrian Resistance groups co-ordinated their efforts, which made it possible, just a few days after the liberation, to form a provisional government comprising Socialists, Communists and members of the People's Party, these being the parties involved in the foundation of the Second Republic. On 27 April 1945 this government issued a Declaration of Independence, which was diametrically opposed to the Proclamation of the First Republic in 1918 in that it particularly emphasized Austria's autonomy and its absolute independence of Germany. This commitment to patriotism and the affirmation of democracy were the foundation stones of the Second Republic, and at this time both the government and the people as a whole manifested an attitude of Austrian patriotism.

From liberation to State Treaty

During the decade 1945 to 1955 successive governments made great efforts to secure the establishment of complete national sovereignty, i.e. through the withdrawal of the Allied forces of occupation. These efforts eventually succeeded with the signing of the State Treaty on 15 May 1955 and the passing of the Constitution Act regarding Austria's permanent neutrality on 26 October of the same year. These two actions in the realm of state law were high points of Austrian self-awareness; they were actions reflecting a national consensus. The overwhelming majority of the population identified themselves with the Austrian nation which, with the State Treaty and neutrality, had now finally come to maturity.

There is no denying the fact that, in the light of the foregoing, events before 1955 called into question the concept of Austria as an independent state.

While one component of Austria's growing awareness of nationhood — the Communist Party — was ousted from national life through the events of the cold war in the late 1940s, it was not long before that arch-enemy of the Austrian nation, Pan-Germanism, raised its head. Thus as early as 1949, a so-called fourth party was founded: the League of Independents (*Verband der Unabhängigen* or VdU), which became a rallying point for many former Nazis and which in the elections of that year received about 10 per cent of the vote, so winning 16 seats. This party rejected outright the existence of the Austrian nation and of a separate Austrian culture. In this period, being preoccupied with the cold war, the two major political parties (the ÖVP and the SPÖ) were neglecting their ideological campaign against Nazism, the result being that the latter found it easy to start disseminating its anti-Austrian ideology all over again. The main evidence for such neo-Nazi subversion may be summarized as follows: many illegal Nazi cells were founded which not only preached 'Volk'-orientated mysticism but also followed this up with overt action: bombings, violent clashes with the police, antisemitic demonstrations with shouts of 'Long Live Auschwitz!' and eventually the murder of a former Resistance fighter, E. Kirchweger, in 1965. A few years later, when Kreisky's Socialist government was fulfilling one of the requirements of the State Treaty, namely the erection of bilingual place name signs (German and Slovenian) in the mixed-language areas of Carinthia, there was a fresh outbreak of German-nationalist feeling: the bilingual signs were removed by force and the so-called Carinthian Homeland Movement (*Kärntner Heimatdienst*) quite openly announced a strategy aimed at the disappearance of the Slovene minority — a strategy still being pursued today.

Neo-Nazi attitudes, permanently at work both underground and in public life, manifested themselves once again in 1984 when Frischenschlager, Defence Minister in the coalition government and a member of the VdU's successor organization the FPÖ, gave a ceremonial welcome to the war criminal Reder upon the latter's arrival in Austria after his early release from imprisonment in Italy. It is true that the Reder-Frischenschlager affair provoked protest from democratic forces in Austria, but at the same time it was clear that many groups of ex-Nazis in the country had still not put the past behind them. The strength of such attitudes, even today, was shown in the election of the Federal President in June 1986, the person elected being ÖVP candidate Kurt Waldheim who, during his election campaign, had claimed that as an officer in the *Wehrmacht* during the Hitler period, he had 'only done his duty'. In saying this he failed to recognize the severe harm he was doing to Austria's international standing, since he was contradicting the official position of all post-war Austrian governments which had stressed that Austria wished to be regarded — and must be regarded — as the first victim of Hitler's imperialism. The contradiction between 'being a victim' and 'doing one's duty' is only too obvious.

In the autumn of 1986 there was yet a further alarm signal indicating the persistence of Nazi ideology in certain circles: at the FPÖ party conference the national wing of the party (and this calls itself the 'Freedom' Party!) carried out what can only be called a putsch against Steger the party leader who was regarded as liberal and who was also Vice-Chancellor in the SPÖ and FPÖ coalition cabinet. The Socialist Federal Chancellor therefore immediately terminated the coalition and called new elections for 23 November 1986, as a result of which the new leader of the FPÖ Haider, whose Nazi and neo-Nazi sympathies can hardly be denied, emerged victorious inasmuch as his party obtained 10 per cent of the vote (18 seats) — exactly the same percentage as the VdU in 1949. One is bound to ask: has Austria learnt nothing in almost 40 years?

The Austrian nation is now firmly established

The repeated neo-Nazi attacks upon the Austrian nation have not gone unanswered. The outbursts of anti-Austrian feeling referred to above have stung the forces of patriotism into action. Even in the 1960s there was serious discussion about 'the Nation' which led to increased national awareness on the part of Austrians. Then the discussion reached the mass media, and progress towards nationhood became a matter of national concern, as was indicated in a series of opinion polls, the results of which can only be summarized here in rounded figures.

In 1956 — one year after the State Treaty — only 49 per cent of Austrians were convinced of their own nationhood while as many as 46 per cent declared there was no such thing as an Austrian nation. In 1970 the number of those who felt themselves to be Austrians had increased to 66 per cent with only 8 per cent against (the remainder being undecided). In 1980, however, about 80 per cent were either of the opinion that the Austrian nation was an accomplished fact or believed it was on the way to becoming so. There were still about 10 per cent against, and it is remarkable that this tallies exactly with the FPÖ's share of the vote on 23 November 1986.

A major contributory factor to this growth in national awareness was the Kreisky era with its unambiguous support for 'the Austrian Way'. However, for Austrian nationhood to become a complete reality, pan-Germanism, neo-Nazism and all the prejudices of a bygone age (ideological/nationalistic, historiographical, etc.) will have to be jettisoned once and for all.

At all events, it is quite clear that the Austrian nation does exist and that hardly anyone in Austria believes it to be, as the pan-Germanists claim, a 'communist or monarchist' invention. The Austrians assume their nation's existence in their day-to-day living and feel it to be the end-product of their common history and their own socio-economic and cultural development, particularly during the past 150 years. There is, furthermore, a will to stay together as a unified body. Even in the contemporary world it is possible for a small state to maintain its sovereignty and freedom of action, to develop its own national economy and, through on-going democratization of all areas of life, to enable its citizens to participate more and more fully in public life and political decision-making.

The relevance and status of the Austrian nation derive from its independence, its neutrality and its pluralist democracy, and from its position at the point of intersection between divergent social systems. Austria must not allow this status to be destroyed by those who persist in proclaiming the glories of pan-Germanism, who still question Austrian nationhood and so wish to bring about a loss of that national identity which has been achieved by Austrians at the cost of so many lives.

The fact that Austria is now a nation in the fullest sense of the word enables it to act as an honest broker between different systems without in the least surrendering its independence or its identity. Provided, therefore, that it continues to carry out this function, the Austrian nation will become a factor contributing to peace and to international stability.

2 From the First to the Second Republic: continuity and discontinuity

Gerhard Botz

In historical thinking, continuity and discontinuity stand in a causal relationship to each other. Just as the long-continued existence of social and intellectual structures is characterized by the absence of breaks or periods of accelerated change, so discontinuities in the historical process always mark the boundary zones between different continuities.

Fascism to democracy

The first question to be discussed here is as follows: what is the precise nature of the continuity and discontinuity between the First and Second Austrian Republics? This problem will be approached from two directions: first from a macro-historical and macro-social perspective, and then from a 'meso-historical' standpoint emphasizing the differences between political groups and the experiences of the various strata and classes within society.

At the macro-social level, the problem can be brought into focus by an approach which, to be sure, is extremely imprecise and even basically inadmissible — namely by asking the hypothetical question: 'What would have happened if . . .?' Thus: 'How would the Austrian economy and Austrian society have developed after 1945 if there had been no interlude of Fascism and authoritarianism (with or without the Second World War)? Would Austria's economic position have been as strong as it is today? Would the close co-operation of the most important interest groups which characterized the Austrian economy after 1957 and became known as the 'social partnership', have developed?'

Most of these questions suggest an answer along the lines of 'Probably not'. As far as the country's economic and social development is concerned, the arguments of social scientists who write from a historical perspective, such as Erich Bodzenta, Kurt Rothschild, Maria Szecsi and Eduard März, would support the following thesis: certainly 1938 saw a structural break (or alternatively a drastic reinforcement of older socio-historical tendencies within Austria), but — and this is the important point — these structural changes remained in being more or less continuously beyond the year 1945.

Some of the relevant factors may be briefly enumerated: the *Anschluss* in 1938 brought with it a boost to the economy which was unexpected given Austria's situation at the time and behind which lay the full weight of the economic and military expansionist policies of the Third Reich. This ended at a stroke the disastrous, deflationary Austrian economic policy of the inter-war period.

The expropriation of the considerable gold and foreign currency reserves of the Austrian National Bank was a serious matter, as was the theft of Jewish property, otherwise known as 'arianization', but at the same time the unused reserves of labour, the low wage levels, the natural resources and the availability of raw materials in agriculture and forestry all attracted German capital to Austria. This led to strong foreign infiltration of the Austrian economy which again, in the medium term, proved to be the foundation for one of the most important pillars of economic and social policy in the Second Republic: the nationalization of the basic goods and power industries and of the banking sector.

A further consequence for Austria of the economic *Anschluss* of 1938 was that during the expansion phase of the Third Reich new enterprises were being established and developed which were of such magnitude that no small state could possibly have initiated them on the basis of its own internal economic resources; these involved the expansion of petroleum production, the iron and steel industry, hydro-electric power, the chemical industry and so on. It is true that many of these large enterprises did not serve to develop the existing organically evolved conditions for growth in the Austrian economy, but rather the particular interests of the economy's German masters. Nevertheless once created, and even when only half-finished or largely destroyed at the end of the war, such industrial plant (together with its infrastructure and its skilled workforce) made possible a further fundamental post-war decision concerning the economy of the Second Republic and the nature of its society — namely the decision to undertake the total reconstruction of heavy industry and to continue with other large-scale investment projects after 1945. There was a third, external factor, however, even more far-reaching in its impact upon social policy: without the Marshall Plan these intentions could certainly not have been realized to their full extent.

The acceleration of industrialization between 1938 and 1945 was also accompanied by the orientation of the Austrian economy towards the West, the further development of the country's tourist economy (specifically adapted to meet war-time needs), and the encouragement of mechanization and increased production in agriculture. The relative shift towards the West which the economy underwent between 1934 and 1951 was one factor behind the decrease in the share of the population within the three easterly federal provinces (*Länder*) (from 54.5 per cent to 47.5 per cent), compared with a slight increase in Carinthia and Styria (1.8 per cent) and considerable growth in the westerly *Länder* (5.2 per cent). During the subsequent history of the Second Republic these trends have not only had sociological results but have also affected voting patterns and the growth of federalism. There is much truth in the thesis advanced by Ernst Hanisch concerning the de-provincializing of the provinces, by which is meant that the structural contrast between province and metropolis is becoming ever less pronounced.

In considering all these structural changes, which can be regarded with approval from the perspective of present-day Austria, we should not forget the monstrous cruelty with which the Nazi dictatorship pursued its political opponents and those whom it called 'racial enemies', murdering them with bureaucratic, machine-like efficiency. Another fact that should not be forgotten is that the Second World War claimed the lives of almost a quarter of a million Austrian military personnel. Nor should we lose sight of the suffering and hardship endured by their dependents, by the wounded and by those injured in air raids, to say nothing of the privations and shock of displacement experienced by the millions of refugees and expellees. Some of these remained in Austria, which was a further factor in the break-up of traditional social structures.

It would not be legitimate, either ethically or methodologically, to draw up a detailed profit-and-loss account for Austria covering the period 1938–1945. Nevertheless one can agree with the view that while the Austrian economy did not benefit directly from the *Anschluss*, the expansionist industrial policies of the Third Reich did give an impetus to that economy which can only be described as a leap, as a discontinuity in important structural features of the Austrian economy. We shall now return to the question under consideration in this section, namely continuity or discontinuity after 1938 and 1945, and examine it from a more individual perspective.

The various stages of the *Anschluss* affair, seen through the eyes of those who lived through them, were no everyday occurrence, and for many areas of Austria this was even more true of the extremely bitter fighting and the chaos associated with the end of the war. The records of every parish, every church and every school must contain references to it. The exit of the top Nazi élite was a political event quite as drastic as their pseudo-revolutionary seizure of power had been 7 years before. There were equally drastic breaks in continuity in the sphere of constitutional law, for 1938 marked the end of sovereignty while 1945 saw its revival. Or was there in fact some deep-seated 'Austria' which lived on beneath the surface brutality of the German occupation? After 1945 this idea was the subject of vigorous theoretical discussion among writers on international law.

It is a fact that even the administrative sub-divisions of the country were so firmly embedded in people's habits, in communications, in the areas of competence — both large and small — of the various bureaucracies, and in the thinking of the Austrian Nazi leadership, that in 1938 the centralists in Berlin were able to change the structures to only a marginal degree. Similar resistance to change was seen in 1945 — only the other way round — in that even comparatively trivial modifications which had been introduced by the Nazi régime remained in force for years, until there was the opportunity or the will to bring about, for example, the reintegration of larger or smaller areas.

Nazi interference in administrative organizations — the logical outcome of the new rulers' desire for integration as well as for bureaucratic efficiency — was of course frequently very serious, particularly in the case of the central administrative authority in Vienna which in fact was incompatible with German Nazi control and which was therefore abolished. But below the highest decision-making level, which in any case had had an authoritarian hierarchical structure even before 1938, surprisingly little change took place in the administration of powerful bodies such as the *Länder-Reichsgau* authorities, the police, the army, the railways, the employment exchanges and the courts. This statement applies more to the basic principles of their actual work and in some cases to administrative and organizational details, rather than to their overall organization and written codes of practice.

According to studies relating to the first few years after 1945, precisely the same situation applied in the western zones of occupation: everyday political and economic administration had surprisingly little difficulty in coping with such massive breaks in the system — even (in conventional military terms) with disasters of the first magnitude! In the interests of day-to-day survival, it probably had to be this way. (In the Soviet zone, adaptation to the new situation was essential, but was largely just a matter of form.) In the eyes of the general public, therefore, most of Austria's administrative structures (reshaped along authoritarian lines in 1933–4) cannot have been essentially different from those of the Nazi bureaucracy, and these in turn were similar to the provisional administration offices, occupation headquarters and federal authorities of the immediate post-war years.

There is, however, one essential qualification to be made: any who failed to fit into the system for cultural, religious, nationalist or political reasons, in other words those who were caught up in the cogs of the control machinery because they were Jews, Gypsies, Communists, Catholic activists etc. — such people found the differences crucial, often a matter of life or death. But what percentage of the population did this directly involve? 10 per cent? 20 per cent? Most Austrians just lived through all the political breaks in the system, showing partial conformity, partial resistance and much indifference, and just wishing they could have been spared the fear, the ever-changing need for a guilty conscience, and what were undoubtedly the terrible hardships of 1945. So it is not particularly surprising that, for example, in 1938 when the Nazis seized power barely 10 per cent of all those employed by the Vienna municipal authority were dismissed on political grounds, including so-called 'racial' grounds. Then in 1945 about 7.5 per cent of employees in the whole of Austria were dismissed (at least temporarily), though this did mean 100,000 public sector and 70,000 private sector employees. In general, however, and apart from the inevitable exceptions, the political climate changed but the government officials (*Beamte*) remained in office. As an ÖVP district councillor said in 1946:

> What happened in 1918, 1938 and 1945? The departmental head came in, called his employees together, told them with greater or lesser enthusiasm that there was now a different form of government, and got them to take the oath. Then they went back to work.

This was the real problem about de-Nazification which in the longer term was only moderately successful. Certainly as far as Austria was concerned the problem was not so much the absence of political will; if there had been a really drastic administrative break in 1945, then presumably the changed rules of bureaucratic procedure and the need for a different kind of expertise would have made it impossible for the administration to fall back upon the specialist knowledge and the routine of its employees to help put it back on its feet — but as it was, such a course of action was totally inevitable. Admittedly the extent to which de-Nazification was carried out varied greatly from one profession and one region to another. In general, however, it would appear that with the exception of the two 'changeover' years of 1938 and 1945, when higher positions were subject to radical purges, the bureaucracies saw no drastic turnover of staff in either case.

By contrast, on the level of the political, administrative and cultural élites (though less so in the case of the economic élite), both 1938 and 1945 are mainly characterized by discontinuity. One has only to consider the high average age of the élites of all political groups before 1938, and add to this the fact that, as activists, many of them emigrated or were annihilated, to understand the wholesale changeover of personnel brought about by differences in political decision-making between the First and Second Republics. The same applies to the cultural élites, whose leadership by Jews of the old Austrian school was abruptly ended by physical mass extermination. This was another area therefore where there could be no continuity with the tradition of the First Republic.

We still know far too little about the political and social-psychological consequences of all these political breaks in the system and sociographical discontinuities within the political, cultural and economic élites of Austria. Nevertheless there are good grounds for assuming that later leadership groups in the Second Republic had learnt some lessons from those earlier changes of régime with their accompanying political persecution. The copious literature showing how the idea was born of a 'Grand Coalition' and of co-operation between social partners 'on the road from Dachau' provides overwhelming evidence of this — though admittedly it carried weight only with those political élites which were interned and decimated in concentration camps such as Dachau. Several scholars have rightly stressed the importance of this learning process for the rise of 'élite consensus', which is basic to the functioning of the social partnership in today's Second Republic.

But how did the broad mass of party members behave, i.e. the old and new middle classes? Once again historical science has not provided any empirical findings, although the methods of oral history would be particularly appropriate for portraying the subjective experiences of the lower and middle classes who were far from the centre of power. Preliminary evidence is provided only by empirical social research which distinguishes three age cohorts (or generations) of Austrians, depending on whether they grew up about the time of the First World War, before and during the Second World War, or in the first decade of the Second Republic. Generally speaking these three age groups still show the general characteristics of the period in which they became politically socialized, i.e. entered adulthood: the oldest generation show an ideological politicization while the youngest show tendencies towards direct and corporate participation. As for the middle age group which was influenced by Fascism, investigation shows that the lower social groups have a negative attitude towards political involvement, having presumably been discouraged from such activity during the years of Fascism, and having been made wary of politics by what they saw at that time.

This situation, taken together with the strongly pro-authoritarian attitudes found particularly in that generation, may explain the political psychology at work in the shaping of the social partnership: an 'enlightened', consensus-orientated political élite finds full allegiance among the (socially and educationally) lower and middle groups, benefiting directly from the de-politicizing experience of such groups and their attitude towards authority. The high degree of electoral and trade union involvement shown by this age group would then not be the product of great democratic maturity but rather of scepticism towards the assurances put out by our democratic political élites: the latter are disbelieved when they claim to be both unable and unwilling to penalize divergent opinions and passive resistance. Discontinuity on the level of the political system and the political élites would then correspond to strong continuity of basic political attitude on the part of the masses who are far from the centre of power and still have their roots in the period 1934/8 to 1945. Both elements appear integral to the functioning of the present social partnership.

The Second Republic

The second question to be examined by this article is as follows: What degree of continuity is to be found in the social and political system of the Second Republic? Are there not periods of change within the period 1945 to the present day which are more crucial than the period of *Anschluss* and the Second World War discussed above?

It seems indisputable that although the relative weighting of continuity and discontinuity in twentieth-century Austrian history varies according to the sector under consideration, the historical 'watershed' cannot simply be placed at the years 1938 or 1945. It is rather the case that the Second Republic in the early years after 1945 showed far stronger continuity with ongoing tendencies from the inter-war period, but also that it has stronger links with the period of the Second World War than has generally been acknowledged. Its peculiar political and social character, which markedly distinguishes it from the First Republic, did not reach full development until the fifties and sixties.

The Second Republic (as opposed to the pre-war period) is generally described as a period showing, *inter alia*, the following characteristics:

(i) stable parliamentary democracy;

(ii) social partnership;
(iii) hardly any political violence and few strikes;
(iv) high economic growth;
(v) no abrupt social changes;
(vi) staunch national consciousness;

There is no doubt that the political system of the Second Republic is characterized to a very high degree by stability. The average parliamentary term of 28 months is close to the theoretically possible upper limit and is more than three times as long as in the inter-war period, the balance of power in parliament does not seriously fluctuate, and the share of seats enjoyed by the two strongest parliamentary parties is almost always very high. The recruitment of *Nationalrat* members has been a relatively continuous process, only the period around 1966 showing any marked generation gap in parliament. Finally the Republic's constitution — taken over, as is well known, from the First Republic — has scarcely been questioned and has not been subjected to any fundamental alterations. On the other hand, even in post-war Austria the forms of government have varied considerably: there have been a 3-party government, a 'Grand Coalition', single-party governments including a minority government, and a 'Small Coalition'. These fluctuations in the political make-up of government, however, are quite normal in any well established democracy and are not a catastrophe as some Austrians would have us believe even to this day. In terms of practical politics such fluctuations are of little significance since they are underpinned by the social partnership.

The latter is well known as a highly developed model of co-operative, non-confrontational decision-making in modern Austria, dealing with most issues relating to the economic and to social policy and reaching negotiated settlements by bringing together representatives of opposing economic interests or interest groups, both sides having equal voting rights. It is based upon the opposing parties being voluntarily prepared to observe certain formal procedures and certain economic and distributional principles without the existence of any written system of rules and regulations. It is quite rightly considered to be the central socio-political institution in the Second Republic.

The social partnership is of interest in this context only as an indicator of the underlying mechanism for resolving internal conflicts, for it is striking that the most important component institution of the partnership — the Parity Commission for Prices and Wages — was created only in 1957 (on the basis of the Raab-Böhm agreement of 1956), since when it has undergone further development.

Before this, however, there had been various attempts at formulating economic and social policy co-operatively between the employees' side and the employers' side, and during the post-war reconstruction period this form of co-operation, which had received particularly strong support from the Austrian Trade Union Federation (ÖGB), was remarkably successful in boosting the economy and curbing inflation. Yet after the expiry of the fifth wages and prices agreement and recovery from the stabilization crisis of 1953 it looked for a time as if both sides of industry would revert to confrontation, regarding themselves — in accordance with tradition — as autonomous interest groups. This, after all, had happened almost everywhere else in the western world.

It is debatable whether the studies currently available on the early history of the social partnership provide justification for speaking of a break in continuity in 1957, or whether one ought rather to speak of a 'formative phase' of the social partnership up to 1957, to distinguish it from the fully developed though constantly changing system of co-operative conflict resolution which we have today. In any event it requires a very considerable historical generalization to assert that the Second Republic shows unbroken continuity in this regard.

The same is true of the widely acknowledged freedom from violence and strikes which the Second Republic has enjoyed: the late forties and the communist-inspired 'October strike' of 1950 (which could have had serious political consequences) were anything but free of violence. The socio-political devastation wrought by the Nazi dictatorship and the Second World War was not easily overcome. Moreover the scale and bitterness of the strike movements during the Second Republic's consolidation phase (up to the mid-fifties) are more reminiscent of the labour disputes of the First Republic. It was only after that point in time, indeed not until the mid-sixties, that the extremely low strike rate, so characteristic of contemporary Austrian society, became established. This is a further indication of the need for greater caution in describing the entire Second Republic as comparatively free of conflict.

Space forbids even a cursory treatment of the structural changes which took place after 1945 within society and in the area of economic development. The general conclusion that may be drawn is that in certain respects the Second Republic can be sub-divided into three phases:

1. First of all there was the reconstruction or recovery phase lasting until about the mid-fifties, marked by the immediate effects of the war and despite rapid economic growth, producing no far-

reaching changes in social structure; it was rather the case that since the world economic crisis of 1934 and in spite of all the disruptions caused by the *Anschluss* and the war, the proportions of social classes and economic sectors had remained surprisingly constant. During this phase, however, the course was set for future developments in political life and in social and economic policy. And in foreign affairs the end of this period was important in that it saw the establishment of Austria as a neutral state.

2 Next came a kind of consolidation phase, again helped by exceptionally favourable economic development but with so much inherent momentum that it became a phase of accelerated social change.

3 Then lastly, in the late sixties, and in common with many western European countries, Austria saw a distinct change in values, epitomized by such phrases as 'the silent revolution', 'post-materialism', 'post-modernity' or 'the post-industrial society'. In practice this expresses itself, for example, in lower standards of self-discipline in attitudes to achievement, greater hedonism and the adoption of a relaxed life-style, and an increased desire to participate in political and economic decision-making.

There was a 20-year delay, or so it would appear, in finally overcoming those ideologies and value systems which produced the ever-worsening conflicts of the inter-war period and caused Fascism in its different forms to spread. The present writer believes that these changes in the intellectual superstructure were essential if that historical turning point was to take place which one writer has identified as coinciding (though not exclusively) with the beginning of socialist rule in 1970. It is only in this recent past that a new national awareness among Austrians has become widespread: as has recently been pointed out, opinion polls in 1956 showed that only 49 per cent were in favour of the Austrian nation, while after 1970 the figures have been 74 to 86 per cent.

For a minority of the Austrian people (not counting the political leadership groups), 1945 represented a break in continuity as far as their search for national identity was concerned, and it is only with the Second Republic's run of political and economic successes that the new national consciousness has now come to be something taken for granted, particularly among younger generations of Austrians.

In summary, the answer to the second question addressed by this article may be expressed as follows: the Second Republic as a whole is characterized by continuity extending beyond the narrow confines of politics but at the same time shows discontinuities and changes of direction which must be duly taken into account particularly if its trends are to be extrapolated in a manner which is both cautious and prognostically useful.

Future developments

We now turn to the third question, that of the longer-term socio-historical prospects which may be seen to lie ahead for the Second Republic. It can be regarded as certain that the Republic's social development is bound up with secular processes of change variously described as 'modernization, secularization or social organization. Such longer-term patterns are also suggested by the trend of annual economic growth rates which strikingly illustrate the special position occupied by the Second Republic in the context of recent economic development. Whereas the annual economic growth rates within the area now known as Austria stood at an average of just less than 1.5 per cent between 1870 and 1913, the Austrian economy stagnated in the subsequent period of crisis up to 1950, during which the average yearly growth was only 0.2 per cent. In the 15 years which followed, the growth rate shot up on average 5.2 per cent, remaining almost as high during the period 1965 to 1980 (4.3 per cent). Austria's economy therefore shows a growth pattern which sets it apart from western European national economies and brings it rather into line with that of West Germany; in quantative terms it has even surpassed the latter during the most recent phase.

Three explanatory models for these quantative results have been advanced but here, of course, it must remain an open question which one will be corroborated by future developments. First there is the model which explains the radical change in economic development after 1945 in terms of a structural break, making the period of the Second Republic unique among periods of economic history. This argument is supported in Austria by reference to the discontinuities, outlined above, in Austria's economic and social development at the end of the Second World War. Without going into the argument in detail one may say that its assumption of a growth rate continuing at an above-average level appears ill-founded, even though the performance of the Austrian economy to date, superb by international standards, seems to support this thesis.

The second approach, known as the theory of the reconstruction period, is based upon the West German experience but can be directly applied to Austria. It states that, after short- or medium-term interruptions, the economic growth process has a longer-term tendency to revert to the norm. In the case of Austria, severely affected by the First and Second World War, the stagnation between 1913 and 1950 was later compensated for by particularly rapid growth;

this phenomenon, however, is coming to an end in the eighties and is being replaced by longer-term normal growth at a lower level.

The third explanatory model is the theory of 'Kondratieff's waves' or Schumpeter's 'long waves of economic development'. This states that industrial economic growth is not continuous but proceeds in a series of oscillations, each of about 50 years' duration. These spurts of growth are long-term reactions to technological innovations, increased investment activity, credit expansion and similar domestic economic stimuli. As yet, however, no unambiguous empirical proof of the theory has been forthcoming despite numerous considerations which appear to be in its favour. As far as Austria's long-term economic growth is concerned, this model would mean that the stagnation phase in the inter-war period (the world economic crisis) corresponds to a trough while the exceptionally favourable economic development of the Second Republic corresponds to a peak, and that the new Kondratieff cycle beginning in 1945 would have reached its turning point around 1975.

Although there is nothing in principle which makes this last-mentioned model preferable to the others, the 'long wave theory' does appear to be relevant, particularly in view of its implications for society as a whole. If one considers the grave political and social repercussions of previous periods of economic decline (the Kondratieff 'wave-troughs'), it is natural to expect similar things in the future. So it is possible to identify the great depression at the beginning of the last quarter of the nineteenth century with the second Kondratieff cycle and the inter-war crisis of the twentieth century, to some extent at least, with the down-turn phase of the third cycle. Both periods were marked by intense conflicts in the area of economic policy and by an increased use of coercive mechanisms designed to regulate industrial relations; both gave rise to a conservative backlash concerned to restore the status quo, and to radical protest movements and scapegoat ideologies such as antisemitism; in both phases democracy and civil liberties were largely curtailed, and the overall result was a tightening control over society as a whole.

Whether the diminished economic growth and alternative values of recent years (i.e. values which are no longer orientated towards quantitative growth) will prove to be a phase coinciding with a fourth Kondratieff downturn must, as already stated, remain an open question. In the context of this article a cyclical wave theory such as this is of significance in that breaks in development and changes of direction, which from a short-term perspective look like discontinuities, come to be recognizable from a higher, long-term viewpoint as historical continuity.

The reference above to a tightening of control over social processes leads on to a further (and to some extent competing) model of the longer-term historical foundations upon which the Second Republic's political and social characteristics are built. Western European and American social scientists have recently made a connection between the thorough-going organization of practically the whole political and economic sector along the lines of social partnership (as outlined above), and the concept of corporatism/neo-corporatism. In this context Austria is regarded as by no means an exceptional case but simply as a country in which the manifestations of corporatist control over politics and institutions are particularly pronounced.

In very general terms these corporatist structures may be defined as organizational forms within the political and economic sphere based upon models of society where co-operation takes place not between individuals or social classes according to their numerical size, but between interest groups or other large groups which stand in a fixed relationship of parity to each other and are consensus- rather than conflict-orientated. Variable factors include the extent of state involvement in such a mechanism for resolving social conflicts, and the degree to which — if at all — the potential antagonists are compulsorily integrated into the system.

On the one hand there have been manifestations of late feudal corporatism ever since the conservative Taafe era under the Habsburg monarchy and the semi-Fascist corporatism of the Dollfuss-Schuschnigg dictatorship, while on the other hand there have been models rather like those of Renner's wartime socialism or Otto Bauer's nationalization plans after the First World War, which reached their highest stage of development only in the neo-corporatism of the social partnership under the Second Republic. The fact that over the last 100 years and more of Austrian social history corporatism has oscillated in type between the poles of liberalism and authoritarianism may be connected — and this is put forward tentatively and merely as a preliminary hypothesis — with the above-mentioned 'long waves of economic development'. The considerable strength of corporatist structures and trends in Austria (obvious not only in the Second Republic but repeatedly in earlier periods too) would then have to be further explained by a theory of Austria pursuing her own path towards social modernization — a process analogous to the social development of Germany. It must be doubted whether this tendency — so apparent in Austria and Germany — towards a thorough-going organization of politics and the economy is the forerunner of general trends within capitalist societies. For the Austro-Marxists noted these tendencies as early as the beginning of the twentieth century, generalizing them in the theory of organized capitalism, yet since then the degree of social organization has seen repeated periods of decline, and one is bound to ask why, in a country like Austria which is relatively backward in terms of industrial capitalism, the development of capitalist society should be the furthest advanced.

In the context of such longer-term cyclical tendencies we must finally return to the development of an Austrian national consciousness, for despite the Austrians' progress towards nationhood under the Second Republic, the relationship between Austria and Germany is subject to such swings of the pendulum that the long-term perspective is far from clear. In this connection the American sociologist Peter Katzenstein has developed a model of communication theory which in Austria, unfortunately, has still not received the attention it deserves. The theory states that within a region possessing a unified culture (in this case Austria and Germany), changing intensity of political co-ordination between the two countries can be discerned. After the period 1848–70 which was marked by Austro-German conflict there came a period in which political autonomy was increasingly surrendered to the German Reich — a process which reached its climax in the efforts to secure *Anschluss* during the inter-war period. With the defeat of the Third Reich the enforced *Anschluss* was made a nonsense so that after 1945 there began another period of growing political estrangement despite the continued existence of many social and cultural links between Austria and Germany.

If this is the case, then the growth of Austrian national awareness which has received so much comment would appear to be ultimately nothing more than the nation inventing its own national tradition in the interests of political autonomy from Germany. Whether this implication is acceptable or not, Katzenstein's model is worthy of detailed re-examination, and modification if necessary, in terms of its compatibility with the 'long waves of economic growth'. At any rate it is not impossible that the periodically variable and complementary rates of growth shown by cultural communication and economic exchange of goods and services between Austria and Germany (the kind of variations which are at the heart of Katzenstein's model) may derive from the long-term fluctuations of economic development. Such a model of Austria's recent search for national identity would have the advantage of avoiding the quasi-determinism inherent in secular theories of state- and nationhood, and of encouraging alertness to the fact that when trends appear to be following an over-rigidly linear path they are quite capable of changing direction.

3 Austria's economic development 1945–85[a]

Eduard März[b]

1945 — a new beginning

Students of recent Austrian history are invariably struck by the contrast between the development of the country after World War I and after World War II. Although the first Austrian Republic (1918–38) remained economically the weakest of all the countries of Central Europe, forever on the brink of total disaster, present-day Austria can look back on thirty years of unprecedented prosperity and stability. To be sure, an important part of the explanation lies in the vastly superior climate of the international economy in the second of these two periods. However, looking back at the immediate postwar situation of Austria, one might have expected even in this more favourable external setting a rather slow and uneven recovery which would put the economy at best on a path of sluggish growth, highly vulnerable to the impact of international recessions. Thus an equally important part of the explanation must be looked for in factors internal to the history of the Second Republic.

The doctrine of nonviability — a self-fulfilling prophecy

Any attempt to identify these factors leads back to the question concerning the causes of the extremely poor performance of the Austrian economy in the interwar period. At the end of World War I the sudden dissolution of the Austro-Hungarian monarchy had left the German-speaking fragment that constituted itself Austria (originally German-Austria) in a state of complete exhaustion and disorganization, its economy cut off from its former supplies of food and raw materials and its former markets for industrial goods. Austrian industry, geared to a vast internal market and already depleted of machinery and materials by a war effort far beyond its strength, saw itself suddenly confronted by high tariff barriers

a We announce with deep sorrow that since this chapter was written Professor März has died (Eds).

b I am indebted to my late wife, Maria Szecsi, and to Hans Kernbauer for their co-operation on an earlier version of this article.

which the successor states erected to build up their own economies and to gain economic as well as political independence from their former master-nation. The desperate situation of the whole country, especially of the starving population of its oversized capital city of Vienna, has so often been described in the literature on postwar Europe that there is no need to discuss it further.

Admittedly, the task of restructuring the economy to adapt it to its new conditions of survival was a formidable one; it would have taxed to the full all the energies of a people united in national purpose and political will. Unfortunately, the Austrian people at that time were deficient in both. What had seemed the natural solution to Austria's economic problems, namely union with Germany, was vetoed by the Allies. The bourgeoisie, moreover, never became reconciled to the democratic Republic. Thus, Austria remained the state that nobody wanted, without a defined national identity and lacking a basic consensus in support of its political system.

It was in this atmosphere that the doctrine of the economic nonviability of Austria took almost universal hold over the minds of the economic and political leaders of the country. The argument was largely based on the smallness of the internal market and the lack of natural resources. The not inconsiderable assets that the country still possessed in the form of industrial capacity and a highly skilled working population were overlooked or belittled, in any case underestimated. Smallness in itself is not, of course — and never was — an obstacle to economic advancement as shown by the example of the prosperous small nations of Northern and Western Europe. But whatever the merits of the nonviability thesis may have been objectively, its psychological effects assuredly were such that it became a self-fulfilling prophecy. In fact, industrial production throughout the whole history of the First Republic barely surpassed the prewar level by a small margin in the prosperous years 1928–9, only to fall far behind in the Great Depression of the 1930s. By comparison, Germany, equally hit by the war and its disastrous aftermath, by 1938 had reached a GNP level of about 50 per cent above prewar level.

The heritage of German rule

What were the new elements in 1945 that made for such a startling difference in the speed of recovery? Certainly the devastations of World War II were, if anything, much more severe than those of World War I. This time there were the heavy direct effects of war as well as occupation reparations, since the Soviets seized what was left of machinery and equipment in their zone. Housing was in a terrible condition, about 177,000 units having been completely or partly destroyed. And once again, Austria was torn away from the larger economic area into which it had been integrated. In these respects, then, its situation was rather worse than in 1918. But there were compensating advantages.

First of all, we can note the complete reversal of the people's attitude toward the existence of Austria as an independent and democratic state. Seven years of domination by Hitler's Germany had cured the great majority of Austrians of their age-old hankering for union with 'big brother'. The 'State that nobody wanted' became almost overnight a state that almost everybody wanted. On the political level the new sense of national identity found expression in the formation of a coalition government between the leading political forces in the country — the Socialists and the People's Party. The coalition held for twenty years. This created an entirely novel psychological, political and social setting in which doubts about economic viability had no place. There developed, on the contrary, quite a lively industrial spirit hitherto foreign to tradition-bound Austrian entrepreneurs.

A second favourable factor, whose significance emerged only in the course of time, was the large industrial complex built up by Nazi Germany on Austrian territory for armaments requirements. Most important was the Hermann Goering Werke, a large iron and steel complex in Linz, an addition to Austria's older one in Styria. Further new capacities had been created in the fields of heavy chemicals, aluminium and machinery; a number of hydroelectric power plants had been built, and others had been left in various stages of completion or planning. To be sure, all of the previous forms of these works had been destroyed in the war and denuded of their equipment; most had not even been finished by the Germans. Hence, it is not surprising that many voices were raised in favour of liquidating the entire complex which seemed so superfluous to Austrian needs and which called for investments far exceeding the needs of the impoverished country. In spite of these weighty arguments, it was immediately decided to rebuild these works and to restructure the Austrian economy around a greatly enlarged basis of heavy industry. Given the uncertain prospects of European recovery at the time, this decision took some courage. As it turned out, the new capacities were well adapted to the needs of Austria's expanding postwar economy, especially in the period of reconstruction but also long after that. As the almost unlimited demand of world markets for steel and steel products lasted, they served as paçemakers of export growth and industrial modernization. In following this ambitious course Austria benefited not so much by the fragmentary remainders of physical plant it had inherited as from a certain transfer of technology and know-how that had taken place during the German occupation. Thus it is perhaps no accident that its most successful innovation, the *LD* steel-making process (named after the steel centres at Linz and Donawitz), which has found world-wide application, originated in the newly built VÖEST mills (*Vereinigte Österreichische Eisen- und Stahlwerke*), successor to the Hermann Goering Werke.

The phase of reconstruction

The reconstruction of the shattered economy after 1945 proceeded at a fast pace, not only compared with the past but also by any absolute standard. In 1946 the indexes of industrial and agricultural production stood at less than half those of prewar (1937), and Austria was once more, according to American observers, the country with the lowest standard of nutrition in Europe. Only three years later the 1937 level was reached; five years after that the peak level of the interwar period (1929) was surpassed. Thus it can be said that by 1952 the reconstruction period was ended; a new phase of development was about to begin.

The Marshall Plan

Unquestionably the Marshall Plan was an essential factor in this economic miracle. There is no need to enter here into the history and motivation of this remarkable enterprise which became known by its initials–ERP (European Recovery Programme). Considering Austria's singular position as a country committed to the West but still in part occupied by Soviet troops, its aid requirements clearly had high political priority for the USA. Even before the Marshall Plan went into effect, recognition of Austria as a liberated country had made it eligible for United Nations Relief and Rehabilitation Administration (UNRRA) aid which set in at the end of 1945 and consisted mostly of food-stuffs. From then on aid was given under various titles until in 1948 the ERP was set up. Altogether, under all programmes, Austria received some 1.6 billion dollars of Allied aid (1.4 billion from the USA). By far the most important economic effects resulted from the so-called direct aid part of the programme, which was principally utilized to create a revolving fund for the purpose of supplying cheap credit to Austrian enterprises. A total of 678 million dollars was spent for this purpose. The system worked as follows: the goods that the US sent as free gifts were sold to the Austrian public at relatively moderate prices. The revenue from these sales was paid into a special account, the counterpart account, from which credits flowed back into the economy, mostly for investment purposes, at subsidized interest rates varying between 3 and 5 per cent according to the priority rating of the project. Although the US authorities retained final control over the utilization of the counterpart credits, basic policy goals were worked out in agreement with Austrian plans. When the Marshall Plan wound up in 1952, the remaining assets in the counterpart account were turned over to the Austrian government. The ERP fund remained an important, though with the progress in inflation a necessarily dwindling, source of investment finance throughout the 1950s. Another significant form of aid — indirect aid to the tune of 284 million dollars — served to cover deficits in the balance of trade, first on a bilateral, and later on a multilateral, basis in the framework of the European Payments Union (EPU).

In the first two years of ERP (1947–8) the bulk of US aid was used to feed a hungry population and to provide coal and other essentials for survival. Starting in 1950 the major effort could be diverted to capital investment in industry, agriculture, and the country's infrastructure. Of the 11 billion Austrian schillings counterpart credits pumped into the economy until 1953, roughly 3 billions went into coal mining and power plants, 4 billions were devoted to industrial investment, 1.6 billions to agriculture, while the rest was expended on the reconstruction of the transportation and communications systems. Over the whole period this source of finance accounted for roughly 30 per cent of net, and 20 per cent of gross investment.

The Nationalization Acts

Another big problem Austria was confronted with in 1945 was the fate of the huge bulk of former German property, comprising not only the aforementioned new industries but also a number of older Austrian enterprises that had been transferred after 1938 to German owners. There were no legal claimants to this property, nor was private domestic capital available to acquire these assets and to get production going. Transfer to foreign ownership was impossible for political reasons even if there had been serious bidders. The problem was further complicated by the fact that the Soviet Union laid claim to all German property under the title of war reparations. In its own occupation zone it had already seized the enterprises falling into this category and established its own administrative authority (USIA). In the Allied zones the claim was not recognized, but there was no certainty about the future settlement of the whole reparations complex. In view of all these open questions, the political parties quickly reached agreement on the only sensible solution — nationalization. Undoubtedly the impulses behind this extraordinary political act were mixed. In the Socialist Party, though it was by no means of a revolutionary bent, ideological reasons strongly supported the practical considerations involved. And even in conservative circles there was widespread scepticism about the chances of revival of the old capitalist order. But the decisive factor was certainly the pressure of the singular circumstances outlined above. The hope of foiling the Russian designs by this expedient of course played a major role.

The Nationalization Acts of 1946 and 1947 transferred huge industrial holdings to the Republic. They covered the extractive industries (coal, iron, ore, oil, aluminium), with the sole but significant exceptions of American- and French-owned magnesite mines, practically the entire steel industry, and most of the large enterprises in the field of machinery, chemicals, and electrical equipment. At the same time the three largest banks in the country, which in turn held considerable industrial assets, were nationalized. Full public property was also established in the field of electric power generation. Since before the war all major public utilities (railroads, gas, communications, etc.) had been run by the state or the municipalities, Austria emerged after the war as the country with the largest public economic sector in the Western world. This fact has decisively shaped its socio-political structure. However, in the course of time, heavy foreign investment occurred which resulted in the creation of an industrial establishment of comparable size by multinational (especially German) concerns, primarily active in more modern, brain-intensive fields such as electronics, chemicals, and machinery.

The reconstruction period also saw the first — though short-lived — experiment in large-scale economic planning on the basis of an investment programme covering the allocation of ERP funds as well as all other public investment. In this way the main structural decisions were implemented, along with nationalization. But in the degree to which private investment strengthened and the nationalized enterprises were able to finance themselves, largely by internal accumulation, the economics of the market prevailed over the concept of planning. Even so, the sheer volume of public ownership and investment made the presence of the state in the economy felt more ubiquitously than in countries with a purer form of capitalism. Altogether, one may characterize the resulting institutional framework as that of a 'mixed economy' with rather strong elements of state intervention on both the macro- and the micro levels.

Economic achievement 1950–85

Inflation and stabilization

As could be expected, the most threatening danger to the economy in the immediate postwar period was inflation with the spectre of a runaway inflation like that of 1920–2 ever present. The strict price and wage controls imposed immediately after the war necessarily broke down as huge price differentials developed between rationed and black-market goods, leading inevitably to upward pressure on wages. The beginnings of a wage-price spiral were clearly visible. By July 1947 even the official price index (including legally fixed prices) stood at 275 on the basis of 1945. This provided the setting for another novel experiment made possible through the close co-operation of the highly centralized organizations of trade unions and employers — the Austrian Trade Union Federation (*Österreichischer Gewerkschaftsbund*) and the Federal Chamber of the Economy (*Bundeskammer der gewerblichen Wirtschaft*). In 1947 the first of five wage-and-price pacts was concluded between the representatives of these bodies with the concurrence of the government. The agreements covered prices of all essential goods and provided for across-the-board flat wage and pension increases, and aimed at controlling inflation while securing at least minimum wage standards. This was the first trial run of the procedures that later came to be known as 'social partnership'.

Although some initial success could be registered after each of these pacts, it was soon recognized that the rising pressure on costs could not be effectively dealt with by voluntary regulation alone. In 1951–2 a harsher course was decided upon; stabilization was enforced by radical fiscal and monetary restrictions with the unavoidable sequel of a severe recession. In 1953 the rapid recovery of the economy came to a halt and the rate of unemployment rose to almost 9 per cent, the highest figure in all of postwar history. However, though its impact was shocking, the stabilization crisis was to be overcome fairly rapidly. Though the price index had already passed the 800 mark, the threat of a breakdown of the monetary system had been removed, and the Austrian economy was launched upon a course of stable growth and high employment for the next two decades.

Top place in the growth race

As shown in Tables 3.1 to 3.3 and Appendices D1, D4–7, Austria was able to maintain a consistently high rate of growth. From 1950 to 1960 the Gross National Product (GNP) increased on average

Table 3.1 Average growth rates (%) — selected periods 1950–85

	1950–9	1960–9	1970–9	1980–5
Gross Domestic Product	6.0	4.9	4.3	1.9
Industrial production	7.2[a]	5.6	4.4	1.9
Real wages (all employed persons)	4.7[b]	5.2	3.6	0.6
Exports	9.3[b]	9.0	7.6	8.5

Source: Österreichisches Statistisches Zentralamt.
Notes: [a] 1951–1959.
[b] 1954–1959.

Table 3.2 International comparison of real growth rates (per cent)

	1955–9	1960–9	1970–9	1980–7
Austria	5.6	4.9	4.3	1.8
Germany (FRG)	7.1	5.0	3.2	1.7
Sweden	3.2	4.4	2.1	1.8
Netherlands	3.6	5.4	3.5	2.8
United Kingdom	2.2	3.0	2.0	1.5
USA	3.3	4.1	2.8	2.0
OECD (world)	3.9	5.1	3.5	1.6

Source: OECD.

by 6 per cent annually; in the following decade by 4.7 per cent, and from 1970 to 1979 by 4.3 per cent. Since population growth was slight, per capita figures were almost correspondingly great. In the same periods industrial production increased by 7.2, 5.6, and 4.4 per cent respectively and real wages have by and large kept pace with the growth of productivity so as to leave the relative shares between wages and profits constant in the long run.

Even though Austrian development has considerably slowed down since 1979, it still compares quite favourably with most OECD countries, and Austria occupies a top place in the international growth league, slightly ahead of Germany. Consequently, the economic distance between Austria and the historically richer

Table 3.3 Per capita Gross National Product (in dollars) — the relative position of Austria

	1955	1970	1985
Austria	100	100	100
Germany (FRG)	133	128	113
Switzerland	200	162	121
Sweden	171	150	122
Netherlands	143	123	98
Belgium	131	115	103
United Kingdom	155	112	95
OECD (Europe)	112	101	87
USA	225	155	130
Japan	52	96	105
OECD (world)	137	117	103

Source: OECD.

countries has drastically diminished although the per capita income (8,805 dollars in 1985) today is still well below that of the very rich countries like Sweden and Switzerland.

The improvement compared with the pre-war era is impressive. Thus, for instance, the per capita income of pre-war Germany (measured in dollars) was two and a half times as great as that of Austria before the German occupation. Today the difference between Austria and the Federal Republic of Germany has shrunk to about 13–15 per cent. Since Federal Germany has overtaken the USA by a small margin, about the same or even a slightly better relation obtains now between Austria and the USA whose productive powers before the war generated an income 4.5 times greater than that of Austria.

Admittedly, the dollar standard in international income comparison has lost some of its validity in recent years on account of the violent fluctuations in exchange rates, but these do not necessarily reflect comparable shifts in real terms. But living standards depend not only on current income alone but also on the accumulated wealth of households in the past. Thus, for instance, housing conditions in Austria are still not quite comparable with those of the advanced western nations. But even when all that is taken into account, a solid advance in Austria's position cannot be denied. Comparisons in terms of purchasing power are always difficult and debatable, but even where they are attempted, they

Table 3.4 Total employment in Austria by broad economic sector — 1934–83

	1934	1960	1971	1983
Agriculture	37.1	22.6	13.5	8.7
Industry	32.1	41.7	42.3	37.5
Services	30.8	35.7	44.2	53.8

Sources: OECD, Historical Statistics 1960–1983, Paris 1985; OECD, Observer 1986.

show at least as good a picture, or even a better one, than those expressed in dollars.

Structural change

Growth of the order of magnitude we are considering implies rapid structural change between the agricultural, manufacturing and service sectors, particularly the various branches of the last two. Sectoral change, following the well-known laws of Fourastié and Colin Clark, results primarily from a large-scale net shift of the labour force from agriculture to services, in which the manufacturing sector increases only moderately. In Austria in the whole post-war period the share of agriculture in the total labour force (including self-employed) decreased from its high starting point of 32 per cent in 1950 to 8.7 per cent in 1983, a figure only slightly above that of Switzerland, which has similar natural conditions for agriculture. Not less than half of this shift occurred after 1970, a fact that points up vividly the special dynamism of the economy in this short period. Since a low agricultural share of employment generally counts as one of the most important indicators of economic development, it may be said that in Austria a full industrial maturity has been reached as Table 3.4 indicates (see also Appendix D3).

The increase in agricultural productivity has been sufficient not only to offset the decline in labour input but to meet fully the rising internal demand and to produce, beyond that, sizable surpluses of milk and cereals. The differential between agricultural and industrial incomes has remained higher, however, than in most fully developed countries. Whether the system of agricultural subsidies plus controlled prices — which is practised in Austria as in most other Western countries — has held back the incomes of this sector or merely failed to raise them sufficiently is a moot question. (At present farmers in the high Alpine regions receive some support, not only on economic grounds but also for reasons of preserving the natural environment.)

Employment in manufacturing fell slightly between 1950 and 1983, fluctuating somewhat with the cyclical movement. Accordingly, the service sector expanded rapidly, from 30 to 53.8 per cent in the same period. Owing mainly to flourishing tourism and the growth of public services of all kinds, this sector has been able to absorb the labour set free in slack times by industry up to the beginning of the 1980s. Its high elasticity of demand for labour has also been an important factor in maintaining employment in times of sudden inflows into the labour market owing to demographic reasons. Fears expressed by some economists in the mid-1960s, when industrial employment decreased for several years, that the shift to the service sector indicated a 'premature aging' of the economy implying a permanent weakening of its industrial backbone, were not borne out by later developments.

High investment and high employment

In view of a practically stable population, high investment was required to sustain growth. Gross investment rose steadily throughout the 1950s to reach 26 per cent of GNP in 1960. It then remained remarkably constant through the entire decade. In the 1970s there was a significant upward push, resulting in an average of 28.4 per cent for the years 1970–9. Among the Western countries, only Norway and Japan have had higher investment rates. (See Appendix D8.) A further characteristic feature is the high share of public investment. Adding together direct public investment and investment in nationalized industries, the public share has been estimated to amount to somewhat less than 50 per cent of total gross investment. This also explains the steadiness of the investment rate which was hardly affected by cyclical swings; the impact of cycles, however, has been much more marked on industrial investment taken by itself. In recent years the rate of investment has diminished although it still remains remarkably high compared with other OECD countries, as Table 3.5 indicates (see also Appendix D8).

There is a certain correspondence between the trend of employment and that of investment. The unemployment rate, which had been over 6 per cent in the first half of the 1950s, was down to 2.9 per cent by 1960 and stayed below 3 per cent throughout the decade; in the 1970s it was below 2 per cent in all years up to 1980. At the same time the number of wage earners rose from around 2 million (1955) to 2.7 million. The point of full employment was reached in 1960–1; from then on, labour shortages made themselves felt increasingly as a restraint on growth. In this situation trade

Table 3.5 Investment rates as a percentage of GNP

	1950–9	1960–9	1970–9	1980–4
Austria	20.5	26.2	28.4	23.5
Germany (FRG)	22.3	24.0	22.5	21.2
Sweden	18.8	21.8	20.8	19.0
United Kingdom	13.5	19.4	19.7	16.9

Source: OECD.

Table 3.6 Labour market trends — numbers employed and percentage unemployed (selected years)

	1955	1960	1973	1978	1985
Employees (1,000)	2,074	2,282	2,608	2,758	2,760
Foreign workers (1,000)			227	177	140
Rate of unemployment (%)	5.4	3.4	1.2	2.1	4.8

Source: Hauptverband der österreichischen Sozialversicherungsträger and Bundesministerium für soziale Verwaltung.

union resistance to the inflow of foreign workers weakened, and ever larger contingents of foreigners, mostly Yugoslavs and Turks, were admitted into the country. Their number reached its absolute and relative peak in 1973 standing at 227,000 or 8.7 per cent of the employed labour force. As everywhere else, foreign workers filled the least attractive jobs in heavy construction, unskilled factory work, and services for tourism (see Table 3.6).

This brief account of the overall economic performance of Austria will be rounded off with a few words about cyclical movements. In general, with the one significant exception mentioned below, business cycles in Austria followed rather closely the European pattern, being of short duration and leading only to a deceleration of growth without marked employment effects. Although the recession of 1957–8 following the boom of the mid-1950s was quickly overcome, leading to another high in 1960, the period between the two following recessions of 1962 and 1967 was one of sluggish growth accompanied by high inflation. The malaise in the first place affected industrial investment and exports, causing a great deal of pessimism concerning the future prospects of the economy. The fear of chronic stagflation was more widespread among experts and businessmen. But in retrospect there was a temporary maladaptation of the industrial structure to the rapid changes in demand that were taking place in the course of the increasing integration of the European and world economies. This could be identified as the root cause of the trough in the growth curve. Its dark forebodings were soon refuted by the course of events. From 1968 to well into 1974, the country experienced the longest boom in its history, bypassing the general recession of 1971–2 which, though not especially severe, was felt in most European countries. In these two years Austria registered growth rates of 5.6 and 6.0 per cent, compared with 3.2 and 3.7 per cent in Germany, its most important trade partner. To the surprise of all, it was possible for the first time to break the link between the Austrian economy and international cyclical movements. This 'miracle', however, could not be repeated in the oil-shock crisis of the mid-1970s. But before we go into the story of these critical years, we will deal briefly with the problem of European integration as it affected Austria.

Austria and European integration

Integration was easily the most widely discussed issue confronting the country in the 1950s and 1960s. This is hardly surprising in a small country with a foreign trade and services share amounting to roughly 40 per cent of its social product. For an industry traditionally accustomed to high protective tariff barriers, the transition to an open economy was certainly fraught with danger. But the risk had to be taken if Austria did not want to forego participating in the rapid progress of the international division of labour. At an early stage the first steps toward liberalization had to be taken in compliance with general international treaties (GATT and OECD). But the real problem arose when two integration blocks, EFTA and the Common Market (EEC), were forming in Europe.

Since the countries of the Common Market accounted for the bulk of Austria's foreign trade (roughly 60 per cent of imports and 50 per cent of exports), a strong export interest was ranged on the side of those favouring association with this bloc. Producers for the domestic market were just as naturally on the other side of the fence. Moreover, there were important political aspects to the matter. On many sides fears of German domination over the Austrian economy amounting to a 'cold *Anschluss*' were expressed. Such a development would, it was feared, jeopardize the delicate balance of Austria's position between East and West based on the State Treaty of 1955. In this dilemma a dilatory course was chosen. In

1959 Austria joined EFTA whose member countries at that time accounted for only 12–13 per cent of its foreign trade. However, with the beginning of negotiations between Great Britain and the EEC, EFTA soon found itself in a state of impending dissolution, and the trend toward an all-European integrated market became irresistible. Thus Austria too approached the EEC in the early 1960s seeking a special arrangement compatible with its neutral status. After a whole decade of difficult negotiations, agreement was finally reached in 1972, providing for a gradual lowering of tariff barriers to zero. The treaty covered generally manufactured goods with the exception of a few 'sensitive goods' for which the transition period was extended. (Later, provisions for some agricultural products were added, but Austria remained outside the EEC Agricultural Market.)

The final step in the integration process, opening Austrian markets to the competition of the strongest industrial powers in Europe, luckily fell into the period of the 'long boom'. The structural difficulties that had caused so much concern in the mid-1960s were quickly overcome, or at any rate overcompensated for, in the climate of a strong export-led expansion. To be sure, imports grew even faster, leading in the late 1970s to a large deficit in the foreign balance. But this development had — as we shall see presently — specific causes not directly connected with free trade.

Integration certainly speeded up the modernization of industrial and export structure which had been taking place slowly in the 1960s. Thus the share of higher-order industrial goods in Austrian exports — machinery, industrial equipment, and finished consumer goods — rose from 18 per cent (1955) to 45 per cent (1985), accompanied by a corresponding decline of the share of raw materials and semi-finished goods from 76 to 39 per cent in the same period. There were also marked changes in the regional distribution of exports reflecting the two-step integration process. Whereas in the EFTA period the export share of this region more than doubled (from 13 to 29 per cent), it fell again after 1973. The share of the Common Market countries moved in reverse order, first falling sharply (from 49 to 39 per cent) and then recovering very markedly. It should be noted that exports to the Eastern countries, always considered of great importance, were maintained more or less throughout at the same level, of about 11–15 per cent.

Main features of economic policy

The basic problem of postwar economic management was of course the same in Austria as anywhere else in the Western world, namely the trade-off between employment, inflation, and the balance of payments — the famous 'magic triangle'. Creeping inflation began soon after the stabilization crisis of 1953 and became a matter of principal concern in the 1960s, when the inflation rate rose higher, threatening to surpass that of Austria's major trade partners. To cope with this problem, fiscal and monetary restrictions were imposed from time to time with the usual doubtful effects. Yet, though the emphasis varied between different periods and governments, on the whole the fear of inflation never dominated economic policy in Austria as much as it did, say, in Germany or the USA.

Priority for full employment

If it is true, as has been sometimes said, that German inflation fears can be traced back to the traumatic experience of the galloping inflation of the early 1920s, in Austrian psychology the trauma of the enormous unemployment of the 1930s seems to have played an even larger part. However that may be, it is a fair generalization to say that Austrian economic policy has consistently given priority to full employment over price stability, whatever the fashionable doctrines of the moment may have been. The socialist government, in power since 1970, explicitly adheres to this principle as a keystone of its entire programme. In keeping with this Keynesian bias of policy, there has also generally been a marked preference for fiscal over monetary instruments of counter-cyclical steering. Among Austrian economists too, especially among those acting as advisers to the government, Keynesianism has retained a stronger hold in the face of the monetarist counter-attack than in most other countries.

The success of this policy hinged ultimately on the support it received from the institutions of social partnership that had been established on a permanent basis in the late 1950s. Suffice it to point out the importance of the social climate engendered by this unique form of consensual conflict settlement for keeping inflationary cost rises in check without resorting to the remedy of unemployment. Specific labour market policies, such as subsidies for retraining and relocating workers set free by the closing down of operations in non-profitable enterprises or branches of production, have also been applied fairly extensively. But measures of this type, although useful in raising the mobility of labour, cannot affect the level of employment significantly.

Crisis management since 1974

In coming to the end of this brief survey, special treatment must be given to the difficult period that set in with the world-wide recession in the aftermath of the oil shock and the breakdown of the Bretton Woods system. The fact that Austria managed to maintain high employment as well as relative price stability in these years, which elsewhere were haunted by rising unemployment and/or inflation, has aroused a great deal of international attention. The initial shock hit Austria no less severely than other countries, though with a certain delay. In 1974 the inflation rate rose to 9.5 per cent, still below the OECD average of 13.5 per cent but uncomfortably high. Belying all forecasts of continuing prosperity, the boom came to an abrupt end; 1975 brought a negative growth rate for the first time since 1953 causing an unexpected jump in the budget deficit. Yet, in spite of the simultaneous fiscal and inflation problems, the socialist government decided on a course of further deficit spending. To cope with the threat of being drawn into the international inflationary trend, it was decided to maintain the exchange rate of the schilling tied to the German mark, regardless of mounting pressure from exporters calling for devaluation and without paying heed to the well-meaning advice of international authorities. This was a risky policy which needed full trade-union backing on the wage front. The government could rely more surely on receiving this backing, since the old habits of social partnership were now reinforced by the political loyalty of the unions to the socialist leadership — an experience radically different from that of the British Labour Government in the same period. Thus the rate of wage increases was brought down successively along with the falling inflation rate, and there were only slight or no real wage gains for a few years. As a result, Austria became the most stable country after Germany and Switzerland, with an inflation rate of only 3.2 per cent in 1985, compared with the OECD average of 4.5 per cent. At the same time employment was kept high, not only by fiscal demand management and public investment but also by selective supports of various kinds. For this purpose subsidies to enterprises in temporary difficulties were combined with the more generous use of facilities provided under the Labour Market Act (retraining of labour). In the Nationalized Industries redundant labour was kept on temporarily, especially to avoid dismissals in the steel industry during the international steel slump. Also some export of unemployment took place as the number of foreign workers was reduced so as to diminish their share in the total labour force from over 8 to about 5.5 per cent. But these were only supplementary remedies which would have been exhausted quickly if the overall strategy had not been, on the whole, highly successful — a fact the more remarkable in view of the specially strong influx of young people into the labour market in this period.

On the other side of the balance sheet the price of this strategy cannot be ignored. From 1972 to 1985 the budget deficit increased in nominal terms from 8 billion to 92 billion AS (Austrian schillings), in relative terms from a little over 7 to nearly 20 per cent of total expenditure. The national debt rose, even so, to only about 526 billion AS, a still fairly moderate amount compared to that of many other countries. But the psychological effects of the steep rise in the deficit, together with the growing load of servicing the debt, set limits to further fiscal expansion. To reduce the deficit — or, at any rate, to prevent its further increase — became imperative. Another phenomenon darkening the horizon in the mid-1970s was the unfavourable development of the balance of trade and invisibles (balance on current account) in spite of a steady rise in tourism and consistently high export gains. This was partly a direct consequence of prosperity, since Austrian consumers tend to spend a disproportionate part of rising incomes on imported goods, especially motor cars. In part, of course, the rising oil bill added to the trouble. In 1977 the deficit reached 35 billion AS. Though it fell considerably in the two following years to 9 and 14 billion respectively, the existence of a long-run structural problem had to be faced. Thus another factor restraining expansive policies came into the picture.

Up to the early eighties, these difficulties could be kept within manageable bounds by various expedients. After this however, the limits of the special 'Austro-Keynesian' practice of crisis management became apparent. A small country with such a high degree of dependence on its foreign trade cannot, of course, remain an island of stability in an unstable world.

Problems and perspectives

The difficulties indicated above arise not only on a technical plane. The rapid changes the world has undergone in the last decade have everywhere raised questions outside the traditional concerns of economists and economic policy makers, whether Keynesian, monetarist, or any other. It is neither possible nor necessary to list here in detail all these new issues that bedevil the governments of the Western world, which are ever more baffling. It suffices to point to the international debt problem, to the growing awareness of environmental restraints, and the increasing political instability in many parts of the world. All of these factors tend to reinforce the stagnation tendencies that, for a variety of economic reasons, seem to have made their appearance on the international scene since 1973. Thus, according to almost unanimous expert opinion, the Western world must prepare for an extended period of slow growth. From these deeper-lying roots of the present social and economic problems Austria is not and cannot be exempt.

Further problems of industrial structure will appear with the accelerating shift of simpler manufacturing processes from Western countries to those of the Third World — already well under way. In spite of the great progress made in the past in the modernization of industry, Austria still has too large a sector of traditional manufactures, too small a basis in modern electronics and other 'brain-intensive' products. Here the consequences of longstanding neglect of research and development — notwithstanding considerable efforts in this direction in the recent past — will make themselves increasingly felt, as much as the persistent risk aversion of Austrian entrepreneurs. Again, the world-wide crisis in the iron and steel sector has severely affected the nationalized branches of Austrian industry.

One of the most difficult hurdles in the transition to slower growth, which seems in any case unavoidable, will probably arise in the social and political sphere. This economic readjustment will necessarily raise issues of income distribution which will put a severe strain on the hitherto smoothly functioning instruments of conflict regulation. As long as the demands of all groups could be satisfied more or less proportionately out of the increase in social product, distributive shares remained — more or less — constant. Dissatisfaction with the existing income distribution never reached a high pitch. This condition may change when the rising expectations of the various social groups, in view of social considerations and the need for public services on a growing scale, can no longer be met in the same measure. Redistribution policies in taking effect are bound to sharpen the edge of social conflict. Whether the problem-solving capacity of the present institutional system of Austria, with its built-in mechanisms of flexibility, will be adequate to these new challenges only time will tell. Evaluation of its past performance perhaps allows some hope that the Austrian model will prove workable even under the highly unpropitious conditions prevailing on the international economic scene in the mid-1980s.

PART II
THE POLITICAL SYSTEM

4 The peculiarities of politics in Austria: the constitution, federalism, parliamentary and social democracy

Anton Pelinka

The constitutional framework

The Federal Constitution Act (*Bundesverfassungsgesetz*) of 1920, supplemented by a major constitutional amendment in 1929 and by numerous further amendments, is the legal basis of the political system in Austria. The 1920/29 Constitution combines parliamentary and presidential elements, so that in terms of constitutional law Austria's political system is not unlike that of the Weimar Republic and the Fifth French Republic — a mixed system similar in many ways to the British parliamentary model and in numerous other ways to the US presidential model.

The presidential component is seen in the separate, direct democratic processes of electing both the Federal President and the National Assembly (*Nationalrat*). The President is directly elected by the people for a period of 6 years and may be re-elected once only. By a separate process the National Assembly, the Lower House of Parliament, is elected by the people for a period of 4 years, though the parliamentary term may be shortened by dissolution. This means that two organs of the constitution, both of which can lay basic claim to the same democratic legitimacy, appear to exist immediately side by side. In this respect Austria's Constitution at first sight resembles that of a presidential system. A closer look, however, modifies this impression: the President is not the head of government, rather he appoints a Federal Chancellor and, at the latter's recommendation, the other members of the government (the Vice-Chancellor, the ministers, and the state secretaries). He is also empowered to dismiss the government or individual members of it. In this way the government would appear at any rate to be subject to the political will of the President.

This dependence of the government upon the President is substantially qualified however, by the fact that the government — though not the President — is politically responsible to the National Assembly. That is to say the Assembly, by a simple majority decision, can bring down either the entire government or individual members of it by means of a vote of no confidence. Hence the government is in a position of two-fold dependence: not only upon the political will of the President but also upon that of the majority in the National Assembly.

The unification of powers enshrined in the parliamentary component of the constitution proves in practice to be stronger than the separation of powers inherent in its presidential component, for it has been normal since 1929, and particularly since 1945, for the President to respect the parliamentary majority's wishes, that is, he appoints as Chancellor the parliamentary nominee for the office and then accepts the Chancellor's recommendations as to other government appointments. The composition of the government is therefore determined not by the President's choice but indirectly by that of the National Assembly. Furthermore frequent use is made of the Assembly's right of self-dissolution which similarly emphasizes the unification of powers inherent in parliament at the expense of the presidential separation of powers.

Ultimately the political system is one which is unambiguously parliamentarian but which has certain formal presidential elements. In practice the President approximates much less to the President of the USA and much more to the British monarch: his main function is to perform official duties; he is an essential part of Austria's political symbolism and lends dignity to the constitution. Effective political power, on the other hand, is held by the government and the majority in the National Assembly interacting in parliament, this being fully consistent with the 'Chancellor and Cabinet' principle which is typical of parliamentary systems.

The separation of powers, largely negated by the relationship which exists between the legislature (parliament) and the executive (President and government), is nevertheless clearly operative in the relationship between these two powers on the one hand and the judiciary on the other hand. The Austrian judiciary, by virtue of constitutional guarantees and particularly by virtue of its right to recruit its own membership, is politically independent in keeping with the traditions of constitutional states. This applies to the individual sections of the judiciary in varying degrees, however: the lower judiciary headed by the Supreme Court, and the Administrative Court as part of the higher judiciary, themselves recruit the members of the judicial Bench, whose appointment by the Federal President on the recommendation of the Minister of Justice is purely a formality; the third principal court of justice is the Constitutional Court (also part of the higher judiciary) and this, because of its potentially great political significance, is much more closely tied to the two other powers.

In terms of formal procedure, the members of the Constitutional Court — which decides in matters of constitutional conflict — are appointed by the Federal President, partly upon the recommendation of the government and partly upon the recommendation of both Houses of Parliament. In practice, however, an arrangement has developed between the political parties whereby some of the judges in the Constitutional Court are informally recommended by the Socialist Party (SPÖ) and the others by the Austrian People's Party (ÖVP). In this way the SPÖ and the ÖVP control the composition of the Constitutional Court, thereby ensuring that it does not become an instrument of biased constitutional interpretation. On the other hand this also ensures that the judgements handed down by the court are very guarded and hence not very political. The Austrian Constitutional Court is an example of the fact that a court of justice, through being politicized, ultimately becomes de-politicized.

The Federal Constitution Act declares Austria to be a federal state. The powers of the state are divided between the federal state and the nine provinces. Compared with the federalism of other countries that of Austria is not very highly developed: only two of the three powers (legislature and executive) are divided between the federal state and the provinces, the latter having their own parliaments (*Landtage*) and governments, but no courts of law under their authority since the judicial system is exclusively a matter for the federal state.

Moreover, the Federal Constitution Act allots areas of competence to the provinces (Länder), particularly in the political sphere. This is admittedly qualified by the fact that the provinces and their administrators also act in the interests of the federal state ('indirect federal administration' or *mittelbare Bundesverwaltung*), so that in this area the provinces indirectly do carry more weight. Nevertheless Austrian federalism may be regarded as under-developed, and Austria itself as a federal state with strong centralizing tendencies.

The real political significance of Austrian federalism, however, lies in its counterbalancing effects. Since the nine provinces are politically less evenly balanced than the federal state, various regional strongholds have developed which ensure that in certain provinces one of the major parties is clearly dominant, irrespective of which major party is in power at federal level. Thus during the Second Republic the provinces of Lower Austria, Upper Austria, Salzburg, Tyrol, Vorarlberg and Styria have established themselves as ÖVP strongholds and hence as a counterweight to socialist federal governments, while the provinces of Vienna, Carinthia and Burgenland since 1964 have been a potential socialist counterweight to ÖVP-led federal governments.

This counterbalancing function is not, however, what federalism was originally designed for. The front line of conflict lies not between the federal state and the provinces but between the major parties, the SPÖ and the ÖVP — federal state and provinces being merely the constitutionally provided levels at which this conflict may be peaceably carried on.

This is seen clearly from the example of the *Bundesrat* or Federal Assembly, the Upper House of the Austrian parliament. According to the constitution the *Bundesrat* has the task of representing the interests of the provinces in relation to the federal state. Its members are not elected directly by the people but are appointed indirectly by the provincial parliaments (*Landtage*). But the *Bundesrat* has little real significance for several reasons:

a) the federal government is politically answerable to the *Nationalrat* alone, but not to the *Bundesrat*; hence party-political majorities are of secondary importance in the *Bundesrat*;
b) the *Bundesrat* may not exercise more than once its right of suspensive veto against any legislative proposal from the *Nationalrat*; hence on any contentious issue the *Nationalrat* can always prevail;
c) the members of the *Bundesrat* collaborate not according to provinces (*Länder*) but along party lines; hence in actual fact the *Bundesrat* presents the same aspect as the *Nationalrat*: both Houses of Parliament are models of the kind of parliamentary system which exists within a state with strongly competing political parties.

The parliamentary system in Austria

The parliamentary system was a late development in Austria. Only from 1867 onwards is it possible to speak of an Austrian parliamentary system, and until 1918 this was half-hearted since under the Austrian monarchy the government was politically responsible to the Emperor alone and not to parliament (the *Reichsrat*). Furthermore, in practice, the emperor and his government could circumvent the legislative authority of parliament by means of emergency decrees.

It was not until 1918 that the Austrian parliament was given those areas of competence which are essential for a modern parliament: legislation and control in terms of the government being politically responsible to the parliamentary majority. However, even this authentic if late parliamentary system had its influence diluted — by the parties and the discipline they demanded.

The Federal Constitution Act of 1920 and the authentic parliamentary system enshrined in it were the result of a compromise between the major parties. Being more deeply embedded in Austrian society than parliamentarianism, the parties dominated parliament from the outset through their strong discipline. Even today it is a foregone conclusion that the party parliamentary groups in the *Nationalrat* and the *Bundesrat* will always be unanimous. This considerably reduces the significance of the individual member, and means that parliament is seen as a forum where debates arising within the 'party state' are carried on.

Another factor which serves to weaken the role of parliament is the importance of extra-parliamentary decision-making. As in other parliamentary systems, e.g. Britain, the initiative behind legislation lies almost exclusively with the government. Most laws are issued by the government as bills for detailed examination in the process of which essential interests — those of the major economic interest groups, of the provinces (and hence also of the opposition) — are already canvassed before parliament itself officially receives the bill. In most cases therefore the political outcome of a bill is already decided before the relevant committee of the *Nationalrat* can even begin to consider it. The strong party discipline then further ensures that the parliamentary majority, which is closely associated with the government, will approve the bill with scarcely any difficulty.

The parliamentary system of present-day Austria is therefore marked by the following characteristics:

a) the importance of extra-parliamentary decision-making in the legislative process. The political course which legislation will take is largely mapped out within the government or by arrangement between the government and other interests (the opposition);
b) the 'party state' system. Strong party discipline ensures that parliamentary decision-making processes are controlled by the parties' central offices or by the government;
c) the importance of interest groups. The close interaction between the parties and the economic interest groups, and the high status enjoyed by the social partnership, particularly at the extra-parliamentary stage of legislation, ensures that interest groups bring strong influence to bear upon Parliament.

These characteristics of the parliamentary system are strengthened still further by the electoral principle of proportional representation as laid down in the Federal Constitutional Act, and by the list system or *Listenwahl*. In Austria members get into parliament via a list drawn up by the relevant party, their parliamentary career is the outcome of their work within the party, and their parliamentary future likewise depends upon the party.

The Austrian *Nationalrat*, the more important of the two Houses of Parliament, has certain striking characteristics from which significant conclusions may be drawn concerning the peculiarities of the political system:

a) the *Nationalrat* is male-dominated. On average only about 10 per cent of members are women;
b) the average age of members is disproportionately high. Members under the age of 40 constitute only a small minority;
c) it contains an excessive number of civil servants (*Beamte*). The latter make up by far the largest professional group among its members;
d) it is a graduate stronghold. The proportion of members with a university degree is far above average for the population as a whole, and continues to rise.

Social democracy

In Austria political affairs are only partly determined by those institutions designated for that purpose in the Federal Constitution Act. Life within these institutions is determined by the parties which in turn, of course, are closely involved with social forces. The resultant Austrian political culture has a characteristic which is in marked contrast to the political culture of many other countries: it is largely consensus- rather than conflict-orientated.

In Austria as a liberal democracy of a neo-corporatist type (consensus democracy) the parties, the economic interest groups and the most diverse social forces play a large part in ensuring that conflicts are dealt with in a remarkably peaceful fashion — or alternatively not dealt with at all. Austrian consensus democracy is the result of the country's social development since 1918. Initially the democratic republic developed as a centrifugal democracy in which the opposing political groupings were given to confrontation, projected hostile images of their opponents, progressively lost the ability to commuicate with each other and eventually fought a civil war which was started by the Christian-Social government. The First Republic collapsed because of a lack of willingness to arrive at consensus.

The Second Republic developed in sharp contrast to the First Republic. The élites of the two major political groupings (those of the Socialists and the Christian-Conservatives) had radically changed their approach, and the clear results of this change were the formation of a Grand Coalition which lasted until 1966 and the gradual emergence of social partnership.

This development from conflict orientation to consensus orientation, from centrifugal to centripetal democracy, presupposed the existence of the political groupings referred to above. Austrian political culture, like the whole of Austrian society, has been and still is deeply influenced by the existence of sub-cultures. In the second half of the nineteenth century there arose two major groupings and one minor grouping which have always stood in opposition to one another: those of the Socialists, the Christian-Conservatives, and the Pan-German Nationalists. In the main, the Socialist grouping has always been socially based, being the organization of the dominant forces within the labour movement, while that of the Christian-Conservatives is above all confessionally based, the expression of a political Catholicism which, though a thing of the past as to its outward form, still makes its presence felt in practice. The Pan-German Nationalist grouping is to a great extent culturally based, arising largely from the enthusiasm for union with Germany which at the beginning of the First Republic was shared by virtually all political parties, i.e. the idea that Austria should be integrated into a German *Reich*. Even though the social, confessional and cultural aspects of the three groupings became blurred after 1945, and even though in particular enthusiasm for union with Germany is now outmoded, the underlying mentality is still a factor which cannot be totally ignored.

The groupings are a combination of political parties and their associated or auxiliary organizations. These largely consist of the groupings which, in close alliance with the political parties, dominate the major economic interest groups and hence the social partnership. The trade union movement may serve as an example: during the First Republic the Free Trade Unions not only constituted the largest group of unions in Austria, they were also closely involved within the Socialist grouping with the Social Democratic Workers' Party. The Christian Trade Unions, a minority group within the movement, were closely allied with the Christian-Social Party in the Christian-Conservative grouping, while the Pan-German Salaried Workers' Union (*Deutschnationale Angestelltengewerkschaft*) was closely linked to the Pan-German People's Party. In the Second Republic the political parties' groupings within the trade unions (*Fraktionen*) are integrated into the structure of the non-partisan (or 'non-party') Austrian Federation of Trade Unions (*Österreichischer Gewerkschaftsbund*), the central organisation of the Austrian unions. In this way the political conflicts and disunity of the trade unions which occurred up to 1945 are avoided.

The whole of Austrian society is permeated by consensus democracy and the politico-ideological groupings which form its basis. Since both the First and the Second Republics have been the work of the parties, social life in Austria is much more strongly influenced by the parties than in other comparable countries. This approach and the sharing of power which has occurred within the framework of consensus democracy have meant that, both in the economic sector and in the field of education, adherence to one of the two major parties and hence to one of the two major groupings has become a decisive criterion when it comes to careers.

This kind of mentality, however, is gradually diminishing. One of the successes of consensus democracy is that to some extent this mentality becomes unnecessary; precisely because the Second Republic has achieved an unusual degree of stability with the permeation of society by the parties and the political groupings, a larger number of social conflicts can now be permitted without endangering this stability. This expresses itself in greater volatility on the part of the electorate as well as in the increased use of referendum techniques. The opposition to the atomic power station at Zwentendorf and to the construction of a dam near Hainburg demonstrated the ability of popular opinion to prevail even over the will of a consensus democracy, and in particular over that of the 'social partners'.

Building upon a constitutional framework which commands general acceptance, and also upon a parliamentary system which is now taken for granted, the Second Republic has achieved a certain maturity. Consensus democracy, which for decades has been the essential characteristic of Austria's political system and political culture, is now not so necessary for the stabilizing of Austrian society. In future this society will doubtless be able to permit itself more conflict than would have been possible in the past, particularly during the immediate post-war period.

5 The Socialist Party of Austria

Melanie A. Sully

Historical background

The Socialist Party of Austria (SPÖ) has played a decisive role in shaping the political format of the Second Republic. With the exception of the period 1966–70, it has been involved in government either alone (1970–83) or as part of a coalition. It has wielded considerable influence on the decision-making process and has come to be associated with the growth of prosperity and stability in post-war Austria. Through the system of social partnership and its links with the trade unions, the SPÖ retained much of this influence even during the years of opposition. It was able to build upon the foundations laid in the earlier Grand Coalition era (1945–66) which provided the two main parties with access to key administrative posts as well as a duopoly of economic control. The Socialist Party has become an integral part of the political scene and a supporter of the country's independence and sovereignty. For some critics this has led to an unhealthy identification with the Establishment unfitting for a socialist party.

The SPÖ is proud of its history and is the successor of the Social Democratic Party founded in 1888–9 under the leadership of a young doctor, Victor Adler. From humble beginnings, the movement began to grow under the Habsburg monarchy championing the interests of the exploited proletariat. As the First World War drew to a close and the empire disintegrated, the Social Democrats were influential in shaping the political norms of the nascent republic. They remained in a powerful position throughout the 1920s largely due to their bastion of 'Red Vienna'. In the capital they pioneered many important social and economic welfare schemes which made Vienna a model for European socialists. The rest of the country, under the reactionary sway of clericalism championed by the Christian-Social Party, remained antagonistic to Vienna, the hated symbol of 'Bolshevik' advances. The irreconcilability of these two large political party organisations ('camps' or *Lager*) eventually culminated in a civil war in 1934 in which the Social Democrats suffered a brutal defeat at the hands of the Dollfuss regime. From 1934 until the German annexation (*Anschluss*), the party was confined to illegal activity which became increasingly difficult after the German occupation. In 1945 a new start was made building on the older traditions of the Austro-Marxists which inevitably faded in the post-war era. Throughout its history the party has striven to adopt a middle way between the extremes of Bolshevism and right-wing labourism. It has adopted compromise as a method of formulating policy and has been brilliantly successful to date in preserving its coveted unity. An example of this penchant for compromise can be seen in the party's programmes and ideology.

Programme and Ideology

The Social Democrats of the First Republic avoided the disastrous split which plagued their German comrades. Austro-Marxism was able to retain the loyalty of moderates as well as members of the radical left. One of its most controversial programmes was adopted at a conference in Linz in 1926. This made unfortunate and ambiguous references to the necessity of a dictatorship if the bourgeoisie should seek to mount a counter-revolution after a socialist victory through the ballot box. This alarmed conservative forces and provided an ideal excuse to attack the Social Democrats. In practice the party was far more reformist than its revolutionary rhetoric suggested. This kind of dualism held the party together in difficult times but created confusion about the precise action it should follow during the critical days of the civil war.

After the Second World War the newly-founded SPÖ was more pragmatic in outlook. Positive statements were issued supporting the state and the democratic system which it was hoped would avoid the misunderstandings of the past. A major revision of party policy was left until 1958 at a conference in Vienna which was designed to project the SPÖ as a modern *Volkspartei*. References to public ownership were toned down for fear of alienating potential voters and the party adopted a less anti-clerical stance. The SPÖ remained committed, however, to the goal of creating a classless society, unlike the German Social Democratic Party (SPD) which went further along the reformist path at a similar time.

The programme adopted in 1958 remained valid for twenty years but was then substantially modified during the Kreisky era. A thorough discussion on party ideology was encouraged at all levels in the SPÖ by Bruno Kreisky who had steered the party through successive electoral victories in the 1970s. This culminated in the formulation of a new programme adopted at a conference in 1978. The reference to a classless society was retained and the party continued to build bridges with Christians to create a just and free society. The new programme bore the hallmark of Kreisky's vision of Social

Democracy which sought to change the decision-making relationships and increase the ability of individuals to determine freely their own future. This was expressed in the programme as follows:

> Social Democracy is being realised by constantly impregnating new areas of society with the ideas of democracy. Wherever possible, people should, guided by a sense of social responsibility, be able to shape their own lives and work, and take part in the decisions which affect them.

Throughout the programme a close identification of socialism with democracy was emphasized. The party has always been keen to distance itself from the negative aspects of eastern European 'socialist' regimes whilst fighting for a new humanitarian and equal society. The 1978 programme recognized the threats to the welfare state posed by capitalism and reminded social democrats of their duty to fight for the restructuring of the 'existing economic order into one more just and less prone to crises'. Under Kreisky the party seemed to strike the right note which was vindicated by the SPÖ's popularity at the polls and reflected in its healthy membership figures.

Membership and Electoral Support

The SPÖ is a mass membership party with 13 per cent of eligible voters organized as members. Membership is direct and individual and there is a high ratio of members to voters. In 1984, 29.9 per cent of Socialist voters were also party members. In Vienna, 40.4 per cent of the party's voters are also members in contrast to 10.8 per cent in the western province of Vorarlberg. According to the official figures party membership totalled 690,533 at the end of 1984 compared with 694,598 the year before. Slight increases were registered in Carinthia, Upper Austria and Styria but elsewhere membership declined. The SPÖ possesses a vanguard of unpaid, specially trained party workers (*Vertrauenspersonen*) amounting to around 10 per cent of its membership. They maintain contact with the rank and file, collect dues and report back to the party headquarters. In recent years discontent has been apparent amongst this corps of the party faithful with regard to the performance and efficiency of the SPÖ machine.

Women traditionally constitute a low proportion of the SPÖ's membership (33.6 per cent in 1984, see Table 5.1). The 1985 conference amended the party statute to allow women wider representation in party posts and as candidates for public office. A quota system was approved to ensure that women are represented at least in proportion to the number of female party officials and in a ratio never lower than 25 per cent of all candidates. The women's organization

Table 5.1 SPÖ profile at end of 1984

Province	Number of district organizations	Women as % of membership	Number of members	% of total membership
Burgenland	7	23.11	30,156	4.37
Carinthia	9	27.03	52,606	7.62
Lower Austria	23	30.86	137,276	19.88
Upper Austria	15	24.47	101,794	14.74
Salzburg	6	28.59	24,961	3.61
Styria	16	28.37	100,112	14.50
Tyrol	9	24.93	14,190	2.05
Vorarlberg	4	26.30	5,193	0.75
Vienna	24	46.04	224,245	32.47
Austria	113	33.62	690,533	100

Source: SPÖ Yearbook, 1985.

had demanded a quota system reflecting the proportion of female party members but this was rejected. Manual workers are becoming less important for the party and formed 29.9 per cent of the total membership compared with 42.1 per cent in 1955 and 38.3 per cent in 1970. White-collar workers have increased from 22.3 per cent in 1955 to 31.4 per cent in 1978. Pensioners are also on the increase in the party, comprising 18.3 per cent of the total.

Whilst in opposition (1966–70) the SPÖ streamlined its organization, modernized its image and changed its leader. Kreisky formed a minority government for the party in 1970 and subsequently led the party to victory in the elections of 1971, 1975 and 1979 when the SPÖ won an absolute majority. After the losses incurred in the 1983 election (see Table 5.2) Kreisky resigned and was replaced by Fred Sinowatz who formed an uneasy coalition with the small right-wing *Freiheitliche Partei Österreichs* (FPÖ). The Socialist Youth had called on the party to go into opposition but this was rejected by the leadership. Kreisky remained as the honorary chairman of the party which now began to be moulded in a different style.

Under Kreisky, the SPÖ campaigned on a successful programme to modernize Austria, ensure stability, prosperity and full employment. Absolute majorities for the party were secured by Kreisky's astute appeal to liberal fellow-travellers and sympathizers of the social democratic movement. This provided a broad electoral base including middle-class elements in addition to the loyal working-class core. At a time of world-wide recession and increasing uncertainty, 'Kaiser

Table 5.2 Election results in the Kreisky era

Year	SPÖ % of votes	SPÖ Seats	ÖVP % of votes	ÖVP Seats	FPÖ % of votes	FPÖ Seats	Others % of votes	Others Seats
1970	48.42	81	44.69	78	5.52	6	1.37	–
1971	50.04	93	43.11	80	5.45	10	1.40	–
1975	50.42	93	42.95	80	5.41	10	1.22	–
1979	51.03	95	41.90	77	6.06	11	1.01	–
1983	47.65	90	43.22	81	4.98	12	4.15	–

Source: Austrian Central Statistical Office, Vienna.

Bruno' offered peace and progress as well as projecting a positive image of Austria on the international scene. Party cohesion remained high during these years of steady electoral progress and it was easy to dismiss internal critics concerned with more long-term socialist objectives. Discontent became more vociferous in the 1980s when the party seemed to be stagnating, clinging to power for its own sake and often in the news for associations with scandals and corruption charges. In the 1983 election, working-class support for the SPÖ held up well but losses were suffered amongst the new middle-class civil servants, salaried employees and the well-educated. Sinowatz's brand of socialism tried to appeal to the 'small man', the average school teacher and salaried employee. This stolid, rather boring image lacked the dynamism and spark of the Kreisky reign and lost the interest of new social movements, centred around youth and womens' groups, just beginning to find their way into the Austrian political scene. The party's electoral hold on the working class has also become less secure, contributing to its reversal of fortunes as the party seems less convincing on the issue of full employment than under Kreisky.

Since 1983 the party has been on the defensive, obliged to share the fruits of office with the FPÖ, itself struggling for political survival. Election results at provincial level and in the 1984 elections to the Chambers of Labour produced heavy losses for the Socialists as fears of rising unemployment mounted. In the Provincial (*Land*) election in Lower Austria in October 1983 the SPÖ lost three seats and four per cent of the vote. A year later in an election in Vorarlberg its vote dropped from 29 to 24 per cent; this was followed by a further blow in an election in Upper Austria in October 1985 when the SPÖ vote went down from 41.4 per cent to 37.9 per cent. The controversial presidential election of 1986 represented the biggest humiliation for the party since the general election of 1966 when it was forced into opposition. The Federal president had throughout the Second Republic always come from the ranks of the SPÖ or at least been a nominee of the party. The 1986 campaign exposed weaknesses in the SPÖ's organization and demonstrated its failure to attract the young and mobilize effectively its working-class vote. This was noticeable in areas facing the prospect of recession and redundancies where high abstentions were recorded. The election was keenly followed outside Austria not so much because of this but due to the interest which was aroused by the unwelcome publicity caused by the Waldheim affair.

After the débâcle, Sinowatz resigned as Chancellor and was replaced by a 48 year old banker, Franz Vranitzky, who was immediately lampooned in the press as the 'pinstripe socialist'. It has yet to be seen whether the new leadership will be able to provide the SPÖ with a second wind in time to salvage its electoral position. Sinowatz stayed on as chairman of the party to maintain some continuity and smooth the transference of power. This was a new departure for the SPÖ since in the past the post of Chancellor or Vice-Chancellor has been combined with the party leadership when in power. The departure of Sinowatz was a prelude to a major reshuffle in personnel both in the government and the party. It was interpreted as signalling a willingness by the SPÖ to consider the reformation of the Grand Coalition after the next election and this, indeed, transpired. The loss of the Presidency jolted the party into a pessimistic, introspective phase which inevitably involved an examination of the party organization.

Party Organization

The SPÖ is a highly centralized structure composed of 3,476 small local units (*Ortsorganisationen* and *Sektionen*) which combine together to form 113 district organizations throughout the nine federal provinces (*Länder*). At federal level, it is the party conference held every two years which in theory wields supreme authority but with over 500 delegates it is too big to fulfil this function effectively. Apart from the Vienna party and the socialist trade union group, individual units of the SPÖ have little autonomy or influence. Delegates to conference come from the women's organizations, the trade unions, the pensioners' league, the youth section and other affiliated associations as well as the district and provincial parties.

One of the main duties of conference is to elect the 56 members of the party executive from a list of candidates prepared by an election committee. The party executive takes the main political decisions of the party and carries out conference resolutions. It is empowered to propose from its ranks the party chairman and his deputies who together constitute the party presidium which has the job of implementing the decisions of the executive. The party executive also appoints the treasurer and central secretaries. In between the conferences of 1983 and 1985 the executive met twenty times, mostly in Vienna. Since 1967 an enlarged party presidium has existed including members of the presidium and representatives from the women's committee, the provincial organizations and the trade unions. It prepares work for the party executive and takes decisions on its behalf if it cannot meet in time.

Much of the blame for the party's failure in the 1986 presidential campaign was attributed to the central secretariat and in particular to Peter Schieder, the central secretary responsible for publicity and propaganda. After the result a third central secretary was appointed, Heinrich Keller, to help improve the management of the party machinery. Cynics are sceptical of such attempts at party reform arguing that they only serve to inflate the bureaucracy.

A party council (*Parteirat*) forms another part of the SPÖ's structure; it can be invoked by the party executive for specific purposes such as the nomination of candidates for the National Assembly and for the Federal Presidency. It is also instrumental in initiating and guiding programmatic debate. Under Kreisky the party embarked on a phase of reform which involved democratizing its structure and opening it up to allow for participation in discussions by sympathizers as well as party activists. At the same time the party constitution was modified to restrict the number of paid political posts held by socialist officials. Under Sinowatz the leadership was criticized for being intolerant of internal debate which deviated from the party line. Further defeats seem to increase the sensitivity of the party to dissent at a time when it could benefit from helpful suggests for reform. As always in difficult times the tendency for the SPÖ is to close ranks and appeal for party unity and discipline to weather the storm.

The party has its own daily newspaper, the *Arbeiterzeitung* (currently in financial difficulties), distributed in eastern Austria. There are also socialist provincials such as the *Kärntner Tageszeitung*, *Neue Zeit*, the *Salzburger Tagblatt* and the *Oberösterreichisches Tagblatt*. The party produces a monthly theoretical journal, *Die Zukunft* and runs its own educational and research organization, the Dr Karl Renner Institute, which organizes courses and conferences and plays host to internationally respected lecturers on a wide variety of topics.

The party offers a comprehensive network of associations to cater for members' recreational interests and hobbies. One of the most popular is the sports' organization ASKÖ with 968,000 members. It is entitled to send seven delegates to the party conference. The Socialist Pensioners' Association has a growing membership which stands at 375,000 and is represented at conference by 10 delegates. The Federation of Socialist Academics (BSA) has a membership of 16,500 and sends four delegates. This forms an important reserve for recruitment to the party élite. The party conference receives reports from the parliamentary party, the executive, the provincial organizations as well as the affiliated associations, and information on party finance. The bulk of the party's income comes from membership dues together with contributions from public funds. The SPÖ receives financial support from the state in the form of a lump sum and on top of this receives money based on its voting strength. Most of the party's expenditure for 1984, according to the conference report, was devoted to publicity and party meetings and conventions.

The trade union connection is an important one for the SPÖ in a country where social partnership allows for a pervasive influence of labour institutions. Formally independent of parties, the Austrian Trade Union Federation (ÖGB) has close links with the SPÖ through the Group of Socialist Trade Unionists (FSG). Fourteen of the fifteen unions in the ÖGB are dominated by the FSG and 73 per cent of the members on the ÖGB executive with voting rights belong to the FSG. In 1979, 77 per cent of delegates at the ÖGB congress were members of the FSG. Similarly Socialists predominate in the Chambers of Labour and in 1984 the party won 58.7 per cent of the vote in elections although this was the worst performance for it in the Second Republic. It lost its overall majority in the salaried employees' (white collar) voting section as well as the Presidency of the Tyrol Chamber to the Conservatives in the Chambers of Labour elections of that year.

The FSG is entitled to send 50 delegates to the party conference and leading trade unionists occupy prominent posts in the SPÖ hierarchy including the ÖGB president, Anton Benya,[1] who is also president of the National Assembly. Alfred Dallinger,[2] leader of the largest union, the Union of Private Employees, has a seat in the cabinet as Minister of Social Affairs. He has often been more critical of the system of social partnership and the preoccupation with economic growth than some of his fellow trade unionists.

One of the chief concerns of the trade union movement has been to preserve jobs through the promotion of economic growth. This has often led to clashes with the small left wing in the party and the youth who have opposed nuclear power and building schemes which could damage the environment. One of the bitterest controversies surrounded the siting of a planned hydro-electric power plant east of Vienna at Hainburg. The mass occupation which occurred to prevent work commencing on the project was broken up by the police. The incident exposed the rift in the party between its intellectuals and trade unionists. As a result of these demonstrations the Hainburg scheme, like the nuclear power station Zwentendorf before it, was shelved leaving the SPÖ's energy strategy in shreds. A prominent trade unionist rebel, Günther Nenning, who was one of the 'green' Hainburg ringleaders, was subsequently expelled from both the ÖGB and the SPÖ causing further uproar amongst the left, outraged by the heavy-handed and arbitrary intolerance of the party.

Defence has been another area where the left and the youth have challenged the unions' drive to export arms to Third World dictatorships for the sake of keeping Austrian workers in jobs. The crisis in the nationalized industries with their colossal deficits, mismanagement and insatiable thirst for subsidies has threatened further the job outlook and will present a dilemma for both the ÖGB and the SPÖ in the future.

The Socialist Youth of Austria (SJÖ) has often been at odds with the party leadership for taking part in demonstrations with other youth movements, including catholics and communists, in support of world peace. The SJÖ has 42,000 members and is entitled to send six delegates to conference. It was critical of the coalition with the national-liberal FPÖ and opposes expenditure on unnecessary defence items such as interceptor jets, preferring money to be diverted to the needs of the welfare state. The SJÖ has been active in maintaining contacts with the growing 'alternative' camp through its 'Red-Green' project. This is designed to discuss alternative energy schemes and increase awareness in the party on environmental conservation.

The SJÖ has a keen sense of history and constantly reminds the party of its origins as a workers' party, of the need to fight Fascism and of its mission to achieve Socialism. It has often clashed with the middle generation in the party referred to as the *Macher* or technocratic clique, devoid of ideological perspectives and concerned only with self-interest. Despite some friction, especially on nuclear energy, the SJÖ seemed to share greater empathy with Kreisky and his generation.

The party did badly with young voters in the 1986 presidential election and seems unlikely to overcome its well-established image as the 'red pensioners' party'. After the 1983 election, the leader of the SJÖ, Josef Cap, became a deputy in the National Assembly but, obliged to follow the dictates of the parliamentary party, his impact on the stultified socialist leadership was negligible. Disillusioned young voters are likely to look to the Alternative/Greens in the future to express their dissatisfaction with the establishment.

Problems and Prospects

The fragile coalition with the FPÖ had not proved a happy arrangement for the SPÖ and after the presidential election in 1986, efforts were intensified to investigate possibilities of a future Grand Coalition. Several incidents damaged the small coalition including the wine scandal of 1985 which gave Austria a bad press abroad. This followed differences of opinion between the then FPÖ Vice-Chancellor and Minister of Trade, Norbert Steger, and the Minister for Social Affairs, Alfred Dallinger. The latter clashed with Steger who wanted to liberalize legally-fixed shop opening times and holidays. Soon after came the Hainburg incident which lost the Socialists support amongst the young, intellectuals and the left. The government's apparent insensitivity for wildlife and the environment further dented Austria's international reputation. An area of great scenic beauty with many species of rare faunae was to be sacrificed and over a million trees cut down. Protesters who had camped in the area were violently removed by the police in ugly scenes.

The consensus, stability and social peace which has characterized much of the political life of post-war Austria has increasingly been challenged in recent years. Noticeably less confidence and optimism is now apparent not just in the ranks of the Socialist Party but throughout the country. The ghosts of the past continue to haunt the small republic contributing to this nervousness. The Reder case, when a former member of the SS was welcomed home as an old soldier, added to the negative picture particularly in America. The FPÖ Minister of Defence went to the airport personally to receive Walter Reder who had been serving a life sentence in Italy for shooting civilian hostages at the end of the war. Some socialist members of the cabinet were on the verge of resignation and party unity was severely strained.

Kreisky's painstaking construction of bridges between the SPÖ and non-partisan, floating voters was exploded after these events. Concurrently electoral volatility has been on the increase and party identification shows signs of weakening. It is not yet clear to what extent this new mobility will affect the old hyperstability of the political system but changes of this kind are potentially dangerous for the SPÖ. Adverse attitudes to traditional parties are on the increase and this has been fused with a mounting sense of frustration and cynicism. Voters seem less happy with political élites, a tendency which will undermine the position of the coalition partners.

Table 5.3 Election results, November 1986

SPÖ		OVP		FPÖ		VGÖ/ALÖ (Greens)	
% of votes	seats	% of votes	seats	% of votes	seats	% of votes	seats
43.1	80	41.3	77	9.7	18	4.8	8

A reaction against what was considered to be socialist arrogance and a disregard for individuals stemming from a long spell in office gradually accumulated. Waldheim's success was in part the by-product of this frustration as well as resentment against foreign intervention in Austrian domestic affairs. The presidential campaign revived old fears and anti-semitic prejudices and further exposed the vulnerability of the Socialists. It was clear that the party had lost credibility with the new middle class and the youth and was even flagging in its working-class strongholds. Party strategy for the future will have to be geared to these new harsh realities. Under the Chancellorship of Vranitzky the SPÖ is likely to take tough decisions on overmanning in the stricken nationalized industries and will call for more efficiency and greater profit orientation. Recent setbacks have pushed the party to the right and it seems disinclined to pursue contacts with the Greens, a policy regarded by many in the party élite as a fruitless exercise.

In the prematurely-held elections of November 1986 the chickens had come home to roost: a further decline in the Socialist vote and a less severe drop for the Conservatives (compare Table 5.2) produced the results shown in Table 5.3. In the light of the results, at the beginning of 1987, a Grand Coalition was formed once more with the Coalition partners distancing themselves from Liberals (FPÖ) and Greens (ALÖ) alike, the latter being represented in the *Nationalrat* for the first time ever.

Since 1984 the SPÖ has been reviewing its programmatic position through a series of debates held under the title of 'Perspectives 90'. This is designed to up-date the 1978 programme to act as an orientation guide to make it more relevant in the modern world. A major concern has revolved around the problem of how best to adapt new technology to ensure humane working conditions and employment. In the first year around 30,000 members participated in the debate which formed the basis for a major policy document. This urged the reduction of the working week, greater direct democracy and a redistribution of wealth. The task of restructuring the welfare state and reconciling ecological and economic requirements also received attention but little reference was made to the all-important system of social partnership. Perspectives 90 was intended to bridge the gap between theory and practice but the progress of these discussions has been fitful and inevitably clouded by the SPÖ's electoral decline.

The party is unlikely to experiment with anything adventurous at such a critical phase and when it has just switched coalition partners. As often in the past the role of theory could be relegated to the status of occupational therapy for would-be party intellectuals. It could be argued that many of the present troubles stem from the Kreisky period when problems were complacently shelved and social welfare and full employment were pursued to the detriment of other economic goals. This would be a tempting but facile excuse for the party's difficulties which are more structural and fundamental. Failure of the party to respond to challenges from the new social movements is likely to lead to a permanent loss of the social-liberal consensus which provided the SPÖ with its absolute majority under Kreisky. The party needs to experiment with some fresh ideas as a means of self-regeneration and in order to shake off accusations that it has become jaded and weary after 16 years in office. Socialist ministers sometimes call to mind Disraeli's comment on the Treasury Bench when he referred to 'landscapes not unusual on the coasts of South America. You behold a range of exhausted volcanoes.' As the twentieth century draws to a close, it remains to be seen whether the SPÖ can rediscover the creative energy and dynamism necessary to conquer Austria's economic and social problems.

Notes

1 Since this was written Anton Benya has retired from all forms of public activity.

2 Alfred Dallinger has retired from his trade union posts but remains Minister of Social Affairs.

6 The Austrian People's Party

Irene Dyk

Historical background

The ideological and practical development of the Austrian People's Party (ÖVP) can be seen as less continuous and uniform than that of the Austrian Socialist Party. The history of the Austrian People's Party, established in 1945, is in part based on the principles of the Christian-Social Party. Likewise, the period from the Christian-Social Party's foundation in the 1880s to the end of World War I shows differences in political objectives, content and style compared to the inter-war period.

The Christian-Social Party and the Austrian People's Party have origins in the Christian social doctrine of the Catholic Church, particularly in the crucial issue of individualism and collectivism. Parallel to the theoretical foundation (whereby the papal social encyclicals played a much more decisive role in the earlier times rather than after World War II) a number of social reform groups and movements organized themselves along the lines of a 'Christian Realism' to which were associated co-operatives and trade unions with a Christian ethos, as well as party-political organizations. From the very beginning in Austria two groupings could be distinguished: a Christian conservative group (the Liechtenstein circle) and a Christan democratic group (the Vogelsang circle). These groupings developed different stances on the labour question as well as on the national question (the multi-ethnic composition of the Habsburg state).

In the 1890s Lueger, who later became mayor of Vienna, and the workers' leader Kunschak — both of whom belonged to the Vogelsang circle — succeeded in uniting the two competing groups by their acceptance of the *Schindler Programme* of 1891. (This programme was regarded as revolutionary and Pope Leo XIII only eventually approved it in 1895.) The newly-founded Christian-Social Party gained its first impressive municipal election success in 1895 in Vienna after a process of consolidation in the provinces. This was followed by a national breakthrough in other parts of Austria in 1907. It was in fact so impressive that the Catholic Conservative wing of Liechtenstein joined forces with the Christian-Socials. Thus the Christian-Social Party assumed national importance within the Habsburg state, not only pursuing modern municipal policies under Lueger and establishing an effective Christian Trade Union organization under Kunschak but also coming to grips with the problems of the middle classes endangered by industrialization.

Personality problems, quarrels with the Emperor, the nationality question (which unlike the labour question had not been solved) all led to a loss of power in Vienna and loss of ground in other areas. After World War I the Christian-Social Party was at an all-time low — organizationally as well as ideologically — the latter resulting from, amongst other things, a rise in nationalism and anti-semitism. Kunschak could not succeed, revered and esteemed as he was by the other political parties, in establishing a lasting coalition government after 1920.

The Annexation Movement which was strong in all the political groupings but especially so in some provinces aggravated domestic conflict which contributed to Kunschak's resignation and his succession by Seipel. The declaration of new party programmes by the two largest parties sharpened their differences and led to new elections in 1927, the result of which was that although Christian-Socials emerged as the largest single party, they could only govern with the support of the pan-German parties. In the 1930 elections, however, the Social Democrats came through as the largest single party so that for a while the Christian-Socials became even more dependent on the pan-Germans (*Grossdeutsche*). As the governing parties began to quarrel, the Christian-Socials were forced to seek closer contacts with the para-military *Heimwehr* (Local Defence Corps) Movement which had won eight seats in the elections and had by this time become even more extreme. This latter organization had not only attempted a number of *coups d'etat* but was allying itself with the Nazis from time to time. But other changes were contemplated: after Dollfuss had formed a new government in 1931 following the appearance of the papal encyclical *Quadragesimo Anno*, the reorganization of the state into a corporate state was considered. The democratic wing of the Christian-Socials wanted such proposals incorporated into the constitution, whereas Dollfuss aimed at a complete constitutional change. Vaugoin, the Christian-Social Party chairman, was as a consequence removed. Next, the Local Defence Corps replaced the Land League as a partner in the government. Following that, an 'all-embracing' political organization called the 'Fatherland (Vaterländische) Front' absorbed all non-socialist political groups in a quasi one-party state. The socialist opposition was suppressed and later in 1934 after the civil war, it was prohibited.

This paved the way for an authoritarian regime which was eventually succeeded by Hitler in 1938.

The democratic wing of the Christian-Social movement was, like the socialists, forced to go underground. Because of the existence of many factions, the Christian-Socials displayed no unity, and apart from a few individuals, had no mutual contact till after World War II. These individuals, however, were the ones who, together with representatives from the Socialist Party (as it became known later) suffered at the hands of the National Socialists in the concentration camps and together made preparations for the democratic post-war reconstruction.

The Austrian People's Party after 1945

As early as 17 August 1945 the Austrian People's Party was founded following the initiative of Kunschak and other leading figures of the Conservative Trade Union grouping such as Weinberger, as well as Figl (Farmers' Union) and Raab (Austrian Trade Association). A federal structure for the organization was proposed. The provincial sections were established by the autumn of the same year. The new name, the Austrian People's Party, indicated programmatic and operational changes which marked a contrast to the former party.

In the provisional post-war government of Renner there already sat important representatives of the Austrian People's Party (among others Figl, Raab, Weinberger). The first post-war elections on 25 November 1945 were now fought and won with an absolute majority by a unified, single party. Despite the Austrian People's Party's majority, a coalition government was formed with the Socialists and Communists, because it was felt that the economic problems of the post-war period and the difficult political situation of the country — still under allied occupation — were features of a situation best to be mastered jointly by all the democratic forces.

Under the new Federal Chancellor Figl notable reconstruction work and the consolidation of state power took place. Preparations for a State Treaty created a favourable climate of relationships with the allied forces which prevented among other things the division of Austria, sparing her the fate of Germany.

The general secretary of the Austrian People's Party, Hurdes, succeeded in stabilizing the party organization, making provision for employee and employer interests within its structure. To some extent this was influenced by two other government ministers: Altenburg, a moderate Christian trade unionist, and Kamitz with his successful economic policies. At the start, Bock, Minister for Trade in the Figl government, was able to pave the way for Austria to join EFTA, which further led to the country becoming an associate member of the European Community (EEC) at a later stage.

In 1953 Raab became chairman of the party and head of the government, and Maleta became party general secretary. Raab stimulated new discussions of programmatic principles and ideological reorientation (with well-known academics and experts acting in a consultative role) in order to deal with the problems of political party demarcation which had arisen during the coalition.

In 1955 the State Treaty was introduced to which Foreign Minister Figl had made a considerable contribution. The political independence of Austria was thus secured, supplemented by extensive economic autonomy as a consequence of the efficient economic policies following the Raab-Kamitz orientation. Education Minister Drimmel carried out educational reforms which facilitated greater access to higher education.

In 1960 Raab was succeeded by Gorbach. During his time in office not only were economic problems solved, but Austria experienced her 'economic miracle' which was manifested by a boom in the building industry. Kotzina, Minister for Building and Construction, reformed the existing building regulations and initiated the Dwellings Assistance Act of 1968. Gorbach, a strong advocate of the Grand Coalition, followed a line of close co-operation with the coalition partner. By his side as party general secretary, however, there was Withalm, a strategist and fighter whose style was more in the way of confrontation on an ideological front with the coalition partner. This strategy was continued from 1964 under party chairman and Federal Chancellor Klaus who had previously been the successful Provincial Governor of Salzburg and Finance Minister in Gorbach's cabinet. It led to a decisive election success for the Austrian People's Party in 1966 but was possibly responsible for the subsequent break down of negotiations with the Socialists which in the end resulted in a single party government of the People's Party. Finance Minister Koren, who is today President of the National Bank, occupied himself with legislation for promoting changes in trade and industrial structure, and as the first woman minister, Grete Rehor (Minister for Social Affairs) acquitted herself with a Labour Market Support Act which successfully combatted the early deficiences in the labour market, an Act which is still today of great importance. All such beneficial changes notwithstanding, the Austrian People's Party lost its absolute majority in 1970 because it was incapable of interpreting some of the signs of the time, e.g. questions concerning the liberalization of justice, even though the party's brains-trust, the so-called *Aktion 2000* which acted as a 'council for the future' (*Zukunftskommission*), had given advance warning of this danger.

The People's Party in opposition 1970–86

Chancellor Klaus resigned after the defeat at the 1970 elections, having rejected the formation of a Small Coalition with the Freedom Party and after not being able to succeed in forming a Grand Coalition. As the Socialists formed a minority government, Withalm became party leader of the Austrian People's Party till he was superseded by Schleinzer in 1971. This rapid change of personnel shows how irritating the opposition role must have been for the 'party which was accustomed to govern'. Together with general secretary Kohlmair, who coined the phrase 'dry dock' (denoting the political revival of the party), Schleinzer initiated talks on the reformation of the party and involved all the individual associations, as well as all the provincial, district and local organizations. These talks resulted in the Salzburg Programme, which is still the party manifesto today.

A few months before the parliamentary elections of 1975 Schleinzer was killed in a car accident. His successor as leader of the party was Taus, who teamed up with general secretary Busek. Both were representatives of the intellectual wing of the party, and came with the intention of advocating a clear-cut division from the Socialists, which manifested itself in a rather liberal economic policy on the one hand and in increased efforts to improve the quality of life on the other. This latter aspect of policy anticipated many of the issues with which the Green and Alternative Parties are concerned today. Furthermore, the discussion at the present time over the future of the nationalized industries and the role of economic subsidies proves Taus, the economist, right on many points albeit in hindsight. Taus was not able to establish himself in the two elections in which he fought against Kreisky who not only had the advantage of being in office but who in contrast to the aloof image of the economic expert Taus was popular with the Austrian people. Since 1979 the party leader has been Alois Mock, who was formerly Education Minister in the governments of 1966–70 and leader of the Federation of Manual and White Collar Employees Association. His close links with the employee organizations of the Austrian People's Party, his preference for the views of experts, and his international contacts as President of the Conservative European Democratic Union and the International Democratic Union, make him quite a different type of politician. Between 1979 and 1983, with the then party's general secretary Lanner — a man who preferred to remain in the background — Mock succeeded in balancing the influences on the party of the individual organizations and associations and in promoting the concept of a single unified party. (This for example postulated the possibility of direct party membership without membership of a sub-organization; this is regarded as an advantage, especially by intellectuals.) The present general secretary Graff in 1983 proceeded to intensify the public relations work which had been neglected up to that time. Graff has often been criticized for his rather aggressive style, but the increasing election successes of the party have given occasion to prove him right. However, it is Mock's ability to integrate and balance regional and interest-group differences, which signals optimism. The parliamentary elections of 1983 showed an increase of votes for the Austrian People's Party and a decrease for the Socialists (see Table 6.1) who had to compensate for this shift in conservative popularity by forming a Small Coalition with the Freedom Party. Kreisky, who had no liking for a Small Coalition, was succeeded by Sinowatz. The Small Coalition did not work to the advantage of the two governmental parties. The elections of the various interest groups as well as for the provincial parliaments — with yet further increased majorities where the Party already did well — were a particular feature.

A change in the leadership of the Freedom Party — a shift from the liberal Steger to the rather nationalistic Haider — in the autumn of 1986 led to the collapse of the Small Coalition. The early parliamentary elections on 23 November 1986 must be seen in the light of the Presidential elections earlier that year in which the Socialist candidate lost and as a consequence of which Federal Chancellor Sinowatz resigned. His successor, Franz Vranitzky, was possibly forced to call for the early elections demanded by the opposition because of the difficult situation of the nationalized industries and the state of the budget.

Party programmes and ideology

From the beginning the programmatic development of the Christian-Social Party was characterized by the controversy between rather conservative groups (for example the Church and the nobility) and movements which aimed at social reform based on Christian beliefs. For the latter the question of labour was of central importance. Their representatives from 1889 onwards met regularly (amongst them Schindler, Gessmann, Lueger), and in 1891 under the influence of the Papal encyclical *Rerum Novarum* they worked out the first Christian-Social Party Programme. Among other things it dealt with questions of electoral reform, labour and social security regulations, and the issues of education (particularly those relating to religious schools). Nevertheless, this first programme was for a long time regarded as controversial by the Catholic Church. In the 'Programmatic Resolution' of 1895 the principles of the Schindler Programme were proclaimed. In 1896, under Kunschak, the first independent 'Programme of the Christian Workers' Party' was formulated, in which the right to work, the legal protection of workers, the reduction of working hours, equal wages and social security for all employees were demanded. In the 'Eggenburg Party Conference Resolution' of 1905, the pressing nationality question was dealt with along the lines of a demand for national autonomy. As regards electoral reform there were similar demands made by the Social Democrats since both parties represented groups excluded from the right to vote.

The 'Election Manifesto of the Christian-Social Imperial Party' of 1907, which included many of the elements of the preceding programmes, proved to be decisive and successful in the elections of that year although it contained the first statements of an anti-semitic nature. After the fall of the Monarchy and the end of World War I, the Christian-Socials in their 'Address to Party Members' in 1918, declared their loyalty to the newly-founded independent state, to the Republic and to party democracy. For the first time, the principles of the Christian-Social doctrine are laid down in a systematic way, listing the following main points: freedom, justice, democracy, federalism, the protection of the family, the subsidizing of the economy and agriculture, education for all, just wages, and labour and social legislation. In addition, questions of property acquisition and subsidies for housing formed a part. Similarly, 'The Action Programme of the Christian-Social Association' made demands even for profit-sharing by employees. In 1918 and in 1919 anti-semitic and pan-German national statements were made, which in 1919 became expressed as the idea of the *Anschluss*.

Of decisive influence on the development of the party as a whole was the 'Party Programme of the Viennese Christian-Socials' drawn up in 1919 and which from today's perspective is a particularly ambivalent document. On the one hand, the party is declared as being 'Christian, German and anti-semitic', and on the other hand some clauses appear very progressive by today's standards: plebiscites on basic issues, extension of universities and student participation, equal opportunities for women in the public sector, and so on. In 1923 the 'Linz Programme' of the Christian Workers of Austria (mainly drawn up by Kunschak) was concerned with family, work, and housing. For the first time a programme called for a 'corporative' organization of society, which emphasized co-operation of employers' and employees' representative bodies, the latter functioning as self-governing organizations with full political rights. These ideas were further developed in 1926 in the 'Programme of the Christian-Social Party' which still envisaged a democratic society. There is no record of any further programmatic development after that since involvement with the Local Defence Corps Movement and the Fatherland Front prevented or suppressed any independent ideological movement within the Christian-Socials' thinking. During the Nazi period and World War II, personalities such as Kunschak, Raab, Figl, Weinberger, Lugmayr and others, who were either original members or closely associated with the Christian-Social Party, tried to develop new principles with the aim of building a new democratic and unified party based on a Christian basis. Already the early stages of the concept of a 'People's Party' were beginning to be discussed.

Party programmes since 1945

After 1945 it became obvious that the changed social and economic situation had to be taken into account, and in step with the Christian-Social doctrine the 'social question' had to be looked at again in a different light.

The 'Programmatic Basic Principles' of 1945, in recounting the nation's experience under a totalitarian regime, advocated party democracy, the rule of law, basic rights and federalism. There was also a decisive refusal to be linked to the Catholic Church, but at the same time a reaffirmation of Christian principles. Independence, private initiative and achievement in economic terms were complemented by social-political principles such as pensions and social insurance for all and an equal and just distribution of liabilities — taking special account of family circumstances. Special claims were made for the right to the fruits of labour and the right to accumulate personal and private property, with an emphasis on the right to buy one's land and home.

In 1952 the manifesto 'Everything For Austria' was issued: the concept of private property was supplemented by suggestions for a broad distribution of wealth; an attempt was made to work out the Austrian variant of a social market economy and to restrict the role of the state (in comparison to the role envisaged in the 1945 programme). The postulate of promoting research and science was new to a party programme and was later to be extended in the Innsbruck Programme of 1958. The latter, called 'What We Want', defines the concept of a society in which education plays a major role and promotes the idea of an active youth policy. In addition to a commitment to the European concept and to Austria's neutrality in international relations, the co-operative aspect of labour and capital was affirmed.

The Klagenfurt Manifesto of 1965 was the result of broadly-based discussions stimulated from 1963 onwards by the idea of reform and the necessity of demarcating the sphere of activity of each coalition partner. Some basic principles have been maintained or slightly amended since 1945. These include the concern for man as an individual, the appreciation of small social groups (as a result of which there are important demands for family policies), commitment to the federal structure of Austria, the basic concept of participation or democratization, the commitment to private property, measures to increase privatization, and the idea of competition and the principle of the 'achieving society'.

Programmes since 1970

The period of entering into opposition launched a discussion on basic principles which took place at all the levels of the party and resulted in the 'Salzburg Programme' of 1972, which is still the current party statement of ideology. In its preamble it refers to the basic principles of Christian social teaching and humanism, and emphasizes the ideological continuity concerning such principles. In the years which followed the drafting of the Salzburg Programme, the Austrian People's Party began to define itself as a party of the progressive centre and as a party of social integration. The basic values of freedom, equality, solidarity, achievement, participation and partnership are seen as influencing the different areas of life such as education, work, leisure, the environment, and social questions, which are to be viewed in the context of important 'target groups', such as youth, the family, women, and senior citizens. Such aims as self-realization and the 'quality of life' play a prominent role, whereby the latter concept anticipates many of the issues of the Alternative/Green Parties years before their appearance on the political scene.

Parallel to the national programmes of the Austrian People's Party, there have always been ideological statements by the individual associations and the provincial organizations concerning their specific problems. In all the programmatic work after World War II, an increasing independence from Papal encyclicals and circulars becomes obvious even though there is an ongoing dialogue over their content. One can say that the Austrian People's Party has been overtaken from the left by some activist groups in the Catholic Church, although recent attitude studies point to the members' views as being conservative.

Party organization, membership and electoral structure

The two main parties in Austria claim to be parties of the people, but there is a major difference between them: whereas the Socialist Party's organizational structure is centralist, the Austrian People's Party is organized on a federal and corporate basis. The provincial organizations (and their sub-groups) are to a great extent autonomous not only as regards matters concerning a particular province (of the nine provinces six have been dominated by them for the last 40 years) but also those relating to national policies. (See Appendix C1.)

This provincial autonomy is not only important for a party which adheres to the principle of self-help and which takes account of regional differences, problems and initiatives, but is surely also a reflection of the fact that among all the political leaders in the provinces there are some outstanding personalities (for example Gleissner, Lechner, Wallnöfer, Krainer, Ratzenböck) who could not and cannot be ignored in any decision-making process at national level; this was especially true in those years when the party was in opposition, since such personalities represented the most convincing proof of the party's ability to govern. Even now in those provinces where the party is in opposition, some politicians (for example Busek in Vienna) have been able to influence the political scene beyond their own domain. It follows that this structure can lead to differences of opinion between the provincial and the national organizations, and that this plurality of opinions in some cases could be misinterpreted by voters.

The second most important element in the structure of the Austrian People's Party is the associations or federations (*Bünde*). They are interest groups within the party representing employees, employers or the self-employed, farmers, women, youth and senior citizens. Dual membership is a feature (and is rather frequent), but individual membership (without membership of an association) is also available and is made use of by intellectual newcomers in particular.

Total membership of the party in 1986 was nearly 800,000 excluding dual membership. Categories of membership of affiliated organizations and on an individual basis in the same year were as follows:

Austrian Federation of Manual and White Collar Employees (ÖAAB)	186,000 members
Austrian Farmers' Federation (ÖBB)	380,000 members
Austrian Federation of Employers and Trades People (ÖWB)	140,000 members
Austrian Women's Movement (ÖFB)	83,000 members
Young Conservatives (JÖVP)	114,000 members

Austrian Senior Citizens' Federation (ÖSB)	220,000 members
Individual members	2,500

The federal structure of the party's organization does not represent a continuation of the structures of the pre-war corporate state but represents, through member organizations, the idea of a party of social integration or a party of the people. Furthermore, it represents the Austrian model of social and economic partnership within the structure of a political party, complemented by a partnership of the sexes and the generations. Although the intention behind this type of organizational structure was inner-party problem solving, it is clear that a combination of all interests cannot always be reached without conflict (one example of which is the case of regional versus national interests as noted above). In recent years, due to structural changes in society, the Federation of Manual and White Collar Employees has grown in importance, and this has been accompanied by a decrease in numbers of self-employed in agriculture, industry, trade and commerce. In addition, due to changes in the party rules, representatives of the women's, youth and senior citizens' organizations have become involved in inner-party decision-making as well as providing election candidates. In some cases this has led to a power struggle which has been disadvantageous for the party which could not always present a united image. The introduction, however, of various models of preliminary nomination ballots by which the idea of choice of the individual candidate is promoted, has reduced the possibility of narrow 'list' selection procedures becoming an issue.

In selecting candidates for elections, apart from the procedures of affiliated organizations, the members and party officials at branch, local, district and provincial levels play a role of increasing importance. In some cases open preliminary nomination ballots (where everybody can take part) have been successfully carried out. Increasingly units on a regional and plant level are involved in discussions of party programmes. At the same time those elected to public office (local councillors, members of the Federal Council or Senate, and the Parliament) have been made 'counsellors' to ensure a closer link between the grassroots membership and the party hierarchy particularly in regard to regional problems. This system of counsellors, however, decreases the importance of belonging to one of the federations or associations because the elected representative is confronted with many conflicting interests. The feed-back for the work of the elected representatives comes from the preliminary nomination ballots, which are used not only as an instrument for selecting, but also for monitoring political performance.

In recent years the importance of the party's own 'Political

Academy' has grown where, apart from research and the analysis of programmes and political actions, training programmes for party officials are carried out. The training programmes are decentralized and organized according to regional needs. The courses provided are well attended, and this system of information and education is supplemented by a number of periodicals and publications.

The party also publishes a daily paper, the *Neues Volksblatt*, which tends to be most highly regarded in the provinces of Upper and Lower Austria. In contrast to the Socialist Party of Austria, the People's Party does not have its own organization for university graduates but some student and graduate organizations, because of their ideological orientation, are closely linked with the party. The Austrian Federation of Academics, for example, with its 10,000 members is closely linked with the party. It does not enjoy the status of an independent association within the party structure, but is mainly a liberal and somewhat critical organization in the political front line.

A very important and a sometimes contentious role is played by the Christian Trade Unions which are closely connected with the Austrian People's Party, but greater support comes from the Federation of Manual and White Collar Employees (ÖAAB) some of whose members enjoy dual membership and the 'cumulation of office'. Of the 1,160,000 members of the non-party political Austrian Trade Union Federation (which is, however, split into different political groupings) 221,000, that is nearly 20 per cent, are members of the Christian Conservative Grouping. The Christian Conservative Trade Union Section is handicapped on the one hand by issues concerning trade union solidarity when it has to follow the policies of the Socialist-dominated Austrian Trade Union Federation, and by party policies on the other; both aspects are not easy to combine. However, since the Christian Conservative Trade Union Section and the Austrian Federation of Manual and White Collar Employees contest the elections of the Austrian Chambers of Labour (of which all employees are compulsory members) on a united ticket (list), electoral success has been significantly increased. The Chambers of Labour of two provinces (Tyrol and Vorarlberg) are now governed by the Conservatives. At the last elections to the Chambers of Labour in 1984 for the whole of Austria, the Conservative list (ÖAAB/FCG) had an increase of 5.5 per cent of the total vote (from 31 per cent to 36.5 per cent) in comparison to 1979, while the Socialists had their overall percentage vote reduced from 64.3 per cent to 58.7 per cent (see Appendix F7).

The Christian Conservative Section is at its strongest amongst employees in the public services and amongst teachers. More and more members of this grouping can be found among skilled workers and white collar workers — which indicates that the Austrian People's Party appeals especially to the new middle class.

Traditionally the Party enjoys its strongest support in the employers' organizations representing the interests of agriculture, trade and industry.

For women who want to be put up for election, the federal concept of the party has certain disadvantages. Strong federations or associations like the Federation of Manual and White Collar Employees, the Farmers' or the Employers' and Trades People's Federations are male-dominated, despite the fact that there is a rise in female membership. The Austrian Women's Movement on the other hand is not strong enough to counter-balance this. Nevertheless, the percentage of women becoming party officials or election candidates is increasing on all political levels. This would reflect women's political attitudes in society at large: as a percentage of the electorate more women vote conservative. The fact that the party in its programmes treats housewives and working women equally, that it demands freedom of choice between family and work, emphasizes family policies and formulates proposals for female part-time employment, seems to appeal to women.

The Austrian People's Party is supported by landowners, the self-employed, by middle management, and by those with educational advantage. It also finds considerable support among the middle aged and the elderly, while even at the other end of the electoral spectrum the very young are more likely to vote for it rather than for the Socialists. As before, the Austrian People's Party dominates in rural areas, but in recent years significant gains have been made in working-class areas.

Problems and opportunities for the future

Election results in 1983 gave cause for optimism among the party's supporters. Table 6.1 gives an indication of gradual increasing popular support for the party at that time. The 1986 elections witnessed a slight falling away of this support, while some comfort could be taken from the fairly disastrous results for the Socialists. A favourable trend has been observed, however, in the results of the provincial parliamentary elections and, to a lesser extent, the Chambers of Labour elections up to 1984 (see Appendix F7).

Between 1945 and 1986 the Presidents of Austria have been the nominees of the Socialists. At the presidential elections in the spring of 1986, however, the Socialist candidate Steyrer, who as the Minister for Health and the Environment enjoyed great popularity, gained

Table 6.1 General Election results in Austria since 1945 (percentage of votes cast)

Year	Conservatives (ÖVP)	Socialists (SPÖ)	Liberals (FPÖ/VdU)	Communists (KPÖ)	Others
1945	49.80	44.60	–	5.42	0.18
1949	44.03	38.71	11.67	5.08	0.51
1953	41.26	42.11	10.95	5.28	0.40
1956	45.96	43.04	6.52	4.42	0.06
1959	44.19	44.79	7.70	3.27	0.05
1962	45.43	44.00	7.05	3.04	0.48
1966	48.35	42.56	5.35	0.41	3.33[a]
1970	44.69	48.42	5.52	0.98	0.39
1971	43.11	50.04	5.45	1.36	0.04
1975	42.95	51.42	5.41	1.19	0.03
1979	41.90	51.03	6.06	0.96	0.05
1983	43.22	47.65	4.98	0.66	3.49[b]
1986	41.29	43.12	9.73	0.72	5.14[b]

Notes: [a] The vast majority of votes under this heading were cast for the Democratic Progressive Party (DFP).
[b] The vast majority of votes under this heading were cast for the Green Party (VGÖ/ALÖ).

only 44.7 per cent of the votes in the first round. The People's Party candidate, Waldheim, centre of controversial news coverage both domestically and abroad, gained 49.6 per cent of the votes in the first round, thus narrowly missing the absolute majority. The other candidates were the former Liberal (though rather nationalistic) Scrinzi who gained 1.3 per cent, and the candidate of the Green Parties, Meissner-Blau, who gained 4.4 per cent.

In the second electoral round, with only the two main candidates, Waldheim gained 53.12 per cent and Steyrer 46.88 per cent. During the election campaign and between the two electoral rounds the allegations against Waldheim concerning a Nazi past were mounted by the Jewish World Congress. The Austrian electors reacted with resentment against foreign interference and the raising of a person's past may have played some part in the final result. The decisive factor, however, was not only the personality of Waldheim and his experience as a former diplomat, Foreign Secretary and UN–General Secretary, but also his views on the traditional values — of integrity, honesty, achievement, social responsibility and patriotism. These views are very much in line with the thinking of the Austrian People's Party.

This successful bid for the Presidency is an indication of the Austrian People's Party being ascendant once again. Recent trends in Austrian politics indicate that the People's Party is still very much a part of Austria's present and before long may very well determine its future. Its participation in the present Grand Coalition is essential to keep Austria on the right path in domestic as well as in international affairs.

7 The Freedom Party of Austria (FPÖ)

Franz Eitzinger

Historical development

The ideological roots of the party known as the *Freiheitliche Partei Österreichs* (FPÖ) are those of liberalism and nationalism. The ideological dualism implicit in the phrase national/liberal continues to characterize the third main political grouping (the so-called 'third *Lager*') in Austria right down to the present day.

In the period up to the beginning of the First World War the loosely-knit groups of Liberals belonging to the tradition of 'early liberalism' were not yet organized as a political party and were being gradually replaced by nationalist groupings. During those years several smaller pan-German nationalist parties merged with the German People's Party (*Deutsche Volkspartei*) to form an umbrella organization known as the German National League (*Deutscher Nationalverband*).

After the War, in an Austria which, compared with the size of the Empire, was now just a small state, thoughts of union with Germany (and hence German nationalism) flourished as never before. The nationalist grouping and its parties were unable, however, to achieve a corresponding numerical size since they still tended to be dependent upon the voluntary activities of a few individuals and were quite unable to match the good, firm organization of the two mass-membership parties. The representatives of the nationalist grouping in the First Republic, namely the Pan-German People's party (*Grossdeutsche Volkspartei*) and the Austrian Agrarian League (*Landbund für Österreich*) could not command more than 20 per cent of the votes between them, and between 1930 and 1934 this grouping was almost entirely taken over by National Socialism.

After the Second World War and the overthrow of the Nazi rule of terror the Allies permitted only three parties initially: the Socialist Party (SPÖ), the People's Party (ÖVP) and the Communist Party (KPÖ). The national-liberal grouping received no licence to form a party. Only after the repeal of the law against National Socialism and after several attempts by nationalist groups to form a party had been blocked by the veto of the government or the Allies did the national-liberals eventually, in 1949, gain a political voice with the formation of the League of Independents or VdU (*Verband der Unabhängigen*). Under the leadership of its two founders, the journalists Dr Herbert Kraus and Dr Viktor Reimann, the VdU fought for the rehabilitation of former Nazis and against the remaining anti-nationalist laws. It described itself as the party of those with no party allegiance (*die Partei der Parteilosen*) or as a non-party and as the representative of former National Socialists, returnees and German expellees. In its early days, however, its liberal leadership gave it a liberal rather than a nationalistic orientation.

It had some initial electoral successes, but in a situation where the internal political situation was settling down, where the rehabilitation of former Nazis was making visible progress and the politicians of the two government parties were gaining ever greater popularity and respect through their skilful negotiations for a State Treaty, the VdU's fortunes rapidly waned.

As a parallel development there were also conflicts within the party over the direction it was to take, and the nationalist wing emerged triumphant. With the resignation of the VdU's conservative-liberal founder Herbert Kraus, and with the formation of a new party, the Freedom Party of Austria (FPÖ), the nationalist takeover of the third *Lager* in Austrian politics became an accomplished fact. Unlike the VdU in its early days, therefore, the FPÖ was at first a markedly nationalistic party. Former Nazis took over its leadership, the first party leader being Anton Reinthaller, a leading functionary in the National Socialist Party.

The very first election fought by the new party, the *Nationalrat* election of 1956, showed that in post-war Austria the FPÖ would have no success if it pursued a purely nationalist course. Of the VdU's 14 seats the FPÖ managed to hold on to only six, and subsequent elections confirmed it to be a small party with a 5–7 per cent share of the vote.

With the accession of Reinthaller's successor Friedrich Peter to the party chairmanship in 1958, the leadership passed into the hands of the generation which had seen active war service. Peter, who had been an SS officer during the Second World War, initially continued Reinthaller's policies, so that in this period the main concerns of the FPÖ parliamentary group and of its party newspapers were to defend the soldiers of the Second World War and praise their achievements, while at the same time discrediting those who had fought in the Resistance.

Very soon, however, Peter recognized that if the party pursued an exclusively nationalist line and saw itself as belonging inevitably to the opposition, it would have no future. The FPÖ became more and more intent on breaking the Grand Coalition which it hated, and forming a Small Coalition with one of the ruling parties. But this could only succeed if the FPÖ changed course in the direction of liberalism. The party managed to escape from its relative political isolation, as a result of the decision by the Federal Chancellor Bruno Kreisky to risk an SPÖ minority government, for which the socialists needed the FPÖ's support. This enhanced the FPÖ's political standing immensely since it now had the opportunity, for the first time, of exerting influence upon the political situation.

The period from 1971 to 1974 may be described as the party's reform phase. The improvement of the party organization, the replacement of long-serving officials by those of the generation born between 1930 and 1940, the formation of what was known as the Lake Atter Circle (*Atterseekreis*), i.e. a political study group of young FPÖ intellectuals, the foundation of a training academy known as the Freedom (Party) Study Group (*Freiheitliches Bildungswerk*), the party's admission to the Liberal International, and the drawing up of the FPÖ's Manifesto on Social Policy (*Freiheitliches Manifest zur Gesellschaftspolitik*) which committed the party for the first time to a long-term political programme — these were all decisive steps towards the creation of a liberal, relevant and contemporary party image.

After scoring a resounding success in the Graz municipal elections the nationalist-conservative Mayor of Graz, Dr Alexander Götz, was appointed leader of the party at national level, but was shortly afterwards replaced by the liberal Dr Norbert Steger, the first FPÖ leader to have had no direct links with National Socialism. With Steger the party was once again on a liberal course.

The image which the party projected under its new leader was that of watch-dog (*Kontrollpartei*) or 'the party with clean hands' (*Partei der Saubermänner*). Power within the party was at last in the hands of the younger generation. After the SPÖ lost its absolute majority, the party achieved it long-held ambition of sharing in government. For the first time during the Second Republic a Small Coalition was formed — between the SPÖ and the FPÖ. With its new role as a government party there also came many new problems: it lost its potential, hitherto so important, of appealing to the protest vote; the party programme had to be adapted to the new situation; and after 3 years' participation in government, the nationalists were seeking to re-establish their own leadership of the party.

Organizational structure

In terms of organizational structure the FPÖ no longer differs materially from the major parties. Among the essential characteristics of parties within the third *Lager* in pre-war Austria were their loose organizational form and their dependence upon the voluntary activities of a few individuals: the fortunes of the political representatives of national-liberal ideology were in the hands of distinguished individuals and political patrons. This in turn caused fragmentation into innumerable groupings and ideological schools of thought, so that at the time when the Second Republic was founded there were almost 20 nationalist groups in Austria. Not until the early 70s, as part of a general process of reform within the FPÖ, was the party able to tighten its organization and so bring it into line with the modern organizational forms of the two mass-membership parties. Even today, however, the party's provincial organizations exercise a decisive influence, which it has proved impossible to restrain, upon the policies of the whole party, this being particularly true of those provincial associations which traditionally have a strong membership: Upper Austria, Carinthia, Styria and Salzburg.

Attempts by the party leader Dr Steger (till recently the Federal Vice-Chancellor) and a few young Viennese office-bearers to give the party a purely liberal image failed repeatedly because of the opposition, backed up by threats of secession, from the much more nationalistically minded provincial organizations in the regions. Then too, prominent individuals frequently oppose the national party, relying upon the numerical strength of their own provincial organizations.

The FPÖ has only a small proportion of the country's political party membership (14 per cent) and though it cannot be described as large by Austrian standards, it is active at every administrative and geographical level in the country. It has a structure which, with a largely top-down chain of command, is relatively strong and basically centralized despite the presence of some strong ideological tendencies towards federalism and decentralization.

Ideology and aims

The ideological roots of the third political grouping in Austria are liberalism and nationalism, both of them bourgeois ideologies. Towards the end of the nineteenth century, liberalism was totally displaced by a type of nationalism which looked towards Germany, and even to this day the nationalistic elements have not completely disappeared from the ideology of the third *Lager*. The first programme of the nationalist grouping, the Linz Programme of 1882, which served as the basis for all pan-German nationalist groupings and parties both then and since, was drawn up by the spiritual father of pan-German nationalism Georg Ritter von Schönerer, a radical protagonist of anti-semitism and of what was known as the *Kleindeutsche Lösung*. The main thrust of the programme, apart from its social demands, was that Austria should return to her natural 'home', the German Reich. Up to the Second World War, union (*Anschluss*), anti-semitism and anti-clericalism were firmly embedded in the programme of every nationalist party.

Although the programme of the first party representing the national-liberal grouping under the Second Republic was liberal rather than nationalistic, it once again revealed a commitment to pan-Germanism. Under the motto 'Justice, Integrity and Achievement' the programme concentrated on former National Socialists, returnees and expellees, opposing, in this context, the judicial system and practice of the immediate post-war period with its People's Courts and retrospective criminal legislation. Other central issues in the programme were attacks on the policies of proportional representation and protectionism pursued by the two major parties and, in the area of social and economic policy, attacks on nationalization, on the formation of cartels and monopolies, and the approval of private property.

In the second programme of the VdU, the Aussee Programme (*Ausseer Programm*), nationalism was again more prominent in order to placate the rebellious nationalist wing of the movement. There were already signs of a nationalist takeover within the third *Lager*, and indeed the first party programme of the FPÖ (known as the Summary Programme of the Freedom Party of Austria or *Kurzprogramm der Freiheitlichen Partei Österreichs*) was unambiguously nationalist in character. Among its 15 concisely stated points was a commitment to pan-Germanism in terms of German life and culture, and even opposition to 'degenerate art'. Nor was anything new added by the party's 'Guidelines' (*Richtlinien freiheitlicher Politik*) adopted by the third party conference in 1957; these served purely to interpret and amplify the briefly presented material of the *Kurzprogramm*.

There was no change of ideological direction until the seventh party conference in 1964 which adopted the Salzburg Declaration (*Salzburger Bekenntnis*) as an amplification of the party's programme. The new party leader Friedrich Peter had realized that the party, with its nationalist line, would never emerge from its political ghetto, and that it had to move away from being an ideological party in order to become, like the two major parties, a people's party (*Volkspartei*), one which appeals to all sections of the population. The objective of smashing the now tottering Grand Coalition and of forming a government with one of the two major parties could be achieved only by liberalizing the party's image, so the *Salzburger Bekenntnis* was pervaded by the liberal idea of freedom. The FPÖ intended by means of this programme to demonstrate its own readiness for government, but for the moment each of the ruling parties merely used the FPÖ, whenever necessary, as a means of putting pressure on its coalition partner.

Nor did the Bad Ischl Programme (*Bad Ischler Programm*), adopted in 1968, contain anything basically new. This was intended as a reaction to a new political situation, namely government by a single party, the ÖVP. There was still no commitment to Austria's neutrality from the point of view of the FPÖ — in fact this did not appear until 1970. Prominence in the new programme was given to the importance of élitism, and to the demand for a European federal state. Subsequently the European idea was increasingly to replace the demand for a pan-German community in terms of life and culture.

Only with the party's Manifesto on Social Policy, adopted in 1973 as an amplification of the basic programme, can the FPÖ be said to have become a party with a long-term programme. The 45-page document gives detailed attention to all social areas, and the German nationalist element had now finally been relegated to the background.

The national/liberal conflict, however, is still not finally settled even today. The recruitment of the younger generation of party leaders from the conservative pan-German nationalist student organization RFS (*Ring freiheitlicher Studenten*) which has cross-links with pan-German nationalist student fraternities, plus the nationalistic outlook of some individual provincial organizations (e.g. Carinthia) and of some individuals, does not greatly favour the FPÖ's prospects of acquiring a purely liberal image.

Even the party's recent programme necessitated by its participation in government and adopted at Salzburg in June 1985 had to make concessions to the nationalists within the party. This highly comprehensive programme, dealing with all areas of life, must nonetheless be described as unambiguously liberal in its basic character.

While in coalition with the SPÖ, whose ideology is diametrically opposed to its own in most things, the FPÖ felt obliged to defend and emphasize its ideological position in order not to be swallowed up by its major partner and in order to maintain its credibility with the voters. The ideology with which the FPÖ counters socialism, is, however, not nationalism but liberalism.

Whether or not the FPÖ becomes a purely liberal party will depend on the nationalist elements within its ranks. At this point in time they would appear to be in the ascendant, being responsible for the dissolution of the Small Coalition in 1986. The new party leader Haider seems to strike a chord amongst the voters of nationalist persuasion and the increase in the Party's representation in parliament after the November 1986 General Election reflects this type of orientation. This means that the essence of the liberal tradition, previously an important factor in the formation of the Freedom Party, is likely in the foreseeable future to become dormant or disappear altogether.

8 The Communist Party of Austria

Jim Sweeney

The Communist Party of Austria (*Kommunistische Partei Österreichs* or KPÖ) is the only remaining Marxist-Leninist political party of any significance in Austria today even though among the electorate its influence can be seen to lag considerably behind that of the other more traditional parties, and even more recently, that of the Environmentalist parties.

Establishment of the Austrian Communist Party

The Communist Party of German-Austria (KPDÖ) was founded on 3 November 1918 by the radical left group headed by Paul and Elfriede Friedländer after the arrest of the leading lights of the Action Committee of the Left Radicals associated with the January strikes of 1918. The KPDÖ's early days coincided with the establishment of the First Republic and the initial problems which that brought in its train. Its early membership groups were largely composed of the activists mentioned above, returning soldiers from the Russian Front who were predominantly active Communists (for example Koplenig, Brodnig, Toman), the Federation of Revolutionary Socialist Internationals led by Rothziegel and Wertheim — who had also played an active role in the January strikes — and left-radical youth groups who had left, or were expelled from, the Socialist Party, as well as other less prominent organized left groups. At its inception, the Viennese section of the Jewish Workers' Party (*Paole Zion*) worked closely with the KPDÖ, and in the course of time, those of its members who remained in Austria eventually joined the Communist Party which, by 1919, had dropped the designation 'German-Austria' and had become simply the Communist Party of Austria (KPÖ).

The First Republic and the Third Reich: initial support and illegal resistance

The fortunes of the new Communist Party were quite varied in the First Republic, being heavily influenced by many factors: the prevailing climate of revolution and uncertainty, the quality of the new leadership, the social strata attracted to their ideas and perhaps the most crucial of all — a factor which continued well into the Second Republic — the vicissitudes of the Social Democratic Party of Austria (properly called the Social Democratic Workers Party — SDAP). The atmosphere of revolution and change which attended the fall of the Habsburg monarchy was, it must be said, favourable to the newly-founded Communist Party. The January strikes of 1918 and the formation of the party, largely composed of radical disaffected elements of the Social Democratic Party, provided the core of early activities and support. As disagreements about the impending social and political crisis took place between the moderate and extreme sections within the Social Democratic Party, a sufficient rift occurred to enable the new party to exploit the opportunities which the uncertainty and alienation of the new economic and political situation brought for it.

The first task was to organize a structure and electoral base for future activities and in regard to organization, the financial means certainly came from abroad. Even though many of the party's leading activists were young and enthusiastic, the party lacked political experience, containing only a few who had lengthy involvement in the Austrian Labour Movement and few intellectuals to enable it to construct radical alternative policies and programmes for mass appeal. Particularly striking was its failure to attract middle rank or leading figures from the Social Democratic Party — with the exception of Josef Strasser — which was crucial to its development of an apparatus capable of attracting members and mobilizing public support. A particularly injurious blow was the refusal of the immensely popular leading Social Democrat, Friedrich Adler, to accept the leadership of the new party on his release from prison in 1918.

In electoral terms, the first failure was the reluctance of the party to contest the first general election in the new Republic. Despite that, certainly till the end of 1920, the Communist Party found some support, mainly among demobilized soldiers many of whom had been prisoners of war, sections of the unemployed and other groups including lumpen-proletarian elements. Accordingly the party's propaganda became directed at the unemployed, the disabled, the sick and returning exiles in what seemed to be the simplest strategy. The party never enjoyed the support of the mass of the workers as was the case with the Social Democratic Party. In industrial concerns, particularly in view of the new form of political/industrial organizations formed under the influence of revolutionary Soviet-type movements in Bavaria and Hungary, things were not particularly bad in the early years. In the elections to the workers' councils (*Arbeiterräte*) in October and November 1919 the party could not compete with the enormous support the Social Democrats attracted; even so it achieved 189 seats (5.1% of the vote) compared with the Socialists 3,462 (93.9%) in the largest firms' electoral category; 602 (to the Socialists 810) in a second — composed mainly of small firms and the unemployed — although it had a parity of representation in many local areas. Generally speaking, apart from six large and medium-sized firms in Vienna and a few locations in the provinces there was no great support. Since a large part of the party's strength lay with the unemployed, as economic activity and employment increased the new organization lost influence and this, to some extent, was reflected in its membership figures. Though numerically weak at the start, it was quite an achievement for membership to increase from 3,000 to 40,000 between February and June 1919. After the initial economic dislocation when life returned to (or became more) normal this membership (as well as its electoral support) melted away. In the short run, however, there was a good foundation for workplace-based policy, particularly when the Social Democrats' credibility ran into trouble for a time but in the medium and long run this could not be sustained, particularly as the international situation improved (although it was never satisfactory) and as threats from without receded with the collapse of Soviet-style governments in Hungary and Bavaria. The demonstration and putsch organized by the party of 15 June 1919 which resulted in the arrest of 130 leading Communists and left 20 dead on the streets with 80 injured was perhaps the last revolutionary act of the new party (until the Second Republic) and from then on its support, considered at one time a sizeable minority, dwindled. By the end of 1919 it was estimated that 10,000 members had left the party, 4,300 in Vienna alone. Its membership continued to fall and it was never above 4,000 for the remainder of the First Republic — although when it was declared 'illegal' it is claimed that there was an increase from 3,000 to 16,000 between February and October 1934.

With the demise of workers' councils (*Arbeiterräte* or Soviets) the little support the Communists enjoyed in workplace representation declined and the establishment of works' councils (*Betriebsräte*) witnessed no reversal of this process. Their industrial support by the middle of the 1920s was extremely marginal. From the end of 1919 a considerable number of splits and internal struggles took place and the party was preoccupied with a good deal of self-criticism. In the four general elections which it contested between 1920 and 1930 in the First Republic, it attracted between 16 and 28,000 votes only and was never represented in parliament.

How does one account for such a dismal electoral performance at this time? In the first place, the Communist Party had no long tradition of political activity in Austria and certainly till 1934 its calls for class struggle and revolution went unheeded and there was a tendency for most Austrians to see it as an extension of a foreign power. It had no base among the significant, solid economic strata in society and had failed to build mass support. The answer also lies in the political competition then prevailing for a party inspired by the ideals of the Soviet Union, and early on it was seen by the masses as less 'German-Austrian' than the Social Democrats, a perception reinforced through the wranglings and internal struggles within the Soviet Union at that period.

The traditional working-class support for the Social Democrats on the other hand remained constant throughout the twenties and early thirties. The clever electoral strategy of the Social Democrats and their 'left' course after 1926 centred around the personality of Bauer created unfavourable conditions for the Communist Party. But to this there must be added the Communist Party's tactical errors. After 1934 when both parties were outlawed it called for a 'United Front' with the Social Democrats. The demand for such a co-operative venture was refused by the latter in view of the 'rigid' attitude of the Executive of the Communist Party and the low regard as a serious political force in which the Socialists held the Communists. At an international rather than domestic level, however, there was a tacit assent to such a call. This situation nevertheless led to criticisms by the Communists of those 'illegal' Social Democrats who had now reorganized into the Revolutionary Socialists. The mistake which constituted such attacks lay in the fact that this was still the party of Adler, Bauer and 'Red Vienna' and the implications of such an error were to continue into the Second Republic. This mistake in the short term was by no means totally disadvantageous to the Communist Party.

The 'illegal activity' after 1934 and its stepping up after the *Anschluss* of 1938 did provide however, despite the rivalry of the SDAP, a temporary 'shot in the arm' for the party. The sharp upturn in membership in 1934 was clearly at the expense of the Social Democrats, as even Otto Bauer admitted, and included the defection of possibly Austria's best known Communist intellectual, writer and editor of the Socialist Party's *Arbeiterzeitung*, Ernst Fischer. By 1938 the Revolutionary Socialists as a revolutionary illegal organization had regained their momentum under bitter criticism from the Communist Party.

The Second Republic: power and disillusionment

The Fascist and Nazi eras brought positive and negative aspects for the KPÖ. We have noted above the defections to it from the Social Democrats; an additional positive aspect lay in the 'image' which had accrued to it such as the 'heroism' of 'Red Vienna', and its association with the non-partisan (*über-parteilich*) organizational network which supported the illegal activity. This gave it the quasi-character of fusion which provided it with a certain kind of influence at the beginning of the Second Republic.

On the other, negative side, the transformation brought about by anti-Nazi resistance also brought about conditions for a demarcation which did not previously pertain and was not evident between 1918 and 1934. This demarcation was a decisive element for the character of the re-established party after 1945 and one of the essential conditions which delineated it from the Socialist Party and thereby affected its electoral support.

The events of 1938–45 had provided no basis for a 'Socialist Unity' party or 'United Front' composed of Socialists and Communists. They did provide, however, for a time, informal Contact Committees with close co-operation in mind. But as for any permanent post-war fusion and organizational merging as far as the Socialist leadership was concerned, the Russian occupation of Vienna and Lower Austria had made such a course unthinkable and popular opinion was a powerful factor in support of that attitude. In recognition of their valuable contributions in the Resistance, Socialist objections notwithstanding, the Communists were invited to join Renner's Provisional Government in 1945 in which they participated with the other two major political parties, but the lamentable results they achieved in the first general election to the Lower House of parliament (*Nationalrat*) on 25 November 1945 was a great disappointment for them. This destroyed any plans or calculations they may have had either in holding a commanding position in parliament as a major political party or any possibility of forming some type of socialist unity party with the Social Democrats (which had now become reorganized as the Socialist Party of Austria — SPÖ) as had occurred elsewhere in Europe. Ideology gave credence to this latter hope: after all, Otto Bauer before his death in 1938 had advocated an 'integrated socialism'. This, however, was not to be. The Socialist Party was now dominated by Renner and the Lower Austrian group who were firmly against the radicalism of the party's left wing or against those whom they regarded as having crypto-Communist tendencies. Even most of the leaders of the Revolutionary Socialists, whether they had been in exile or in the underground movement, were opposed to any kind of fusion. Many of those in the resistance had opposed the Communist slogan of the People's Front during the Nazi era, and to these were added the voices of those in exile who had come under Anglo-Saxon influences. The Labour Party's victory in Britain in 1945 also gave an added impetus to those searching for a new view of democratic socialism which sharply contrasted with totalitarian tendencies. Moreover, the perceptions of those who had daily experienced life in the Third Reich felt strongly on the matter and the new post-war wave of enthusiasm for democratic life demonstrated a high value on new-won freedom; whilst those returning from exile in the Soviet Union or from the German army expressed similar sentiments. The tight discipline of the Socialist Party was little affected by issues of personality or the tactics of the Communist Party. On leaving the Coalition Government the Communist Party attempted to demonstrate by industrial action what it could not achieve by popular confidence — hence the General Strike of 1950 to bring down the Socialist Party/People's Party Coalition provided the complete testimony to the ideological cul-de-sac into which the Communist Party had now run; it also provided the complete testimony to the solidarity of the entire Austrian Socialist community with the SPÖ before the world. Simultaneously it demonstrated a devaluation of ideology, particularly if one considers the rhetoric and contentious atmosphere of left-wing policies in the pre-war era. For now an anti-fanatic, conciliatory and pro-democratic climate predominated in which perceived extremes had no place.

Party programmes, electoral support and the structure of the modern Communist Party

The immediate post-war period brought many changes in the ideology, policies and the approaches of the traditional parties, now reconstituted. The only exception to this was the Community Party which remained traditionally orthodox (in the Soviet sense) and whose structures continued as before. The period after 1945 denoted a greater willingness to co-operate and a consensus between the two large groupings which was exemplified in the social partnership but this did not necessarily or immediately freeze out the Communist Party. Indeed the party had the opportunity as well as the capacity to adjust to the unfavourable situation in which it found itself. Its period of participation in the Coalition Governments brought some gains and it commanded a degree of legitimacy among the electorate which it had previously not enjoyed; it was represented in the Senate (*Bundesrat*) with a single seat from 1949 to 1954 and between 1945 and 1959 had between 3 and 5 of the 165 seats of the Lower House of Parliament (*Nationalrat*). In the longer term, however, it lost popular support as Table 8.1 indicates.

Table 8.1 indicates a much more favourable situation for the Com-

Table 8.1 Representation by absolute votes, percentage of total cast and seats in Austrian parliament (Nationalrat) 1945–86: Communist Party of Austria (KPÖ)

Year	Votes	% of votes cast[a]	Seats
1945	174,257	5.4	4
1949[b]	213,066	5.1	5
1953[b]	228,159	5.3	4
1956	192,438	4.4	3
1959	142,578	3.3	–
1962	135,520	3.0	–
1966	18,636	0.4	–
1970	44,750	1.0	–
1971	61,762	1.4	–
1975	55,032	1.2	–
1979	45,280	1.0	–
1983	31,912	0.7	–
1986	35,104	0.7	–

Notes: [a]The total electorate between 1945 and 1986 ranged from 3.5 to 5.5 millions, 90% of which actually voted.
[b]In 1949 the Communist Party contested the elections under the designation Left Bloc (*Linksblock*) and in 1953 under Austrian Peoples' Opposition Electoral Community (*Wahlgemeinschaft Österreichische Volksopposition*).

munist Party compared to its experience in the First Republic. Whether one chooses seats gained or percentage votes polled this is certainly the case. At the same time one can observe the high points of the party's fortunes in the democratic process between 1949 and 1953 as well as the depths thereafter.

From the table it is not particularly apparent that the events of the Hungarian uprising in 1956 or the Czechoslovakian invasion of 1968 made much difference to a trend which already was set in electoral decline. The slight upturn in the popular vote between 1966 and 1970, however, is surprising. To obtain some understanding of this and later developments one has to turn to membership trends and party policy. By 1946 the party had 132,268 members — 33 times the 1930s' average. Between 1954 and 1956 this had increased to 155,000 but there was a dramatic fall to 60,000 by the end of 1957, a downward trend which continued, reaching 36,408 in 1964, plummeting to 26,000 in 1970 and is thought to be about 17,000 at the present time.

It is not to be forgotten that since the Communist Party was unequivocal in its demand for Austrian independence while remaining a loyal supporter of the Soviet Union, the year 1956 had a two-fold significance: Krushchev's denunciation of the Stalin personality cult at the twentieth congress of the Supreme Soviet in the spring was followed by the Hungarian uprising in October. These events (particularly the destalinization of the first) occasioned mass defections while a few years later the party leadership continued to square the circle as it was later to do again over the Czechoslovak invasion. On the face of it the Czech affair was more serious; the majority of the Central Committee condemned the Soviet intervention and this curiously enough split the party almost in two. The following year, 1969, Ernst Fischer probably the best known intellectual advocate of Austrian Communism, spoke against 'Tank Communism' (*Panzerkommunismus*) and was expelled from the party. Twenty-seven members of the Central Committee followed him which caused a crisis in the party.

In the following year difficulties occurred with the Communist Trade Union group, the Youth Section, the student organization and a doctors' section. In the case of the Prague Spring before the Russian clampdown, it was claimed that the Austrian party principles were beyond those which the Czechs were laying down and this afforded sympathy with the Czechs' demands. This was followed later in 1971, however, by a decision to lift the judgement of the Central Committee — made against the Soviet invasion — and the party thereby returned to its orthodox stance while ostensibly judging subsequent actions in the light of whichever programme could be invoked according to political expediency.

Austrian Communist Party programmes (or manifestos) have never been in any way extensive or comprehensive. There was a relative paucity of manifestos in the First Republic, and in this sense, the tactics they then executed or their specific slogans may have served as substitutes for the strategies or policies which manifestos generally outline. In the Second Republic such manifestos, though more abundant, have been limited to the following:

1946 Programmatic Guiding Principles (*Programmatische Leitsätze*)

1954 The Way to Secure and Safeguard the Independence of Austria (*Der Weg zur Erringung und Sicherung der Unabhängigkeit Österreichs*)

1958 The Austrian Road to Socialism (*Der Weg Österreichs zum Sozialismus*)

1965 Programmatic Guiding Principles (*Programmatische Leitsätze*)
1974 Political-Ideological Guiding Principles (*Politisch-ideologische Leitsätze*)

The essence of these manifestos — despite their general tone — is that there is a great deal held in common with Communist Parties elsewhere while containing much which is specific to the Austrian context. The general substance, however, is that of western Communist orthodoxy and which by the same token has formed the main base of criticism against the Austrian Communist Party, namely that it is an outpost of the Soviet Union. The usual phraseology and shibboleths are contained within these programmes — class consciousness, class struggle, the ruling system, dictatorship of capital, state monopoly capitalism, exploitation, peace, freedom and peaceful co-existence. Little or no space is given to the discussion on such currently important issues as education (in any form) or educational policy, health, leisure, defence, the United Nations, youth concerns, family life or old age.

Women's equality is discussed only in the context of capitalism (creates a double exploitation for women in education and career development) whilst with respect to international problems there is no mention of the South Tyrol question — which is understandable — and nothing on civil rights and minorities — which is not. The defence of democratic institutions is bound up with class representation, i.e. Communist representation, in parliament; while the function of democracy is to 'put pressure on the crisis of bourgeois democracy' and is 'essential to socialism', while freedom is considered in the narrow context of freedom from exploitation. Equality relates to the aim of a classless society 'through the establishment of the workers' power' while ecological issues relate to 'pace of work' and the need for 'culturally necessary activities'.

For the matters which specially relate to the Austrian domestic situation nothing more substantial is proffered. The institutions and their locations in and for the Labour Movement — workplace, Chambers of Labour, trade unions, legislative bodies — 'must be harnessed to make the Labour Movement strong'; the party should 'fight with all determination' the People's Party (ÖVP) and the Liberal Party (FPÖ) which are described as reactionary parties — the latter as 'Nazi' — while the Socialist Party is 'sham' about its progressive aims and is the main obstacle for a successful working-class policy. The 'struggle against the economic system must recognize that state monopoly capitalism belongs to the traditions of institutions such as Cartels and Chamber systems' and the prevailing economic policy is such that the capitalist economy cannot exist without increasing state support and one form of this is the Austrian State Holding Company (ÖIAG) which, with its constituent parts, represents 'the influence of domestic and foreign big business' — a growing influence. Again, the social partnership has in growing measure served to shift the functions of big business on to the leaders of the Austrian Trade Union Federation (ÖGB) who 'misuse the unions'; co-determination (*Mitbestimmung*) is relegated to an irrelevance, and nationalization is seen as an 'excessive misuse' in which foreign capital and European Community policies can be deposited.

Finally, even neutrality is seen as part of the international class unity of the Austrian bourgeoisie with United States imperialism and West European monopoly capitalism. These omnibus manifestos appear more useful as warnings and admonitions than guides to action and it is small wonder, if one compares them with the much more improvement-oriented and proactive programmes of some of the other European parties, that they appear unconstructive.

At the organization level, how does the Communist Party of Austria operate? Figure 8.1 gives an indication of the overall organizational structure. The party's first general secretary, Koplenig, elected in 1924, was succeeded by Muhri in 1965 who is still the incumbent. Its official organ is its daily newspaper — a quality one by Western standards — the *Volksstimme*, which as might be expected, has a limited circulation.

Mention has been made of the Communist Party's lack of representation in the national parliament. It is, however, occasionally represented at local level and, much more important, industrially — at workplace, trade union and the Chambers of Labour levels where it is at its strongest. At the present time for example it has 7% of the seats on the executive of the Austrian Federation of Trade Unions and, if we take the two Communist groupings (traditional and European Communists) together, they hold 8 of the 840 Chambers of Labour Council seats in the country.

Conclusion

What can be said of the significance of the Communist Party in modern Austria? There is no doubt it has little influence today compared to the early days of the Second Republic. It is argued that at the birth of the First Republic, when parallel developments elsewhere made the Austrian political situation uncertain, political opportunities might have had more potential for it as a revolutionary party.

Secondly, external events have largely dominated and restricted the scope for action and limited any movement towards an *Austrokommunismus*; such forces it would appear have restricted its

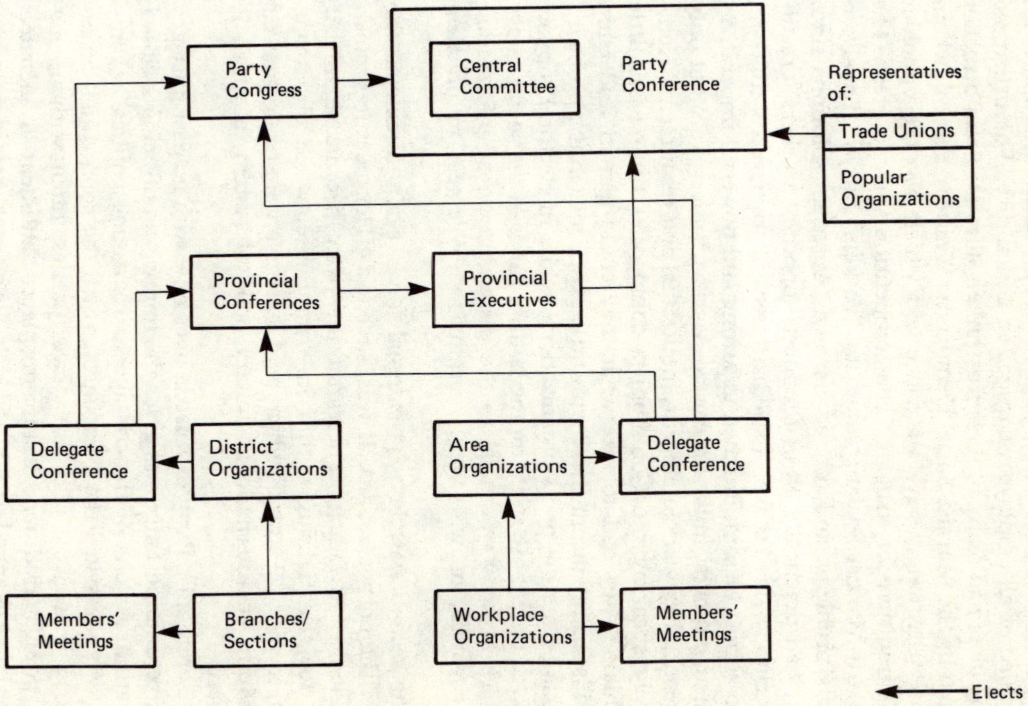

Figure 8.1 Organizational structure of the Austrian Communist Party (KPÖ)

flexibility or its capacity to develop a creativeness by which Austrian responses to Austrian situations might have been appropriate.

A third fundamental and related factor lies in the development of the Austrian working class. Even by 1920, when the Communist Party made a late entry onto the Austrian political stage, there was still a third of all employees engaged in agriculture. The urbanized working class had many of their frustrations alleviated and demands mediated by the Marxist Social Democratic Workers' Party to whom they overwhelmingly gave allegiance and which was the upholder of their traditions of struggle. The competition was too great. The old Austro-Marxist Social Democratic Workers' Party had analysed Austria's problems and offered its own 'Austrian' solutions since 1889; it had practically all of the most important workers' organizations closely allied to it as it still has today. Working-class children, it could almost be said, imbibed its strong and powerful imperatives with their mothers' milk. Its Austro-Marxist leaders were not only courageous, they were intelligent, intellectual and resourceful. Comparatively speaking the Communists could offer the masses little or nothing. They had to take what they could get; in leadership terms this mainly meant those with little experience in the problems of working-class life or its organizations, while in electoral support it attracted only those strata on the bottom rungs of the social ladder who were in no way crucial to the dissemination of information or propaganda, or who were marginal with respect to practical politics.

At the second start in 1945 external forces again dominated the scope of the party's actions. It was forced to effect measures which were doomed to failure. Thereafter the party became significant mainly for fire fighting within its own house, while the strong external ideological strands which held it captive were being gnawed away within an international unitary political system of which it was a part.

The Communist Party of Austria lives now with its past mistakes in relative unimportance and gives the impression of being a closed organization. As one of the courageous remaining political organizations which resisted the Fascism to which the country fell prone after 1934 it seems a pity that newer parties, often without any kind of popular tradition, capture misplaced sentiment or alienated discontent in a changed society and look like overtaking it in influence and importance in Austrian political life.

9 Alternative political movements

Joe Weidenholzer

Modern Austria has long been characterized by a situation of 'political oligopoly' in which three political parties have enjoyed popular support and have dominated the parliamentary scene.

The Communist Party has, from time to time, occupied a marginal position with respect to the other major political groupings, and has occasionally entered into electoral alliances with disaffected and splinter groups from the major parties to make a breakthrough but with little success. In 1949 for example, it joined up with the Association of Progressive Socialists (*Vereinigung fortschrittlicher Sozialisten*) led by the former general secretary of the Socialist Party, Erwin Scharf, and this for a time may have helped it to sustain the little momentum it had in the immediate post-war years; later on, however, its somewhat more questionable alliance with the group led by the former Christian-Social (Conservative) Minister Dobretsberger, called the Democratic Union, in 1953 made no significant change in the electorate's solid preferences for the parties of the centre.

There have been all sorts of activities and organizations in post-war Austria which have styled themselves 'movements' and which have been independent of the mass parties. Many of these might hardly be political in the sense that they would aspire to change social structures or run the affairs of state. In this category, nevertheless, would be such diverse activities as tax boycott groups, civil disobedience campaigns, amnesty international, peace and religious groups, student groups and the like, whose aims are too disparate to appeal to either the idealism or self-interest of the voter and which might be more appropriately called pressure groups. One exception to this in the 1960s and one which lasted (albeit with much less appeal) till the early 1980s was the political organization led by the former Socialist Minister and Austrian Trade Union Federation ex-President, Franz Olah — the Democratic Progressive Party (*Demokratische Fortschrittliche Partei* or DFP). This party fought general elections from 1966 supported by many young people who were demanding a shift to the left, thus signifying to some extent a dissatisfaction with the Socialists with the aim of becoming the radical alternative to the Conservatives in the long run. Much of its drive and enthusiasm, however, were absorbed by the effective, idealist and dynamic election campaigns of the Socialist Party under Dr Kreisky in the early 1970s. Kreisky eventually succeeded in winning back leftish elements to the party's mainstream activities and formed a majority Socialist government.

There is no doubt that the potential for the emergence of a credible alternative political party which could muster a fair degree of public opinion was made possible by the referendum in the summer of 1978 on whether or not the nuclear power station at Zwentendorf should be brought into operation. The result of the referendum was a narrow defeat for the Socialist government thus occasioning the abandonment of nuclear energy. There is no doubt about the part in the anti-nuclear campaign played by a large number of small groups with quite multifarious aims. The campaign also demonstrated that temporary alliances for specific purposes could, should the dissatisfaction be great enough, form a platform to harness the latent idealism of many sections of the population, and bring a new constellation of political forces into being. It is also true to say that most of the vociferous criticisms ranged against the Socialist Party came from significant sections of the membership as well as those inimical to it. It is also true to say that once again in 1979, by means of skilful psychological tactics, the Socialists managed to secure the loyalty of such groups, but the issues that would one day lead to separation were now plain for all to see.

The events leading up to Zwentendorf show that the protest potential of the Greens comes from two quite different sources. On the one hand there were middle-class groups who could not identify with the 'collectivist' trade unions, while on the other hand there were one-time members of the student movement and the left-wing tendency which emerged from it. It was these left-wing groups in particular who now found themselves at odds with the interests of big business and who initially formed the activist core of the future Green Movement.

An important step towards the establishment of a fourth party was the formation of the Peace Movement which emerged in Austria at roughly the same time as elsewhere in western Europe. The Austrian Peace Movement reached its highest point in May 1982 when it succeeded in mobilizing the largest mass of people ever to have been brought together in the country's recent history, bringing them right into the heart of the federal capital to demonstrate for peace. Zwentendorf 1978 and Vienna 1982 are two important dates in the history of the Second Republic, which clearly show that the attachment of the Austrian people to the two major political *Lager* is by no means permanent, and that the development of an autonomous movement outside the confines of these *Lager* had now become a possibility.

It has taken less than a decade since Zwentendorf for these movements to coalesce into a parliamentary force and an alternative to the three main political parties. The entry into parliament of representatives of the Green-Alternative Party in November 1986, however, had been preceded by vehement arguments between the supporters of its two broad streams which had by this time formed an electoral pact. It is important to mention this since there is some confusion concerning the united aspect of the movement, the importance of which, as will be shown, might be somewhat exaggerated. The fact is that the Green members of parliament are from that strand only of the United Green Party of Austria (*die Vereinten Grünen Österreichs* or VGÖ). The VGÖ stands in the traditional middle-class environmentalism and was founded by the Viennese geologist Alexander Tollman who had made a name for himself in connection with the anti-nuclear movement. He was supported by the Salzburg actor Herbert Fux and by Josef Buchner who as Deputy Mayor (*Vizebürgermeister*) of Steyregg, a town adjacent to Linz in Upper Austria, had achieved national prominence. After a series of personal quarrels over the leadership and various escapades in the election campaign of 1986, Buchner (a political realist) emerged victorious. The VGÖ sees itself as a group in the political centre and as a protest movement for environmental protection and, to some degree, civil rights. Although radical in their attitudes to the problems which they confront, members of the VGÖ are concerned that all their activities should remain within the framework of existing institutions.

The other stream, the Alternatives (*Alternativen*), is in many ways fundamentally different. They are themselves an amalgam of a number of small groups which united to form an electioneering organization under the title Alternative Ticket of Austria (*Alternative Liste Österreichs or ALÖ*). They came to prominence in the controversy over the Hainburg dam in the winter of 1984 when they prevented the construction of this hydro-electric power station in conjunction with VGÖ led by Freda Meissner-Blau. Meissner-Blau, as the Greens' nominee for the Presidency in mid-1986, quite clearly profited from this activity with the effect that she received 5.5% of the first round votes. The Alternatives, it must be said, are different in their approach to politics and can be said to be (despite the name) more akin to the Greens in Federal Germany than is the VGÖ. As a consequence of this, just before the General Election of November 1986, a quarrel took place between the leaders of the Alternatives and Frau Meissner-Blau concerning the placing of their joint candidates on the 'list' (that is, those who would be of their joint candidates on the 'list' (that is, those who would be elected should the 5% threshold of votes be attained). The upshot of this issue, widely reported in the national media, was that the Alternatives fought on a separate basis under the name of the Green Alternative Democratic Ticket (*Die Grünalternativen Demokratische Liste*). By then Meissner–Blau had a sufficiently successful electoral campaign, with far better media coverage than her erstwhile election allies, so that the Green (VGÖ) entry onto the parliamentary stage was assured. The difference alluded to above raises certain questions not only about the nature of the relationships between the two wings of the Green Alternative Party, as its common platform label has it, but also about objectives and whether there could be any basis for a permanent fusion. This can best be answered by looking at some fundamental structural characteristics.

The Alternatives' leadership is of a collective nature and the organization functions on the common themes relating to problems upon which campaigns are built. These initiatives are quite often of a moral-ideological nature, for example strict price regulation and the banning of South African goods in Austria. Even the issues they share with the VGÖ reveal a quite different perspective. If we take the case of the environment, they are more concerned with the interface between the environment and man rather than (as in the case of the VGÖ) having a mere preoccupation with the natural world. These issues can be said to form the basis of the Alternatives' manifestos since they do not promulgate formal declarations as such. Apart from meetings or demonstrations, the Alternatives have a newspaper called 'Network' (*Netzwerk*) and an occasional members' news-sheet entitled *Alternativer Rundbrief* whereas the VGÖ has no news medium as yet. Their party membership is on an individual basis and estimated to be around 600 which, though relatively insignificant compared to the long-established parties, is reckoned to be higher than that of the VGÖ; their organizational structure is informal and decentralized with each provincial organization having a considerable degree of autonomy.

The ALÖ has a radical view of parliament as well as its representatives, since they are by no means averse to extra-parliamentary action should the occasion demand it. The member of parliament by this token is seen in a different light: he or she is accountable to, and subject to the control of, the party — a delegate voting according to party instruction rather than according to individual conscience. Parliament is seen as one of many institutions — in no way superior to others — which is in service to society rather than being superordinate to it.

In a real sense the ALÖ is the heir, in the Austrian context, to the student movements of 1968. They draw their support from a number of miscellaneous groups — Eurocommunists, peace movement advocates, students, schoolteachers, the young and those relatively new to politics. The VGÖ on the other hand is composed of the older generation, particularly those who are disenchanted with, or are disaffected elements from the Conservative and Socialist parties. Viewed from such a standpoint, therefore, the Alternatives can be considered left-wing and radical whereas the VGÖ would be a left-of-centre party.

In view of the differences to be found between the component parts of the Green-Alternatives it is no wonder that there appears to be no progress towards a permanent union. Despite their undoubted electoral success, in the light of the reservations expressed above, it is still too early to judge whether or not the trend which favoured them in November 1986 will continue. This question can only be answered by reference to long-term developments. What is much more probable is that the combined forces of the VGÖ and ALÖ will benefit in the short term at the expense of the right and left wings of the Socialist Party and occupy the niche in political life which the Communist Party had at one time, but without offering a real alternative to the main political parties.

PART III
ECONOMIC AND INDUSTRIAL STRUCTURES AND INSTITUTIONS

10 The Austrian economy and the structures of industry

Ewald Nowotny

Macro-economic indicators

Austria's gross domestic product (GDP) amounted to 1,371 billion schillings in 1985. Its per capita GDP was 181,518 schillings, putting it in 13th position among the OECD states (15th in terms of purchasing power parity). Behind these figures lies a long process of catching up in which Austria, from being an economic straggler, has gained a place among the affluent industrial nations.

The Republic of Austria, which came into being upon the collapse of the Austro-Hungarian Empire after the First World War, was regarded by many as being economically non-viable. And certainly, apart from brief periods of stable growth, it had to contend with massive economic problems throughout its history. The Second Republic, which was established after the Second World War, was likewise faced with severe economic difficulties at its inception but by building upon the foundation of a radically altered political and psychological approach, taking advantage of the increased industrialization brought about by the union with Germany, and making use of foreign aid (particularly the European Recovery Programme) the country was able to achieve an economic development which, in terms of dynamism, surpassed that of most European industrial states. During recent decades, even after the end of the immediate period of reconstruction, Austria's real economic growth has exceeded that of the European OECD countries and this has greatly reduced the original prosperity gap.

In 1985 unemployment in Austria stood at 4.7 per cent, well below the average for the European OECD countries and the 8 per cent of West Germany. These differences arise primarily from the fact that after the first oil crisis (1973–4) Austria was able to avoid a massive rise in unemployment. Since the second oil crisis the rate of unemployment in Austria has moved roughly parallel to that of West Germany, but Austria's 'head start' in terms of employment has been maintained.

In 1985 Austria's inflation rate was 2.9 per cent, below the average

Table 10.1 Macro-economic indicators (average values), expressed as annual percentage rates

	1970/75		1975/80		1980/85	
	A	OE	A	OE	A	OE
GDP growth rate	4.5	3.3	2.8	2.3	1.8	1.3
Unemployment rate	1.3	2.6*	1.9	4.3*	3.4	7.6*
Inflation rate	6.8	8.9	5.8	11.6	5.2	9.7
Current account balance as % of GDP	−0.9	−1.1	−3.5	−1.1	−0.7	−0.3

*excluding: Denmark, Finland, Greece, Iceland, Ireland, Luxembourg, Portugal, Turkey
A = Austria
OE = OECD Europe
Source: OECD, Economic Outlook, various years.

for the European OECD countries (6.4 per cent), but above that of West Germany. Over a longer period too, Austria has been among the countries with the lowest inflation rate though Austria's have generally been slightly above those of West Germany.

Labour market and income distribution

Austria's working population of 3,352,000 is made up of 487,000 self-employed and 2,865,000 employed persons. Unemployment rates are, as already indicated, considerably lower in Austria than in most other industrial countries. In absolute terms, the average number of unemployed in 1985 was 139, 447, compared with 22,265 vacancies. Unemployment rates vary widely from region to region; they are comparatively low in the provinces to the west (e.g. 2.7 per cent in Vorarlberg) but relatively high and rising in those to the south-east (e.g. 8.9 per cent in Burgenland). Differences between local districts are even more marked. This must be regarded as an indicator of widening disparities in the labour market and in income distribution — a process observable both in Austria and in other countries, and resulting from the general deterioration in labour market conditions.

In terms of the functional distribution of income (as measured by the share of wages and profits in the national income) the share of wages shows a long-term tendency to rise. However, since the proportion of employees expressed as a percentage of the total work-

Table 10.2 Wages as a proportion of national income 1960–85

	unadjusted	adjusted share of wages
1960	59.8%	55.5%
1970	64.0%	55.2%
1980	73.5%	58.2%
1985	71.0%	55.4%

ing population has increased, the share of wages is constant when adjusted for these changes in the structure of the labour force (see Table 10.2).

Within the share of profits there have been considerable variations in recent years. The proportion of income from company profits has grown more slowly (from 29.7 to 34.5 per cent during the period 1975–84) than the proportion of income from interest in the national income (from 3.0 to 5.9 per cent during the same period). With regard to personal income distribution (per capita distribution of national income), very few empirical investigations have been carried out in Austria. As far as primary distribution is concerned (as measured directly by labour and product markets) there has been some reduction in sex-specific income differences, but long term the changes have been relatively minor. The effect of government redistribution measures, on the other hand, has probably been in the direction of an 'egalitarian secondary distribution' of incomes. As has been demonstrated in other countries, the expenditure side of budgetary policy, particularly in terms of transfer payments, has probably had the effect of equalizing distributions (via social security payments, minimum rent supplements, allowances, etc.), while the total distributive effect of the tax system is considered to be proportional rather than progressively redistributive.

Economic structure

In terms of production and employment, Austria's economy (like that of other countries) has undergone massive structural changes during recent decades (see Table 10.3). In particular the importance of agriculture and forestry has sharply declined, the number of those employed in these sectors having fallen by 792,000 in absolute terms between 1951 and 1982. Since the mid-70s there has been a falling-off of those employed in industry and small trades viewed as a proportion of the total workforce, while during the period 1975–85 the total

Table 10.3 Economic structure: proportion of total employment

Year	Agriculture and Forestry	Industry, Mining and Small Trades	Services
1951	32.6%	37.6%	27.8%
1961	23.0%	41.4%	35.6%
1971	15.0%	42.2%	42.8%
1981	8.5%	41.0%	50.5%
Proportion of GDP			
1980	5.8%	51.2%	43.0%

Source: Österreichisches Statistisches Zentralamt

number of industrial employees fell by 16.3 per cent. (See also Appendix D3.) These developments are in line with the international trend, though Austria still has a considerably higher proportion of agricultural workers in relation to its total labour force than some other highly developed smaller countries (for example, Belgium: 3 per cent).

In the agricultural and forestry sector the main emphasis is on livestock production. In 1980 there were 302,579 farms and forestry units, of which about 113,000 were hill farms. Approximately 60 per cent are run as a second business. In terms of agricultural products, Austria is 95 per cent self-sufficient, though in some areas of the market severe problems exist as a result of agricultural surplus production; disparities in income from one region and from one sector to another also constitute a serious problem.

Milk and grain production are subject to government-backed market regulations linked to a highly comprehensive, centrally controlled production programme and to a system of price equalization. This, together with other measures designed to promote agricultural investment and exports, as well as the pursuance of a social policy in relation to agriculture, calls for massive public subsidies, the funding of which is becoming increasingly difficult.

The industry and small trades sector is characterized by the prominence of small and medium-sized firms. Forty-three per cent of all industrial companies in Austria employ less than 5 persons, though on the other hand companies employing over 1,000 account for 26 per cent of the total number of employees (see also Appendix D10). The most important areas of the industry and small trades sector are metals, engineering and allied industries, building and construc-

Table 10.4 Sectoral distribution of employees 1985

Sector	Employees
Agriculture and forestry	30,737
Energy and water supply	34,239
Manufacturing	1,039,021
including:	
Production of food, drink and tobacco	102,914
Production of textiles and textile goods	46,083
Production of clothing and footwear	58,186
Production of chemicals	71,175
Woodworking and -processing	85,014
Metals, engineering and allied industries	374,540
Building and construction	206,651
Services	1,636,420
including:	
Commerce and warehousing	377,180
Hotels and catering	129,424
Transport, mass media	209,290
Finance and banking	99,355
Health and welfare	87,452
Education and research	115,487
State administration, social security, interest groups	434,336

Source: Österreichisches Statistisches Zentralamt.

tion, and the food industry (see Table 10.4). Despite the fact that the overall numbers of employees are rising, those employed in industry and small trades have decreased in number during recent years after reaching a peak of 1,224,000 in 1977. This decline has particularly affected the raw materials and heavy industries, in which nationalized companies are strongly represented and which in the future will have to face considerable structure changes. The most important areas of the service sector, apart from the public services, are commerce, transport, hotels and catering.

A particularly significant feature of final aggregate demand is the high level of export demand (see Table 10.5), though the export ratio in the wider sense is below that of some other small industrialized countries (e.g. Netherlands: 50 per cent). One characteristic of Austria is a high investment ratio (compared with other industrialized countries), which has to be seen in the context of the

Table 10.5 The components of aggregate demand (1985) (in billions of schillings)

Private consumption	775
Public consumption (Federal Government)	94
Public consumption (rest of public sector)	161
Private gross investment	297
Investment (Federal Government)	14
Investment (rest of public sector)	28
Changes in stocks etc.	35
Domestic demand	1404
Exports	549
Imports	545
GDP	1408

exceptionally high long-term growth rate of the Austrian economy (see also Appendix D8).

Foreign Trade

As a small industrial nation Austria has considerable and rapidly expanding foreign trade connections. Its export ratio in the wider sense (exports of goods and services as a percentage of GDP) rose between 1964 and 1985 from 25.5 to 40.0 per cent, while in the narrower sense (export of goods only) it rose from 16.5 to 29.3 per cent during the same period.

Import ratios (similarly classified) rose from 25.5 (21.5) in 1964 to 39.7 per cent (32.7 per cent) in 1985. The balance of payments on current account showed a passive balance of almost 2 billion schillings in 1985. In the same year, of total exports worth 549 billion schillings, finished products accounted for 43 per cent, including consumer goods (28 per cent). In the case of imports (545 billion) the most important single categories are energy, vehicles and machines. In terms of geographical distribution, Austria's foreign trade shows a very strong concentration on western Europe: in 1985 65 per cent of its total exports and 70 per cent of its total imports went to or came from western Europe, while the corresponding figure for eastern Europe was only 11 per cent in each case (see also Appendix D9).

Austria's most important foreign trade partners are West Germany (proportion of total exports in 1984: 29.6 per cent), Italy (9.4 per cent) and Switzerland (6.9 per cent). Austria's share of total world trade was about 0.9 per cent in 1983, though in more recent years it has been possible to increase this figure. Since 1959 Austria has been a member of EFTA, and since 1973 a free-trade area treaty has existed between Austria (together with the other neutral states) and the European Community which gave rise to a complete dismantling of tariffs on industrial goods up to 1 July 1977. Austria is also a member of GATT and OECD.

Monetary and exchange-rate policy

The authorities mainly responsible for monetary and exchange-rate policy are the Austrian National Bank (*Österreichische Nationalbank*) and the Federal Government, represented by the Federal Finance Minister. The National Bank Act of 1955 provides for the independence of the bank, though the latter 'in fulfilling its functions must take into account the economic policy of the Federal Government'. Half the share capital of the Bank belongs to the Federal Government, and the other half belongs to organizations of the 'economic and social partners'. The government's monetary functions are largely governed by the Credit Act (1979/86) which deals with matters relating to the supervision of the banks and to the control of the money and credit markets. Austria's credit system is characterized by the strong position of the (partially nationalized) joint-stock banks and other clearing systems (the municipal savings bank sector, the *Raiffeisen* sector, and the *Volksbanken*). Austria's monetary and banking system is closely linked to the international money and capital markets, and this integration has increased rapidly in recent years. The country's monetary policy is unlike that of other countries in that it sets no money-supply targets; Austria prefers to set a stable exchange-rate target in relation to other stable currencies, particularly the Deutschmark.

This 'hard currency policy' is based upon the premise that maintaining the external value of the schilling helps to preserve its domestic value also.

The public sector

The central government plays a greater part in Austria's public sector than it does in other federal states such as Switzerland and West Germany. However, as Table 10.6 shows, the Federal Government accounts for less than half of all gross public expenditure; (it also accounts for only 41.6 per cent of total revenue.)

On the revenue side, taxes and social security contributions together accounted for 42.2 per cent of GNP in 1985, of which taxes made up 30.7 per cent. This places Austria somewhere in the middle as far as OECD states are concerned (see Appendix E3). Austria has a strongly developed system of transfer payments.

Table 10.6 The public sector — gross expenditure in 1985 (in billions of schillings)

Federal Government	463
Länder (apart from Vienna)	119
Local authorities (apart from Vienna)	83
Vienna	72
Social Security	212
Others	44
Total	994

Source: Österreichisches Statistisches Zentralamt.

In the case of an employee's family (one wage earner with 2 children) the direct burden of taxation and social insurance as a proportion of gross income was 22.9 per cent, but the net burden, when the various social security payments are taken into account, came to only 9.6 per cent. This is the third-lowest figure for all OECD countries (OECD, 1986).

In 1986 the Federal budget showed total expenditure of approximately 457 billion schillings (495 billion schillings including debt repayments), and total revenue of approximately 389 billion schillings or 4.5 per cent of GDP — a gross deficit of 107 billion schillings. The largest expenditure items are those for social welfare and health (122 billion schillings, including 47 billion schillings for social insurance subsidies, and 37 billion schillings for social security benefits), debt servicing (82 billion schillings) and educational services (40 billion schillings). The defence budget is considerably smaller than in other countries (18 billion schillings). In contrast to what happens in other countries, the Federal Railways and the Federal Post appear in the Austrian budget, with their gross income and expenditure (88 billion schillings). In 1986 the Federal Government's most important sources of income were turnover tax in the form of value-added tax (129 billion schillings), the tax on income from employment (*Lohnsteuer*) (98 billion schillings), assessed income tax (28 billion schillings) and the net operating profits from the railways and the postal service. Overall, indirect taxation in Austria is greater in proportion to direct taxation than is the case, for example, in West Germany and Switzerland.

The gross revenue obtained from the major taxes is divided up between the provinces and the local authorities in accordance with the regulations governing financial equalization. While the provinces depend for their income almost entirely upon this redistribution of taxes, the local authorities also have the benefit of some important taxes of their own, for example commercial rates, payroll and land taxes.

During the past decade Austria's economic policy has been characterized by the philosophy of 'Austro-Keynesianism'. In addition to the pursuit of a comprehensive incomes policy together with the hard currency policy mentioned above, and a structural policy largely based on promoting investment, this approach is marked by a degree of commitment to employment on the part of the public sector which is stronger than in other countries. This has led to lower rates of unemployment and higher growth rates than is the case elsewhere, though it has also produced larger deficits in the Federal budget. (See Appendix E5.)

Institutions and decision making in economic policy

Basically a market economy, Austria is an example of an economic system emphasizing public welfare in which private co-operative and government bodies work together. The ownership structures of the Austrian economic system show some exceptional features, particularly in respect of the significance of foreign capital and of the co-operative and public sector. As a rough approximation one may say that in the realm of industry, one third respectively of all employees work for companies under foreign ownership, under domestic ownership and under co-operative or public ownership.

The co-operative/public sector employs a total of about 470,000 people (18 per cent of all employees). In addition to a large co-operative sector (which is of particular importance in agriculture, house building, banking and commerce), and the sphere of the public service industries (railways and post), there are also the directly and indirectly nationalized companies. These mainly cover the area of the state-run Industrial Holding Company (ÖIAG), operating particularly in the iron and steel industry, the electricity industry which is in federal or provincial ownership, and the mainly nationalized big banks with their groups of companies.

One unique feature in terms of decision-making structures within the field of economic policy is the Austrian system of Social Partnership. This, in essence, is a form of voluntary incomes policy covering the whole economy and backed by the interest groups representing the employees' side (the Trade Union Federation and the Council of Austrian Chambers of Labour, the latter having public-law status), the employers' side (the Federal Chambers of the Economy), and finally agriculture (the Presidential Conference of the Chambers of Agriculture), assisted by those members of the Federal Government who are responsible for economic affairs. The heart of this system is the Parity Commission with its sub-committees for Wages and for Prices and its Advisory Council for Social and Economic Affairs. The fact that all these associations are so strongly involved in a great deal of decision making within the field of economic policy has undoubtedly helped to produce the high degree of economic stability and freedom from conflict which is characteristic of Austria. The average length of strikes during 1985, for example, was 3.8 minutes. (See Appendix F11.)

Fresh issues, many as yet unresolved, are of course posed by lobbies whose interests impinge upon the area of economic policy but which are not represented in the social partnership, e.g. in the realm of energy policy. There are also new challenges arising from the growing international involvement of the Austrian economy which in the future will make it more difficult for Austria to implement economic policy strategies of its own in the face of developments abroad — as is the case, for example, in the field of employment policy.

11 The Austrian economic chambers

Herbert Reiger

The first Austrian Chamber of Commerce was founded in Vienna immediately following the liberal Revolution of 1848. Since that time the Chambers and their specialist organizations have continued to expand, to the point where today they exercise considerable influence upon the political life of the country. After the Second World War the Chambers of Commerce Act (*Handelskammergesetz*) of 1946 brought about a further development in, but at the same time a tightening of, the Chambers' organization.

From the beginning, the Chambers have operated on the principle of compulsory membership, as is the case in some other European countries. In Austria this principle is gaining ground also in the case of all the other Chambers, namely those representing employees, farmers and the liberal professions (for example lawyers, doctors, architects). Compulsory membership is of considerable importance for the Chambers of Commerce in particular, for whereas the other Chambers (especially the Chambers of Labour) have the task of representing essentially parallel interests, the Chambers of Commerce are daily faced with many conflicting interests. Achieving a proper balance of these interests benefits not only industry and commerce but also the community at large. The world of industry and commerce would ultimately collapse if it failed to reconcile its conflicting interests, and without compulsory membership individual groups, particularly the most financially powerful ones, would try to avoid the necessary give and take by threatening to resign. In addition, compulsory membership ensures for the organization the highest possible degree of representation in economic affairs, and this in turn improves its chances of success.

Each of the nine federal provinces has its own Provincial Chamber of Trade and Industry (*Landeskammer der gewerblichen Wirtschaft*), while the body responsible for the country as a whole is, since 1946, the Federal Chamber of the Economy (*Bundeskammer der gewerblichen Wirtschaft* or *Bundeswirtschaftskammer*). Also since 1946 the official branch organizations have been integrated within the Chambers, so that the Federal Economic Chamber for example has six sections, representing respectively Craft Trades (*Gewerbe*), Industry, Trade,

Finance (including Credit and Insurance), Transport, and Tourism; and within these sections there is a total of over 130 professional associations. Analogous arrangements also exist at provincial level. All these professional associations, like the Chambers themselves, are public corporations (*Körperschaften des öffentlichen Rechtes*), and similarly have compulsory membership. They possess limited autonomy within their own sphere of operation.

The Chambers have a comprehensive membership: companies of all sizes belong to them, from the one-man business to the large industrial concern; type of ownership is also immaterial so that membership includes not only private firms but also those in public ownership. The Chambers have a total of about 260,000 members.

Although the Chambers and their professional associations are public corporations, they enjoy a high degree of autonomy vis-a-vis the state. The relevant government bodies can exercise their right of supervision only in order to ensure that the Chambers abide by the law, but they have no authority to direct Chambers in the exercise of their own affairs. To a limited extent the Chambers also act on behalf of the government by assisting the latter and ensuring that the real needs of industry and commerce are taken into account, and in such cases government directives are a possibility.

The internal organization of the Chambers is based upon the voluntary principle. The individual Chambers and their professional associations are not entitled to tell their members what to do, and the same applies to the Federal Chamber in its dealings with the *Land* Chambers. Things are done through the power of argument and the art of persuasion.

The Chambers and their professional associations have no monopoly of representation, so that private associations are also permissible. Generally speaking, the latter have a positive relationship with the official Chamber organization — one of co-operation and rarely of competition.

Each Chamber is headed by a president who also chairs the various decision-making committees. All bodies are elected democratically every five years, with direct elections to the professional associations in the provinces and indirect elections in every other case. There is a fairly good average poll of about 70 per cent. In the Federal Chamber the full-time staff are under the direction of the General Secretary, and in the provincial Chambers are responsible to the Director or Chief Executive (*Kammeramtsdirektor*).

The work of the Chambers and the professional associations may broadly be categorized as looking after their own members' interests, and representing these interests to the world outside. The former involves the provision of numerous services for the benefit of members, the Chambers and professional associations operating at provincial level being the ones to which members usually turn for assistance.

The external representation of members' interests involves having dealings on the one hand with other economic groups, particularly those representing employees, and on the other hand with parliament, with the government and with the other administrative authorities. This is where the Chambers' right of consultation is of great importance. The drafts of all new laws and regulations, insofar as they have a bearing upon economic interests, have to be submitted to the Chambers in good time so that the latter may give their assessment. Their organization is represented on numerous commissions, advisory boards and similar bodies, and also sends assessors to certain courts, such as those hearing commercial and civil cases.

Areas of competence within the organization are divided up according to the principle of self-help. All matters affecting the interests of only one professional group at provincial level fall within the competence of that group. Matters involving more than one professional group within one and the same section are dealt with by the section concerned, while anything with wider implications is a matter for the Provincial Chamber. An analogous situation exists at Federal level between the professional associations, the Federal sections and the Federal Chamber. (See Appendix F10 for a diagram of the structure of the Federal Chamber.) Matters with no relevance beyond an individual province are dealt with by that province; otherwise responsibility rests with the Federal organization.

Within the Parity Commission for Prices and Wages, which is made up of the main economic interest groups and works in co-operation with members of the Federal government, the Federal Economic Chamber looks after the interests of the non-agricultural sectors of the economy. The system of social partnership has developed gradually in Austria since the Second World War and has held its own under all governments. Although not explicitly enshrined in the Constitution, it has proved highly efficient in ensuring peace within society and providing industry and commerce (and also foreign investors) with a secure framework. The fact that strikes are almost unknown in Austria is attributable to the stabilizing influence of the social partnership.

In this context it is important to note that the Chambers and their professional associations are competent to engage in collective bargaining, i.e. to draw up agreements with the trade unions on wages and salaries, as well as on contracts of employment. These collective agreements become an integral part of individual contracts of employment, though may be supplemented by local arrangements which may be more beneficial to employees.

In addition to its various specialist sections each Provincial Chamber has its own Institute for Vocational Advancement (*Wirtschaftsförderungsinstitut*). These Institutes are the largest institutions for further professional training in Austria, providing both employers and employees with an immense range of opportunities for training and further education. Their courses are attended by about 200,000 people each year. Numerous other activities are also undertaken by the Institutes, such as providing member companies with advice on rationalization, export promotion, public relations, etc.

The vital importance to Austria of exports is reflected in the fact that the Federal Economic Chamber has its own foreign trade organization. Throughout the world there are 90 foreign trade delegations acting as offices for the Federal Economic Chamber, i.e. providing support for the efforts of Austrian industry to sell abroad. The Federal Economic Chamber does not regard foreign trade as being all in one direction, however; hence the trade delegations also give information to foreign businessmen with regard to opportunities for selling to Austria.

The Economic Chambers are committed to the system of the social market economy with its cornerstones of freedom, performance, private property, competition, private enterprise and social justice. The Chambers subscribe to the view that this system, with its decentralized decision-making structure, offers the best opportunities for achieving the fulfilment of many individual interests in a way which promotes the common good. It is a system which, to encourage competition, needs the entrepreneur — the person for whom profit and success are the measure of (and the motivation behind) economic self-fulfilment.

The Economic Chambers have considerable political influence. Many employers and managers who hold office in the organization, as well as members of its full-time staff, belong to parliamentary committees, and its political involvement is also considerable at local authority level. Finally, depending upon the political balance of power, representatives of the organization hold office in the Federal government and/or in the Provincial governments.

12 The Austrian trade union movement

Alfred Ströer and Jim Sweeney

The modern Austrian trade union movement is not only a successful model of organized employees' institutions but also one which exerts great influence in the social and political life of the country. In organizational terms it is a movement which has in membership a high proportion of the country's employees (around 60%) in a highly centralized structure. At a political level it is a movement whose views on most of the current social and industrial issues carry great weight in the processes of political decision-making.

The economic success of Austria, particularly the strides taken after the Second World War, has been the subject of admiration in many countries and it is a success in which the Austrian trade union movement has played a significant and decisive role. This recent role is one which has been tempered and moulded by historical factors and experiences — often in the form of great shocks. The collective solidarity Austrian trade unionists display is even more remarkable in a country which is traditionally rich in ethnic, cultural and language differences as well as one in which the 'animal spirits' of free enterprise, as Keynes called them, abound if one views the proportion of the working population which is self-employed. At the same time Austria is a country in which political ideology has been monopolized by two large political parties, particularly since the Second World War, and these parties have sections which permeate an enormous variety of organizations whose major functions are far from the world of politics. At the same time it is a nation in which consensus or compromise politics is a seemingly perennial feature.

The mixture of collectivism and individualism is not sufficiently volatile to create instability, since the country's recently founded (or rediscovered) national consciousness is a powerful bond against destructive division and irrationality. An indication of this bonding can be seen in the low level of industrial relations conflict to be found in Austria compared to other industrialized countries. Not that this has led to complacency and smugness; in Austria, as in other democratic countries, there is always a controversy over the role and purposes of trade unions by friends and enemies alike and some of the more recent criticisms will be considered towards the end of this chapter.

But this pacific climate of industrial relations in Austria was not always the case as historical events before 1945 attest. Before looking at the country's modern trade union movement, therefore, some examination of its antecedents and the problems with which they were beset is called for.

Early beginnings to the events of 1848

In Austria, as elsewhere, it is difficult to disentangle those factors of an economic, legal, social and organizational nature which constituted the drive to create early industrial groupings in the wake of the industrial revolution. There were always 'push' and 'pull' forces at work. The response to market needs for industrial and commercial locations, urbanization, political stability and the ease of greater communication were among those relating to the pull or facilitating factors in the development of attitudes of new common interest; while, at the same time, class and status differences, exploitation, inequality of power relationships, the periodic and violent swings of trade or business cycles, political oppression, hunger, poverty and war were among those which pushed workers to change the *status quo* and which characterized their early struggles for unity. The context of such processes has to be seen in a society changing from one based on feudal relations to the rise and eventual triumph of capitalism. In Habsburg Austria the progress of capitalism was slower than among contemporary major countries of nineteenth-century Europe with the exception of Russia.

The early rudimentary forms of union organization are to be found in the journeymen's gilds (*Zünfte*) and with some exceptions it might be said these represented the earliest stage in craft-interest group formation in Austria before the early eighteenth century. Such craftsmen or journeymen (*Gesellen*) sought employment in predominantly industrial pursuits in the houses of masters, themselves formerly journeymen, in the appropriate trades. This work was often of an itinerant nature. The masters themselves were socially and politically disadvantaged by the feudal nobility who restricted their opportunities to engage in business and earn a living.

The first forms of organization in the period of transition to trade unionism proper are to be found among the fraternities (*Bruderschaften*) of journeymen and early mineworkers (*Knappschaften*). The activities of these organizations were restricted by the feudal and monarchical state machinery as well as being inhibited by the widespread location of workplaces, but their activities must have intensified as the opportunities for journeymen to become masters on their own account decreased.

As more journeymen became wage craftsmen (*Lohnhandwerker*) these scattered fraternities grew in importance — an importance which increased as capitalist modes of small-scale production (at a point at which the profit motive was not fully developed) grew. These craft journeymen tended to see themselves superior to such groups as manufacturing wage earners or domestic servants who in turn, in their restricted perception of freedom (from the landed nobility), regarded the craftsmen as slaves (*Knechte*).

As capitalism grew and became settled, for example when manufacturing became more widespread, the Habsburg monarchs (particularly the more enlightened ones), looked more favourably on it, within, however, the framework of mercantilist policies. Unemployed journeymen were increasingly joined by landless labourers and propertyless town dwellers to become the manufacturing wage earners or proletariat. At this point in time the gilds' influence declined sharply. The Tradesmen's Patent Regulations (*Handwerkerpatente*) of 1731–2 finally deprived them of the right to combine (*Koalitionsverbot*) and they were dissolved. The printers alone remained an exception, and this only because they came under the aegis of the universities, and even then only till 1765, but they displayed little solidarity with other manual occupational groups. The printers' benefit societies (*Unterstützungsvereine*) however, did form a bridge to later trade union activity and when factory organization proceeded apace many of the printers' leaders became the first trade union officials. The continued growth of large-scale capitalist enterprises with large numbers of craftsmen absorbed into the proletariat, and with worsening working conditions, began to give great cause for concern. In Vienna, Graz, Steyr and Wiener Neustadt outbursts of 'Luddism' occurred. Benefit societies burgeoned, however, with support funds (*Fabrikskassen*) for mutual self-help among workers. These latter were declared illegal in 1845.

The period leading up to the Revolutions of 1848 (known in the German-speaking world as *Vormärz*), with the political and legal repression of Metternich's police state, was a period in which working class attempts at organization were not conspicuous. The events of 1848, however, presented an opportunity to secure some basic rights. The manufacturing middle class were at that time, like the workers, without the vote. Their demands for enfranchisement and a constitution were supported by the workers and, as events of 1848 took a violent turn, this support took the form of armed struggle. That which occurred on the outskirts of Vienna on 13 March cost the workers dearly in lives and repression. This identity of interest did not last long; the middle class were granted the right to vote and detached themselves from the workers. But they lived to regret it: within a short space of time the monarchy revoked its promise and restored its absolute rule (neo-absolutism).

Nevertheless, 1848 has a central significance for Austrian trade unionism. The first workers' union organization was set up by Friedrich Sander — the Vienna General Workers' Society (*Wiener allegemeine Arbeiterverein*). This was the germ from which all subsequent union organization can be traced. The leaders of this organization wanted to extend its base to embrace a 'Committee of all the trades', the first attempt at a central, co-ordinating peak organization. Though this was not realized, the General Workers' Society organized a demonstration against pay cuts and rising unemployment as the depression of 1848 took hold. In the bloody repression which followed in the summer of 1848, eighteen workers were killed and 152 seriously injured.

The Vienna General Workers' Society's main function was regarded as providing education and learning for workers, by means of the publication of written material and the holding of lectures. Karl Marx himself addressed it in Vienna at the end of August 1848 on the theme, 'Wage Labour and Capital', in a lecture in which, by his analysis of the events of 1848, he urged the working class to conduct its own struggle against the powers of absolutism without relying on the bourgeoisie. In March 1849 the General Workers' Society was forcibly dissolved along with the new parliament with which, co-evally, it shared a brief existence.

Neo-absolutism and the workers' search for a philosophy of emancipation 1849–67

After 1849 any association of working men was forbidden and attempts to organize combinations were strictly controlled and punished by summary police jurisdiction. The social and industrial conditions of the workers worsened, many strikes took place out of frustration and despair (*Verzweiflungsstreiks*) and assassinations became commonplace.

Now and again benefit societies were formed (of printers and consumers for example) and after 1852 under the influence of events in Germany, particularly the Kolping movement, Catholic journeymen's associations were founded. But the legal restrictions on union organization did not prevent combination and a substantial part of organizational activity went underground. The Trade and Labour Regulations (*Gewerbeordnung*) of 1859 exemplified the Habsburgs' stiffened resistance to the idea of trade unions: they considered many trade union activities as violations of the Penal Code and expressly forbade any concerted action aimed at increasing wages or withdrawing labour (e.g. strike action) with the purpose of improving working conditions.

By 1861 the middle class had achieved representation in the Imperial Parliament as a separate voting class ('estate' or 'curia') of direct tax payers. But the question of labour (*Arbeiterfrage*) remained high on the agenda. In 1862 a consumers' co-operative was formed by non-manual employees and another in 1864 by weavers. This was the time for a serious debate on working-class emancipation and the means of achieving it.

By that time the influence of the German working-class leader and political thinker, Lassalle, was quite strong in Austria. The argument now centered around some socialist type of society as an ideal but there was contention about the means of achieving it. In this respect two contrasting notions were advocated: self-help as against state-help (or 'state-aid'). The former had been presented in the ideas of producer and retail co-operatives as advocated by another German, Schulze-Delitzsch.

Lassalle had already had a considerable influence over the German working-class movement at a theoretical level. His economic analysis of capitalist society had included such concepts as 'The Iron Law of Wages' (*ehernes Lohngesetz*) but here he turned his attention to something quite different. Space does not permit the fine points of argument but the substance of the argument on 'state-aid' was as follows: since the capitalist state had permitted the exploitation of workers, it was necessary for the workers to capture the state machinery or exert an influence on it, to effect a transformation of the state in order to correct the evils of capitalism. To that end the first hurdle to be overcome by the working class was to win the struggle for universal suffrage, and from then on use all endeavours to secure a comprehensive programme of social legislation.

Apart from the experiments advocated by Schulze-Delitzsch, the rudimentary formulation of the Roman Catholic Church's *Subsidiaritätsprinzip* (principle of self-help) then prevailing and popular among Catholic workers, was also weighed against the Lassalleans, whose views nevertheless prevailed and had a great lasting influence on the early Austrian trade union and labour movement. It is still argued to this day whether or not the influence of Lassalle was greater than that of Marx. The former's influence certainly continued well into the twentieth century even though Austrian social democracy came under the influence of Marx in many other respects. In the meantime, however, the unions needed organization as a forum within which such ideas could be examined.

1867–1918 Habsburg constitutionalism, war and political democracy

The demands of technical progress highlighted the problems of illiteracy in Habsburg Austria, many of which were overcome by the determination of the workers themselves. Their awareness of being disadvantaged grew as industrialization accelerated. The Constitution of 1867, while granting a number of civic rights to workers as citizens, accorded them little else. They had neither the vote nor an end to the discriminatory treatment which was their common lot. It did, however, provide an important step forward in the formal granting of the right to combine and associate freely. This right was not entirely given from humanitarian considerations, but rather in view of adoption of the ideas of economic liberalism and the demands of international competition which required a degree of geographical and occupational mobility as well as an educated workforce. To a considerable extent this change came about as a result of working-class pressure. Accordingly, the first workers' organizations to emerge towards the end of 1867 were the workers' educational associations (*Arbeiterbildungsvereine*). The first one appeared in Vienna — the Gumpendorf Workers' Educational Association — and this was quickly followed by the foundation of organizations of the same type elsewhere in Habsburg Austria (Cisleithania). Such societies with educational objectives were fundamental to the discussion and the dissemination of the ideas of freedom and political expression — and this was important for the objective of trade union solidarity.

It was still nevertheless a time of ultra-conservative or reactionary imperial governments: despite the seeming liberal reforms, the new workers' educational associations were restricted to remaining local organizations and were constantly under police surveillance and control. Moreover, the notion of 'state-aid' was regarded as treason in government circles and since such ideas were the political currency of socialist (*sozialdemokratisch*) workers' educational associations, they became automatically suspect. Many members of these organizations were arrested but the workers found ways, albeit clandestinely, to extend their activities. In the process many educational associations were influenced by liberal ideas about education, for example those which emphasized the development of the individual worker, and this might have deflected from the priorities of the moment, although many later writers have regarded this as a positive aspect of trade union development. The long working hours and harsh working conditions were the matters of immediate concern.

The educational associations began to develop trade sections (*Fachsektionen*) within their structures, under the guise of educational activities, and these sections soon became preoccupied with organizing and co-ordinating strike activity. The associations also made full use of an article of the Constitution — the right to petition — for which, in order to express this right, meetings were essential. Organized workers, impatient with the restrictions still imposed on them, used the power of petition to address the government on their social and legal disabilities. Despite the Government's unease and alarm at the growth of the educational associations, it lifted the restrictions on freedom of association and right to organize in April 1870 under pressure from workers' demonstrations, including one of 20,000 which assembled before the parliament building in December 1869.

Another stage in trade union metamorphosis occurred with the formation of trade union societies (*Gewerkschaftsvereine*) which espoused the socialist cause and formed the basis of the later free trade unions (*Freie Gewerkschaften*). This socialist tendency was naturally anathema to the Habsburg state apparatus which attempted at the outset to take administrative measures against the new unions; when these failed, it arraigned the leaders of the unions in July 1870 on a charge of high treason, a charge levelled against those who had fought for freedom of association (*Koalitionsrecht*) as well as those who had supported the First International. They were found guilty and sentenced to six years' imprisonment. At the conclusion of this trial most workers' educational associations and trade union societies were dissolved. The workers responded with widespread demonstrations and strikes. The government was forced to relent and permitted worker organizations to exist but under stringent conditions. In the 1870s and 1880s many were dissolved and many prosecutions took place.

In 1873 the Stock Exchange crashed and heralded an economic crisis. The following period of stagnation created difficulties for trade union recruitment due to heavy unemployment. There were divisions within organized labour, and a general split between moderate and revolutionary socialists occurred while a growing number of activists gravitated towards the ideas of the anarchists, who by 1882 had become influential among the workers. Trade union organization had reached a low ebb. Assassinations became common and martial law was declared in many areas where unions were strong. Emergency powers were introduced and used, quite arbitrarily, against socialists and anarchists alike. Although the first trade union journal *Der Gewerkschaftler* (*The Trade Unionist*) appeared in 1877 many trade union information sheets were seized by the authorities around this time.

There were some unexpected gains however. The provident funds set up by the workers' educational associations after 1867 were extended all over Austria. These prompted the state in competition to set up an employees' state compulsory sickness and accident scheme in 1883 as had occurred in Bismarck's Germany.

Workers' pressure for political representation was kept up. One important issue of the time was the demand for a Chamber of Labour as a legal institution of employees' rights, the equivalent and equal of the Chamber of Commerce which had constituted one of the electoral voting classes (curia) for the middle class to the Cisleithanian Parliament. It was inevitable that working-class organizations should demand a similar provision for workers. This demand for the time being was unsuccessful.

The Socialist Party (*Sozialdemokratische Arbeiterpartei Österreichs*) was founded under the leadership of Viktor Adler at the Hainfeld Conference of 1888/9 and this served as a catalyst to unite many disparate elements as well as effecting the reconciliation of the radical and moderate sections of the workers' organizations. The party programme of measures, aimed at the establishment of a socialist society, gave a new impetus to the Austrian trade union movement. This resulted in less internal strife and a concentration on the extension from local organization to national, thus occasioning the adjustment and fusion of trade unions and party which Viktor Adler later likened to 'Siamese twins'. The birth of these twins meant that a specialization of function could now take place. The unions could now concentrate on workplace issues to a greater extent.

From 1890 the struggle for the 8-hour day began. Between 12 and 16 working hours were quite commonplace in Habsburg Austria and both wings of the newly established labour movement campaigned vigorously for this demand under the slogan 'eight hours' work, eight hours' recreation and eight hours' sleep'. This demand had also been articulated at the Socialist International (Second) of 1889 attended by Viktor Adler.

The 1890s were an important decade for co-ordinating the structures of the trade unions. Union membership rose and, just as significantly, in addition to the large numbers of local union associations, by 1892 there were 10 national individual union organizations each of which had organized a good proportion of the workers in particular trades or industries. In the same year a new umbrella organization was founded — the Provisional Austrian Central Council of Trade Unions (*Gewerkschaftskommission*) and in 1893 the First Congress was held establishing the Council proper and its elected executive with Anton Hueber as First Secretary. This Central Council (known synonymously as the organization of the 'Free Trade Unions') embraced 194 local and national associations with a total membership of 50,000. The individual membership increased to 89,000 by 1895 but this was only something above 1% of all employees in Cisleithania.

Even then there was no single purpose or tendency and religious, ethnic and nationalist differences prevented the complete integration of the workers in one organization. Encouraged by the papal encyclical *Rerum Novarum* in 1891, a Christian (Catholic) Workers' Trade Union Association was founded by Leopold Kunschak in 1892 which became closely associated with the new Christian-Social (Conservative) Party which had been founded in 1887. In 1906 a Central Council of Christian Trade Unions was formed to which 30 organizations were affiliated, with a total affiliated membership of 11,164. Under the great strains and tensions of the 'national question' in the Dual Monarchy, the Czech or Bohemian sections of the Austrian Central Council (Free Trade Unions) broke away in 1897 and formed their own independent Czech Trade Union Council. In 1905, 50,000 workers were members of the Czech Council but the overwhelming majority now belonged to the Free Trade Union Movement which by then numbered 323,099.

Many workers also came under the influence of German nationalism (advocating union with Germany under the Hohenzollern dynasty or the establishment of a German-speaking Republic) and there was a growth in workers' movements of this persuasion in the 1890s. At a conference in Leitmeritz in 1906 a Central Council of German Trade Unions (*Deutsche Gewerkschaftskommission*) was adopted; and again in 1908, at a conference in Vienna, a Central Council of German Employee Associations (*Zentralkommission der deutschen Arbeitnehmerverbände*) was founded. These two organizations no less than the Free and Christian movements were mutually antagonistic and never achieved unity. Later, the nationalist tendencies in Austria and in Czechoslovakia (where there were Bohemian and Prague divisions) made for difficult and complicated ideological and organizational developments.

The struggle for freedom of association having been won, the vital issues which remained for the labour movement were universal suffrage, lower working hours and higher remuneration. Between 1901 and 1903 another economic crisis occurred and the resulting social and industrial dislocation and distress made social legislation an urgent matter for the Free Trade Unions. In 1897 a fifth electoral voting class for men, based on a taxable income of five guilder, called the 'general voting class' (*allgemeine Wählerklasse*) was established and allocated 72 seats in the imperial parliament. In the general election of the same year the Socialists captured 14 of these seats, and with the upturn in trade after 1903 and the granting of universal suffrage by the Czar of Russia in 1905, more pressure was put on the monarchy as a large demonstration of 250,000 workers in Vienna in the same year illustrated. Consequently men achieved the vote without property or fiscal qualification for all parliamentary (provincial and national) elections in 1907, in which year 89 Socialists were returned to the imperial parliament, many of whom were trade union officials.

Many problems under the monarchy appeared somewhat intractable, particularly those of employment relations. Since the enacting of Trade and Labour Regulations of 1859 it was the requirement of every worker to possess a work book (*Arbeitsbuch*), a kind of labour permit. It had been a common requirement elsewhere for much of the nineteenth century although it had been abolished in Prussia in the 1860s and in France in 1881. This requirement was a curious incursion by the state into employment matters at a time when the ideas of economic liberalism were being accepted, since it represented a measure which was mercantilist in nature. In itself it militated against freedom of association, since no worker was permitted to enter into a contract of employment without it. Its importance for working class organizations lay in the fact that it was used covertly by many employers, to compile a black-list of trade union members through the insertion of secret marks or codes. Despite a weak legal amendment in 1874 to the 1859 Trade Regulations this pernicious aspect of labour law continued to flourish and it is curious that there appeared to have been no systematic or collective united action on the part of the workers to have it removed before 1918, even though the Austrian High Court in 1906 had described the employers' misuse of this document as immoral.

The workers were successful nonetheless in securing some forms of legislation which were favourable to them before World War One, such as the Clerical Workers' Pension Act of 1906. Similarly some improvements were achieved through voluntary action, such as progress in the field of collective bargaining. Up to 1910 the number of collective agreements rose and the 10-hour day was implemented. By 1912, however, all improvements in social legislation came to an end and in the years immediately preceding the First World War the cost of living rose sharply and a great number of demonstrations took place as workers' living standards deteriorated.

At the outbreak of hostilities, as was the case elsewhere in Europe, a war hysteria broke out. The Free Trade Unions were opposed to the war since they held the workers would suffer most. Mobilization for the war effort and the suspension of legislation favourable to the unions left them helpless; all they could hope for was the ameliorization of the harsh working conditions demanded by the war effort. The drafting of many workers into the munitions industries and 'essential work' weakened the unions. By 1916 they had lost 60% of their members. In those factories producing war materials, wages lagged behind the rate of inflation and workers were being paid 'soldiers' wages', while yet other workplaces were 'state protected' or placed under military administration.

The pent-up frustration of the workers became more manifest as the war began to go badly for the Central Powers and defeat looked imminent. The withdrawal of Russia from the war and the Russian Revolution in 1917 created a great deal of uncertainty and encouraged many who were impatient at the length and conduct of the war and the deprivations it had brought in its train to advocate industrial action. Between 1917 and 1918 a number of strikes took place in the metal-working trades (munitions factories) and things began to look serious as food shortages became acute. Particularly serious was the strike which started in the Daimler works in Vienna in January 1918, was taken up by other firms in the area and eventually spread to Wiener Neustadt, lasting 8 days. The government intervened directly and handled the negotiations with the workers' representatives over the grievances. The outcome was better working conditions in the munitions factories.

In the autumn of 1918 the monarchy collapsed and Czechoslovakia and Hungary proclaimed their independence. Of the 'Dual Monarchy' (Cisleithania and Transleithania), all that was left were the German-speaking provinces of Austria which had a population of almost 7 millions, in contrast to an empire which had previously encompassed 53 millions.

1918–1938 The First Republic: achievements and near-extinction

Despite the terrible economic and social consequences of the war — internal as well as international — for the new republic, the power and influence of the unions, particularly the Free Trade Union Movement, were enhanced at the cessation of hostilities. This had, of course, much to do with the ascendancy of the Socialist Party. The war had swept away much of the discrimination and arbitrary treatment to which the trade unions had been subject since their inception. The period 1918–20 represented a high water mark in the history of social legislation in Austria and is particularly associated with the first Republican Coalition Government headed by the great socialist lawyer, economist and sociologist, Dr Karl Renner.

The new republic was established under a provisional Constitution drawn up by Dr Renner (the first proper Federal Constitution was drafted by Hans Kelsen and adopted in 1920) and elected a parliament by universal suffrage (women receiving the vote for the first time) which had to wrestle with the various tremendous problems of the post-war era. These included: the conclusion of a peace treaty with the victors (conducted at St Germain-en-Laye), alarming inflation, unemployment, hunger and poverty. Although the Socialist Party was the largest single party at the first general election of the new republic its number of seats was not sufficient for it to govern alone. Despite this, its vast programme of social legislation was steered through parliament by Ferdinand Hanusch the new Minister of Social Welfare, himself the secretary of the Textile Workers' Union and a member of the Executive of the Central Council of Austrian Trade Unions. The appointment of Hanusch started a practice of Austrian socialist governments which has continued down to the present day — the office of Minister of Social Affairs being held by a leading trade unionist.

The programme of legal measures between 1918 and 1920 included those which related to the eight-hour day, the regulation of night work for women and young persons, the prohibition of children at work, the abolition of the work book, the legal status of collective agreements and, at an institutional level, the establishment of works' councils and the Chambers of Labour. This extensive programme survived until 1934 and was reintroduced, consolidated and updated after 1945. Less successful were the measures for the *Sozialisiering* (nationalization) of certain industries, an important policy aspect of not only the Socialist Party, but also of the other parties.

The Renner coalition governments were succeeded by Christian-Social (Conservative) ones since the Christian-Socials had become the largest single party at the 1920 general election. They followed a course of financial orthodoxy and austerity and accepted the conditions of the nations' creditors as demanded by the Geneva and Lausanne Agreements, which among other things included currency reform and a re-organization of public expenditure and employment in a programme of reconstruction (*Sanierung*). While the Socialist Party remained a major political party, no attempt was made to dismantle the social policy measures of the Renner governments although some of their provisions were changed, such as old age pensions, sickness benefit and unemployment pay for example. The growth of union membership from 400,000 in 1918 to 1,080,000 in 1920 always represented a countervailing power to the right-wing politicians and the business élites in the new state.

In 1928 the Trade Union Council changed its name to become the Federation of the Free Trade Unions of Austria (*Bund der Freien Gewerkschaften Österreichs*), took the first steps to restructure itself by introducing a greater degree of centralization, and laid down affiliation of membership on the principle of industry groups. By 1934 for example there were 34 affiliated unions, now all national bodies.

In the post-war period the other trade union centres had increased their membership. By 1920 the Christian organizations had 79,000 and those in the nationalist bodies numbered 45,000. Employers too began to organize their workers into unions ('yellow' unions) which in the early post-war years numbered about 40,000. These became involved in a nationalism of a para-military nature — the Local Defence Organization (*Heimwehr*) and they became known as Local Defence Unions (*Heimwehrgewerkschaften*). By the time of the *Heimwehr* putsch of 1934 they had about 70,000 members. In May 1928 another group, the 'independent' unions, was founded as a counter to the Christian trade unions, but these were later exposed as a *Heimwehr* cover. (For these centres and their political tendencies up to 1931 see Appendix F1; for membership of the Free Trade Unions 1872–1932 see Appendix F2.)

As economic and social conditions worsened in the 1920s powerful tensions arose between the political parties and their respective trade union wings as their programmes and policies became polarized. The parties of the right became even more nationalist (pro-German) and anti-semitic, while by the mid-1920s the Socialist Party appeared to have moved away from its unusual creative brand of Marxism (Austro-Marxism) to a more orthodox stance as it became faced with a Government clearly advocating the interests of capitalism. This change of perceptions was due in no small part to Otto Bauer who was without a doubt the most influential leader of Austrian social democracy from 1924 till his death in 1938 and who, it is curious to recall, shortly after the birth of the new democratic republic advocated an ideological position in which the state held the balance of class interests, that is, acted as some kind of referee between capital and labour. However, as the political situation in Europe worsened, the nationalist *Heimwehr*, encouraged by the success of Mussolini in Italy, became virtually a private army in the late 1920s, with little attempt by governments to control it, especially when it turned to murderous assaults on socialists. The events which occurred in Schattendorf in 1927 and the events of July of the same year which included the burning of the Courts of Justice in Vienna (resulting in 89 deaths) caused the Socialist side to form their own defensive organization, the Republican Defence Corps (*Republikaner Schützbund*). Not only were the nationalists violent and aggressive but so also were the monarchists who were mainly associated with the governing Christian-Social

Party. The nationalists now had seats in the government under the name of the new 'Citizens Group' (*Bürgerblock*).

The shift to the right as the depression deepened in 1929–33 had effects on the membership of the Free Trade Unions. By 1931 numbers fell to 583,000 while the Christian Trade Unions' figure stood at 108,000; in 1934 the numbers had altered considerably and stood at 480,000 and 130,000 respectively. Support for the Socialists and the Free Trade Unions among the populace still held up however, and in the last 'free' election in 1930 before the Second World War they emerged as the largest single party. The time for compromise such as had occurred in the early years of the Republic had now passed.

As the nationalist groups grew stronger, with the 'Greater Germans' (*Grossdeutsche*) represented in the Cabinet, the government became less and less tolerant of the Left, and the growing Austrian fascism typified by the Heimwehr and the appearance of National Socialism, imported from Germany, presented even greater problems of public order. In 1932 the Christian-Social Party thought they had found a solution when Dollfuss became Chancellor. Like his more liberal Christian-Social predecessors he too came under constant pressure from the *Heimwehr* and National Socialists, who were becoming increasingly encouraged by events in Italy and Germany. In March 1933 he was able to take advantage of a parliamentary crisis to abolish democracy and replace it with the 'Corporate State' (*Ständestaat*).

In the industrial sphere Dollfuss withdrew collective agreements and reduced wages and salaries. The new state gradually dismantled the social welfare provisions achieved in the immediate post-war years and placed the self-administering independent Chambers of Labour under a Government-appointed commission.

Worse was to come. The tensions between Right and Left had now reached an intolerable level and in February 1934 civil war broke out. Dollfuss's repressive regime eventually triumphed over the belligerents and brought about a form of social peace which entailed the heavy price that the workers' leaders involved in the struggles were executed. Socialists and representatives of the Free Trade Unions were deprived of their posts on works' councils and employers were given greater powers to dismiss. (Strikes had already been prohibited in 1933.)

Political and governmental decisions were henceforth the prerogative of the 'Fatherland Front' (*Vaterländische Front*), an organizational construct introduced by Dollfuss into which the parties of the right were now constituted (with the exception of the National Socialists), but economic and business decisions were regulated by the new 'corporations'. The Free Trade Unions were abolished and on 2 March 1934 a decree was issued which permitted the only union for employees — the United Trade Union (*Einheitsgewerkschaft*) into which were merged 'yellow', *Heimwehr* and Christian-Social workers' organisations. In July of the same year 'works' unions' (*Werksgemeinschaften*) were formed from among members of the United Trade Union to replace works' councils; their function was to join with the employers in settling workplace issues, but their decisions alone were illegal unless approved by the employers. After the murder of Dollfuss by the Nazis in the same month, union demands for self-administration and voluntary action were still being articulated, but without effect. In the meantime the illegal Free Trade Unions were accepted as the representatives of the Austrian workers by the International Confederation of Free Trade Unions. Political events in Central Europe had taken a turn for the worse and the days of the corporate state were now numbered as these same political events now threatened Austria's independence.

1938–45: annexation by Germany and World War Two

Many of the leaders of the Free Trade Unions and Socialist Party went into exile abroad after 1934 where they formed the Revolutionary Socialist Party under the initiative of Bauer, while in Austria others quietly remained and attempted to work for the restoration of their rights. Dollfuss's successor, Schuschnigg, appeared less inflexible than his predecessor and a token indication of this was that, as a result of a series of strikes in 1936, he introduced regulations for the elections of shop stewards in the works' unions. On the whole, however, the Free Trade Unions met with no success in restoring their legality. Austrian Fascism of the corporate state under pressure of international events came to an end in March 1938. An authoritarianism of a more virulent kind replaced it when German troops marched into Austria and annexed the country as a province of the Third Reich. Both Chambers of Labour and United Trade Union were swept away and Nazi concentration camps henceforth contained Austrian trade unionists of every conceivable type of political and religious persuasion. Those who managed to avoid arrest joined the underground or fled abroad. The Nazi Labour Organization, the German Labour Front (*Deutsche Arbeitsfront*) replaced trade unions. This in fact was a workplace recruitment agency for the Nazi Party. Most matters relating to wages and conditions of work were decided upon by the Reich's ministers in Berlin and administered by the Nazi governors of Austria, now a province of the Reich and renamed Ostmark.

The Second Republic and the rebirth of Austrian trade unionism

In early 1945 the 'Greater German Empire' of Hitler came to an end. As the Allied Powers were jostling for military territorial occupation, steps were already being taken for the restoration of democratic life in Austria. In Vienna, part of the Russian zone of occupation, two prominent Socialists had already assumed high office: Theodor Körner was installed as Mayor of Vienna on 17 April and Karl Renner, as history appeared to repeat itself, was appointed Chancellor of new provisional government on 27 April. The former political parties, excluding the National Socialists, reorganized themselves and assumed new names. The Social Democratic Workers' Party with the Revolutionary Socialists, became the Socialist Party of Austria (SPÖ), the Christian-Socials became the Austrian People's Party (ÖVP) and those of national or liberal beliefs (*Grossdeutsche*, *Deutsch–Bürgerliche*, etc.) formed, first of all, the League of Independents (*Verband der Unabhängigen*)which was later renamed the Austrian Freedom Party (FPÖ). The small Communist Party (KPÖ) recommenced its activities, and was particularly favoured because of its role in the resistance to Nazism. It was represented in the new provisional government along with the representatives of the SPÖ and ÖVP. These preliminary steps to the restoration of democratic life were approved by the Allied Occupying Powers. The first act of the new government was to restore the Constitution of the First Republic as it stood in 1928/9 and repeal all laws subsequent to the annexation by Germany.

While the battle for Vienna was being waged the leaders of the Free Trade Unions and of the other conservative unions were making plans for a new trade union movement. The resultant blueprint was for a federal structure (as with the political administration of the country) yet strongly centralized (along the lines of the restructuring of 1928) incorporating all political viewpoints, but stressing the non-party (*überparteilich*) nature of the organization while declaring itself *not* to be non-political (*unpolitisch*). This unified structure could contain the different political tendencies within rather than wage battles with each other without, as was the experience of the early years. The new Federation (*Bund*) was to provide a structure at provincial (*Land*), district and local levels representing within these geographical areas 14 (later extended to 16) industrial trade unions. On 15 April 1945 this new umbrella organization became the Austrian Trade Union Federation (*Österreichischer Gewerkschaftsbund* or *ÖGB*) and its first President was Johann Böhm. Very soon works' councillors (*Betriebsräte*) and shop stewards (*Vertrauensleute*) were elected at workplace level pending the appropriate legislation, and for this interim purpose the provisions of the 1919 Works' Councils Act were utilized. The close connection between government and unions was restored when Böhm joined the provisional government (and then the elected government) as Minister for Social Administration, thus continuing the tradition begun by Ferdinand Hanusch in the First Republic. Immediate steps were also taken to restore the Chambers of Labour. Unemployment benefit, in view of the dreadful economic situation of the post-war period, was also restored.

In the period of national reconstruction after 1945 the new Trade Union Federation played its part. After the first general election in 1946 which resulted in a coalition government, the Federation acted as co-ordinator of union wage policies in order to achieve economic growth and in return its influence and expertise in social policy were accepted. The Federation's participation in the first Wage and Price Agreements was a solid foundation for the later Social Partnership of the Parity Commission of 1957 — a voluntary external form of worker participation (*überbetriebliche Mitbestimming*). This was later supplemented by steps towards workplace participation (*innerbetriebliche Mitsbestimming*) based on legal norms. The new Federation also participated in the work of the many joint commissions set up and played an active part in the co-ordination of the efforts to bring foodstuffs to the starving population. Not all workers and sections of the movement were in favour of the orderly, conciliatory and co-operative stance adopted by the Federation as the many wildcat strikes which occurred at the time seem to suggest. Real wages lagged behind retail prices by the time of the Fourth Wage and Price Agreement of 1951. The Communists, for example, who were represented in the early post-war governments withdrew their support in 1949 and attempted to mount a general strike in 1950 in opposition to the 'class collaboration' of the unions. This failed and with it perhaps the last vestiges of any regard the majority of the people may have had for the Austrian Communist Party.

Stimulated by the Marshall Plan and international aid, the Austrian economy (in marked contrast to the First Republic) gradually improved, albeit haltingly; with the Russians there were always difficulties, particularly over the many private concerns confiscated by the Germans in the name of the Third Reich. This led to strains between the Allies and the Russians on the one side and the Austrian government and the Russian authorities on the other. The Austrian government nationalized these concerns with the approval of the Western Allies and the disapproval of the Soviet Union. Protracted negotiations took place and finally by the State

Treaty of 1955 with the Allied Powers, in return for the freedom and neutrality of the Second Republic, the 'German assets' were returned to the Austrian state, at a price, however, of considerable reparations in cash and kind to the Soviet Union (the Western Allies neither demanded, nor received, anything).

The foundation of the ÖGB was important for the establishment of the modern Austrian welfare state. The distinct strategy of the ÖGB with respect to social policy had been envisaged in three phases:

1 The re-enactment and improvement of social legislation before 1934.
2 Return to participation in international conventions and consideration of comparative social security developments.
3 The complete codification and unification of social and welfare legislation in a comprehensive set of measures.

To achieve the objectives which these phases entailed, economic growth was necessary and within such a framework, collective agreements had to play a part. The Collective Agreements' Act of 1947 was drawn up outlining the role of the affiliates of the ÖGB with the exception of agricultural workers. In the same year the Works' Councils Act was enacted in accordance with the ÖGB's specifications. These Acts constituted the legal foundations of the collectivized and centralized nature of Austrian industrial relations and provided a modicum of stability till they were replaced by that more comprehensive measure, the Works' Constitution (Labour Code) Act of 1973.

By 1955 social welfare legislation covered agricultural workers, outwork, childrens' allowances and old-age pensions. In the area of work-related social security a change in the system came about. The institutions were taken out of the hands of the state and reformed along the lines of self-administration (*Selbstverwaltung*) through joint management in structures composed of employers' and employees' representatives. Trade union power and influence in the sphere of social legislation was further enhanced when, in 1956, Karl Maisel succeeded Johann Böhm as Social Minister. This coincided with the unification process of social legislation in the passing of the General Social Insurance Act (ASVG) in the same year.

By 1960 the membership of unions affiliated to the ÖGB rose to a new record — 1,501,047. The number kept rising and by 1981 the figure stood at 1,677,265. By this latter date the proportion of organized workers had reached 60% — one of the highest in the world and the total number of unions was now fifteen. (See Appendices F3 and F4.)

Johann Böhm was succeeded as President by Franz Olah, who in turn was succeeded by Anton Benya in 1963. In the early period of Benya's presidency of the ÖGB the earlier priorities of economic growth, the voluntary social partnership and improvements in working life were continued. By the early 1970s, however, unemployment began to rise, and though the level was in no way comparable to Austria's earlier industrial history, it was now significant enough to rank as an important problem — particularly in view of the possible political significance should the situation worsen.

In 1970 the Federation participated in the reforming of the nationalized industries (the former 'German property') and in their running under a state holding company (ÖIAG) which became the supervisory and controlling organ. The effect of this was to enhance the influence of the works' councillors, as representatives of the ÖGB in the industries, particularly in certain sections, e.g. *VÖEST* — the steel concern, which was also the largest company in Austria. After 1972 certain economic and management problems began to occur in the nationalized concerns which were to last for some time.

Through its sensible economic and social policies, with problems notwithstanding, by 1970 Austria had become a model of social peace particularly in view of her negligible strike record compared to other industrialized countries. To many it was felt that a setback occurred in welfare legislation when the Grand Coalitions of the post-war years came to an end with the success of the People's Party in the general election of 1966. Whatever deficiency may have occurred it was certainly corrected in the trade union view by the victory of the Socialist Party under Dr Kreisky at the polls in 1970, and the period of the socialist majority government which followed ushered in, according to the view commonly expressed in Austria today, a 'golden age'.

The structure of collective bargaining in the post-war period also changed markedly. Collective agreements became settled at two levels. Under general collective agreements the ÖGB with its negotiating partner the Federal Chamber of the Economy (*Bundeswirtschaftskammer*) negotiated issues concerned with social betterment, such as working hours and holidays. These general agreements were essentially voluntary in nature but certain aspects became law (for example working hours) after the partners had agreed. This had been the case from the introduction of the 8-hour working day in 1945 and will certainly be the case over the demand for the 35-hour working week in due course.

At the second industry level, all agreements concluded are legally binding. These agreements are negotiated between the individual unions and the relevant sections of the Economic Chambers but are always countersigned by the ÖGB. Over and above that, such agreements allow for adjustments to be negotiated at workplace level.

Other legislative achievements have included protection for works' councillors, paid educational leave, representation of employees on company supervisory Boards, the setting up of Youth Councils in workplaces, minimum pay, severance pay, provision relating to equality and sex discrimination, and more recently a measure concerning those engaged on night and heavy work. These measures have been accompanied by the ÖGB pursuing a policy of the 'humanization of working life' (*Humanisierung der Arbeitswelt*), a theme stretching in a continuum from health and safety to the more recent challenges of new technology.

Trade union structure and finance

Appendix F5 sets out the overall structure of the Austrian trade union movement in its constituent parts outlining the administrative and decision-making structure from branch (*Ortsgruppe*) or local level to district, provincial and finally to national level. Each of the fifteen industrial unions has a similar structure (with some slight modifications) where the Union National Conference (*Gewerkschaftstag*) is the sovereign policy-making body, and is paralleled in the case of the Austrian Trade Union Federation's four-yearly Congress (*Bundeskongress des ÖGB*).

The organizational structures are much more simple than in many other countries largely because there are fewer unions, but they differ from most by their in-built party political tendencies. At workplace level there are distinct differences where works' councils constitute a legal provision for employees (rather than for trade unionists only, although some 95% of all Austrian works' councils are unionized). Unionized works' councils are accountable to the local branch of the appropriate union, although there may also be mechanisms where works' councillors from different firms meet at a local level. The works' councils within the same concern but in different locations also form higher tiers of authority (*Zentralbetriebsräte*) which, for example in the case of VÖEST, can be very powerful indeed.

Works' council elections are fought on a party ticket with the main political parties having 'fractions' or political-industrial groups campaigning on party policies. Such representation operates at all levels from individual workplace all the way up to union national level and ultimately in the ÖGB. The electoral system of proportional representation is a feature of most elections in Austria including those at workplace (works' council) level. Individual unions may elect *Vertrauensleute* (union representatives) as possible substitutes

Table 12.1 Party representation of group seats on ÖGB national executive and works councils — 1979 (%)

	FSG (Socialist)	FCG/ÖAAB (Conservative)	KPÖ (Communist)	FPÖ (Liberal)	Partei-Unabhängige (Independent)	Sonstige (Other)
Works Councils	67.7	13.0	0.6	0.6	18.5	–
ÖGB National Executive	72.2	14.8	3.7	1.9	3.7	3.7

Source: Nick, R. and Pelinka, A, *Bürgerkrieg — Sozialpartnerschaft*, Munich 1983.

for their members sitting on works' councils, where in the case of death or resignation for example, such a substitute will fill the vacant place till the next election or, where the union has few members only, such *Vertrauensleute* will be the union spokesmen in the workplace to ensure that union policies are communicated. At the workplace level there can never be more than two unions, one for white-collar, and one for manual employees. This means that in fairly large concerns there may be two works' councils — one for each category of worker, although this normally pertains to manufacturing industry. Table 12.1 indicates the political representation by seats on the National Executive (*Bundesvorstand*) of the ÖGB and of works' councils following the elections of 1979.

These elections are vigorously contested by the political parties as is also the case with the other institution of employee representation in Austria, the Chambers of Labour. The Socialist Party has a considerable majority of seats in these institutions in a country which is highly politicized in a structural sense compared to her industrial neighbours despite frequent complaints of political apathy.

The Austrian trade unions are financially very sound and the position of the ÖGB is strongest of all in this regard. Finance too is centralized. Union subscriptions are gathered in the first instance by the ÖGB who in turn remits an amount to the individual unions in accordance with their needs. Table 12.2 sets out the percentage expenditure of the ÖGB in 1984.

Many of the items of expenditure in Table 12.2 have considerably changed over time. The Austrian welfare state, largely achieved through trade union activity, means that expenditure on support services of the ÖGB (unemployment, death, etc) is lower than previously. Remittances are also much lower than in the immediate post-war period but the percentage devoted to organizing activities

Table 12.2 ÖGB expenditure 1984 (approximate %)

Contributions to 15 affiliated unions	16
Administration, personnel costs	28
Members' financial support and benefit funds	7
Youth, recreation, sport	3
Education, cultural activities	5
Organizing activities, information	17
Affiliations, international associations	2
Scientific, travel and vocational training organizations	4
Educational activities of party political groups (*Fraktionen*)	1
Renewal and maintenance costs	14
Strike fund	1
Other costs	2

Source: ÖGB Tätigkeitsbericht, Vienna 1985.

has remained consistently high. The central strike fund of the ÖGB is estimated to run into billions of schillings (although only two people know what the actual figure is), is a powerful negotiating weapon and provides a sense of security and solidarity for trade union members. The ÖGB is the main shareholder in the Bank for Work and Economy (*Bank für Arbeit und Wirtschaft*), the successor to the former Workers' Bank founded by Karl Renner in 1923, and is nowadays an important bank in Austria. The Federation also owns a publishing house which is utilized for the documentation and literature it produces in accordance with its aims. Union subscriptions in Austria are high compared with elsewhere although some unions impose a maximum amount. The average subscription is calculated at about 1% of the ordinary member's annual income.

Education and training have a priority in Austrian trade union thinking. Most works' councillors training is undertaken by the ÖGB and the Chambers of Labour jointly in an impressive array of courses and events, although the individual unions do themselves provide a great deal on their own, and some possess extremely fine educational and recreational centres. Thus the dictum that 'knowledge is power', rooted deep in the Austrian worker's past, is a present and constant reality. The outward-looking expression of the Austrian Trade Union Federation is reflected in international activities and its membership of many bodies — the International Confederation of Free Trade Unions, the European Trade Union Confederation and the International Labour Office in particular, and is in keeping with Vienna's modern role as an international centre. Moreover, relations with eastern bloc countries, despite the events of two wars, are smooth and have made the ÖGB an advocate for good international and fraternal relations with their trade union movements.

Future prospects

The history of the Austrian trade union movement has been one of great struggle in the face of considerable obstacles. In a sense the difficult conflict-torn period of the inter-war years was the anvil on which the new movement was forged after 1945. The Austrian 'economic miracle' was due in no small part to the efforts of the new Trade Union Federation which also was part of, and participated in the process of, forming a new 'national consciousness'. The new movement, which had already taken steps to restructure itself before the Second World War, grasped the needs of the new era concretely and responded with a structure which is highly centralized, non-party but not apolitical and which, through the extension of economic and social policy measures, became incorporated into the finely-enmeshed institutional framework of the Austrian Second Republic.

Despite the great achievements and the great men of vision who have guided Austrian trade unions from their beginnings to the present time, there have been criticisms. These are not so much of policies, which in a time of unemployment and economic problems command a high degree of confidence and consensus, but relate quite often to certain trade union activities and practices. To some extent unpopular political decisions produce criticisms which rub off onto the trade union movement due to its close association with the Socialist Party. Recent criticisms, however, include those which relate to the 'cumulation of office' by many trade union officials, and the number of salaried jobs this entails, corrupt commercial practices practised through misuse of privilege, and an arrogance and imperviousness to accountability which critics characterize as features of bureaucracy and of life-styles reminiscent of the upper classes under the Habsburg monarchy.

But the priorities are right. The trade union movement can only remain healthy if the economy is healthy and for that it must place itself in a position to cope with the many current challenges. These include the decline of the old staple nationalized industries, manifesting a growing inability to compete in world markets, and the demands of new technologies in a situation in which the unions now need the social partnership more than employers do, even though many criticisms are aimed at the wages freeze aspects of the decisions of the Wages and Prices Parity Commission. Thus, there are strains on the new consensus and the trade unions, being in the front line, experience these deeply.

Trade unions in Austria are rational, stable and democratic in their structures and are well able to meet modern challenges. They have learnt the lessons of the past. For the future, responsible united action is vital, and they still have a lot to do. The changing nature of work is already having an impact and they still need to attract workers in small firms and from among minority groups. Women employees present particular problems. By the end of 1984 women constituted only 30% of all union members while they made up about 44% of the employed labour force (see Appendix F3).

Whatever the present problems, on balance the lesson is clear: trade unionism in Austria can be commended as a successful model, and one to which trade unions elsewhere should give considerable thought. Trade unions are not perfect institutions. They are representative of the hopes and desire of working people whose interests they serve. They still have much to achieve and those in Austria are in a better position than many elsewhere to do this.

13 The Federation of Austrian Industrialists

Herbert Krejci

Within the intricate network of interest groups and other associations so typical of the institutional scene in Austria, the Federation of Austrian Industrialists (*Vereinigung Österreichischer Industrieller*, or VÖI) has a specific part to play in terms of representing industry. It represents the interests of private manufacturing industry as well as of those companies which, in providing services, make use of industrial methods. Thus the VÖI also has within its membership numerous credit institutions, insurance companies and large retail concerns. Membership is on a voluntary basis. As a result of historical developments after the Second World War the VÖI does not represent the interests of companies within the nationalized sector.

Membership

Of the approximate total of 560,000 who are currently employed in Austrian industry, just under 100,000 work for the nationalized sector. Of the remaining 460,000, around 85 per cent are employed in private-sector companies which are members of the VÖI, so that in terms of the number of employees the Federation has a very respectable level of membership within the private sector of Austrian industry.

The contributions paid by individual members to the Federation generally depend upon the number of persons currently employed within their companies, or upon wage and salary costs. At the present time just under 2,400 companies make up the membership, employing about 420,000 people. The Federation is organized on a regional basis having its own office in each province. The easterly provinces of Vienna, Lower Austria and Burgenland are looked after from Vienna, though in terms of their legal status they count as separate entities. Within the Federation's central office there is no subdivision according to branches of industry; its work is divided among specialist areas of economic and social policy, with public relations work in the narrow and the broader sense constituting a significant part of its activities.

Over 4,500 employers (both owners and managers), together with other leading figures in Austrian industry, are currently organized in the VÖI. It is also responsible for various auxiliary organizations whose task is to bring together under the Federation's umbrella people with specific interests. There is for example the organization known as *Junge Industrie* which specifically looks after the interests of younger industrialists while through the agency of *Gruppe 1031* the Federation gives its members an opportunity to study at some depth fundamental issues of economic and societal development, either at an academic level or through the development of practical and professional skills. This latter group also carries out some of the recruitment to official positions within the Federation.

As the successor organization of the employers' associations existing under the Austro-Hungarian Empire, the VÖI carries on the traditions and has inherited a valuable asset in the form of a prestigious building which, opened on 25 March 1911 by Emperor Franz Joseph, has been the seat of Austrian industry ever since despite all the vicissitudes through which Austria has passed. This building (*Das Wiener Haus der Industrie*) is a valuable capital asset and not merely in a material sense. The VÖI makes use of its genteel ambience not just for work connected immediately with the Federation's affairs but also for public meetings, seminars and discussions. The work of the VÖI is carried on in accordance with the classical principles of employers' interest groups, in that there is an organizational division between the secretariat (i.e. full-time staff who are experts in various specialist fields) and the numerous committees which between them involve hundreds of members or representatives of member companies serving in an honorary capacity. The organization is headed by a Presidium consisting of the president plus four vice-presidents.

The next highest body is the Presidential Council comprising not only the members of the Presidium and the presidents of the various provincial associations, but also the chairmen of the seven statutory committees of the organization. The statutes of the VÖI require that the Federation shall have committees for Economic Affairs, Foreign Trade, Taxation and Finance, Social Affairs, Educational and Social Policy, Legal Affairs and Public Relations. The Board (*Vorstand*) of the VÖI is the forum for the formation of opinion at national level. It currently has a membership of just over 100, these being representatives sent by the autonomous provincial associations in numbers dependent upon the size of their membership.

In the above-mentioned specialist committees, which are also empowered to set up sub-committees as working parties or study groups, there is extremely fruitful dialogue between experts drawn from the practical world of industry and the full-time secretariat staff.

Each provincial association likewise has its own Presidium and Board, so one can be certain that there are currently between 300 and 350 industrialists in immediate, direct contact with the Federation, the result being that the individual member feels a very strong attachment to his organization — to which, after all, he belongs of his own volition and not by force of law. This undoubtedly accounts for the VÖI's power as an interest group. The fact that resignation is a possibility at any time also means that the individual member's wishes and concerns probably receive faster and more thorough attention from the Federation's full-time staff than might be the case in interest groups with compulsory membership.

Within Austria's network of interest groups, referred to above, the VÖI is a recognized institution which enjoys a reputation of professionalism and articulateness from a clearly-defined socio-political standpoint. Its functions are two-fold:

a) on the one hand it sees itself as an organization which very definitely supplies a service by making information and other services in the area of know-how speedily available to member companies;
b) on the other hand it is an interest group with lobbying responsibilities. It plays a full part, for example, in the decision-making process which precedes parliamentary action, and is an indispensable pillar of that system of social partnership which is such a tried and tested feature of Austrian affairs. This social partnership (i.e. the informal but highly intensive co-operation between employers' and employees' interest groups) is the foundation of the level-headedness and good sense which characterize the country's social climate, strike movements and bitter social confrontations being virtually unknown.

Across the country as a whole the VÖI currently employs about 140 people, a very large proportion of whom, by the very nature of the work involved, are highly qualified specialists, a relatively high number being academics. The organizational structure is strongly federalist in character which makes it possible to be very active even at grass-roots level and also to ensure that the interests of industry carry weight in the economic policy of individual provinces.

The main points of the Federation's programme

The VÖI sees itself primarily as a group representing the interests of industrialists, irrespective of whether the latter are such by virtue of ownership or by virtue of appointing decision makers. It is committed to pluralism, to parliamentary democracy and particularly to the system of the social market economy. It regards itself as responsible for upholding and extending as far as possible the liberty of the individual. It is explicitly against collectivism, paternalism and levelling down in social policy, and also against the excessive bureaucratization of public life and over-regimentation of responsible citizens. It is non-aligned politically though committed to a clearly defined ideological position.

14 The Austrian Chambers of Labour

Jim Sweeney

The Chambers of Labour as the name might suggest are the counterpart to the Chambers of Commerce or Chambers of Trade and Industry (Economic Chambers, as Austrians translate it into English) which implies that they represent in some way the interests of employees or labour in much the same way that Chambers of Commerce represent capital or business. In the Austrian context (there are also employees' Chambers in Luxembourg and certain of the states or provinces (*Länder*) of the German Federal Republic), the actual title is Chambers for Manual and Non Manual Employees (*Kammern für Arbeiter und Angestellte*). Austrian standard practice is to refer to them as Chambers of Labour (*Arbeiterkammern*). The plural is generally used because there is actually a Chamber for each Austrian province and one umbrella organization, the Austrian Conference of the Chambers of Labour (*Österreichischer Arbeiterkammertag*). Here we shall use the term Chambers of Labour unless a specific provincial Chamber is referred to. The treatment of the Austrian Chambers of Labour here will deal first with the historical development, then the search towards the concept of such an institution, followed by their establishment in the First Austrian Republic and their re-establishment in the Second, their modern structure and operation and will conclude by a brief evaluation and comment on their future prospects.

Historical development: the search for a concept

The earliest idea of Chambers of Labour appears to have come from France towards the end of the first half of the nineteenth century when the famous revolutionary Louis Blanc suggested a 'project d'organisation du travail' as a means for workers to participate in the affairs of the State — a sort of workers' parliament. In Austria the idea of Chambers of Labour took root about the same time, particularly after the revolutionary years of 1848–9, although the demand took on a more practical, strategic form where workers demanded the same rights as the manufacturing middle class who, in 1854, were granted the right by royal ordinance to set up Chambers of Commerce (*Handelskammern*) which in 1868 functioned also as a new 'estate' or voting class for the Cisleithanien (Austrian) Parliament of the Habsburgs. Accordingly, the demand for Chambers of Labour then became a strategic contrivance for achieving workers' suffrage. There were similar numerous developments in Europe outside the 'Dual Monarchy' towards the close of the nineteenth century and Chambers of this genus were started in Belgium in 1887 and in Holland in 1897, while in France in 1900 the Ministry of Commerce was empowered to set up a *Conseil du travail* in the country's industrial areas.

In the third quarter of the nineteenth century Chambers of Labour were a prime object of attention of the Austrian Free Trade Unions and Austrian Social Democratic Workers' Party (Socialist Party), which saw their importance as providing an extension of the political influence of the working class even though for some time there was no unanimity on the means to be employed in achieving them, or to their place in a socialist society. The division among trade unionists took on an acute character when Oberwinder, leader of the moderates within the trade unions, submitted a memorandum to the Ministry of the Interior and to parliament in 1872 suggesting the establishment of Chambers of Labour with parliamentary representation, with the purpose of informing on the labour situation, having rights of consultation on working conditions and relevant draft laws and submitting reports on the situation of the working class. This was attacked by the leader of the radical wing led by Scheu who adopted a more Marxist stance on the question of 'co-operation', and regarded this as a 'betrayal'. His supporters thereafter contemptuously referred to the Oberwinder group as the 'Party of the Memorandum'. It is interesting to note that part of Oberwinder's notion envisaged the Chambers as a referee and conciliator in disputes between employee and employer over working conditions. In the years between 1886 and 1890, the issue was further taken up by the Liberals in Parliament (by Plener and others) on debates on the condition of labour (*Arbeiterfrage*). Their object was to promote a bill to establish Chambers of Labour to perform (among other things) conciliation and arbitration functions in working life and to provide the basis of an 'estate' by allotting it 9 votes in the Cisleithanian Parliament (*Reichsrat*). Such a scheme was not, however, acceptable to the broad spectrum of Social Democrat and Free Trade Union opinion and a resolution at the Hainfeld Social Democrat Party Congress in 1889 finally dissociated the labour movement from the piecemeal proposals of the Liberals.

Despite the principled ideological rhetoric of the Free Trade Unions and Social Democrats towards the end of the nineteenth century a close association developed between the workers' organizations and the monarchical-capitalist state through the establishment of a Labour Advisory Council (*Arbeitsbeirat*) in 1898 as a section within the Ministry of Commerce. This Advisory Council had the essential function of providing information, including that of a statistical nature, on the conditions and issues of the working class. A third of the members of the Advisory Council were worker representatives. It is fascinating to observe such an early development, nevertheless, and to note that it was a contributory strand of the later social partnership. It is also interesting to note the pragmatic stance taken by Free Trade Unions and Social Democrats in the late 1890s despite the opprobrium heaped on the head of Oberwinder almost three decades earlier. True, most of the Free Trade Union (*Gewerkschaftskommission*) Conferences after 1900 occasioned criticism of the Labour Advisory Council; in 1905, however, its work was extended and this process further continued in 1908 when a social policy section was set up within the Ministry of Commerce. This latter point is significant when we observe the Chambers of Labour after 1920 and see how through this precedent the work of the Chambers became linked to the state bureaucracy — a feature which to some extent has persisted to the present day.

There were other intellectual influences of a political nature at work inside Austria on the idea of Chambers to which some brief mention should be made. In Catholic social teachings, largely under the powerful advocacy of von Vogelsang, the idea of an *Arbeitskammer* was mooted. Here the functions were envisaged as being quite different. In this structure workers and employers would sit together in a bilateral chamber and settle the issues between them relating to contracts of employment. This view accords with much of the Catholic, Conservative anti-capitalist thought developed in Germany and Austria towards the end of the nineteenth century, inspired by the papal encyclical *Rerum Novarum* in 1891, but opposed nevertheless to the Marxist view of irreconcilable interests based on class struggle. Other motives are also apparent. To sections of the ruling élites including the bureaucracy, liberal economists and business strata, an institution representing workers was deemed highly desirable since within such an institution the workers could be tamed to serve the ends of the State. Such ends were perceived in a much more enlightened way than either the Habsburg monarchy or the nobility could contemplate.

For the majority of the working class, expressed through the views of the leaders of the Social Democrats and Free Trade Unions, the 'workers' parliament' as an expression of freedom had a much more realistic meaning — a device for securing the vote. As workplace issues increasingly played a greater part in the lives of workers the demands for such things as labour exchanges and intermediation mechanisms for labour market issues became greater, so the objective of Chambers of Labour became more and more seen as an institution of employees' instrumental interests. Instead of a 'workers' parliament' related to broad social and political rights they became seen as a '*labour* parliament' in which those aspects which directly impinged on people at work were most significant and about which demands could be articulated, and it is this meaning of Chambers of Labour which gradually predominated after 1900, particularly after 1907 when all males were granted the right to vote.

On the other hand, some sections of the middle class, particularly those in the lower echelons, while opposing workers on universal suffrage, might have welcomed such an institution for the purpose of co-operation in view of the conflict-laden industrial and political atmosphere of the times. For the workers, therefore, the Labour Advisory Council could be seen as a practical mechanism in which the demands of the working class could be brought to the forefront of the state's social policy development. It provided a 'behind the screen' way of representing employees' interests at a time when they were denied access to formal avenues of political power owing to the absence of political rights. Some historians believe that the idea of the Labour Advisory Council was more widely accepted than was originally thought and since it was particularly active at the time of the boom conditions after 1903 it favoured workers' interests. It enjoyed the 'certain influence' which Viktor Adler regarded as a necessary condition for its existence. The willingness of many socialist politicians of the time, who were by no means 'revisionist', to negotiate matters of social policy by this medium in the period before universal suffrage, represented an important phase in the development of Austrian social policy and highlights the state's social imperative in acceding to the claims of the workers. It might be said to form a starting point in the transformation of workers' expectations which culminated in the explosion of legal measures at the beginning of the First Republic. At a less obvious level it was also a move towards the integration of the trade union movement into the machinery of state which was favoured by many socialists despite the strictures of Marxist theory (compare, for example, the views of Engels and Lenin).

This form of co-operation, however, was not subject to any fundamental criticisms from the labour movement at the time. Indeed, the most vociferous critics of the Labour Advisory Council were the employers and then, not on point of principle, but on the Council's composition. It might also be argued that the Council's existence represented an attempt at invigorating the state through subjecting its bureaucracy to industrial problem-solving in the manner which might be called 'democratic Josephism' (*demokratischer Josefinismus*) by invoking the parallel of change by 'enlightenment from above', characteristic of the reign of Joseph II (1765–90). Within the framework of constitutionalism, the bureaucracy sought to envelop and socialize working-class leaders by means of the Council to a new situaiton through which the workers' leaders would legitimize, and respond to the authority of, the State (*Obrigkeitsgefühl*). As long as the monarchy lasted, however, the demands for the Chambers of Labour were denied. It is only after its collapse and the establishment of the First Republic that we see their installation according to the workers' specifications. The last demand in this direction occurred when the Central Powers were facing defeat. Once more the Austrian labour movement placed the Chambers of Labour high on the political agenda. The famous article by the socialist politician Karl Renner (shortly to become the first Chancellor in the new Republic) in the Socialist newspaper *Arbeiterzeitung* on 11 July 1917, entitled 'The Necessity of the Chambers of Labour in the Transitional Economy', represented a powerful advocacy for the importance of such an institution for the Austrian working class. This appeal stressed the participation of the working class in post-war reconstruction and their integration into the future democratic life of the nation.

The Chambers of Labour in the First Republic

Although Renner's vision was important in galvanizing the efforts of the labour movement to the idea of Chambers of Labour in the new Republic, the socialist deputies Ferdinand Hanusch and Franz Domes, both prominent trade unionists, engineered the careful preparation for the legislation relating to them and their implementation. Hanusch, as Minister of Social Welfare in Renner's government (1918–20), steered the legislation through the Austrian parliament and became the *Direktor* (Director-General) of the Vienna Chamber in 1921, while Domes became its President.

The role of the Chambers in the First Republic was not without controversy. Once universal suffrage was achieved the question arose: what should this role be? Were they to be an alternative form of employee representation to the unions? The traditional arguments, likewise, had been conducted in terms of wage earners (*Lohnarbeiter*) and excluded salaried groups. But Austria, like other developed economies in the early twentieth century, was now composed of various occupational groups including those of the service classes, employees not traditionally envisaged by Marxist theory.

The unions tended to look at the Chambers of Labour as instruments of support, since the workers' struggle for economic emancipation was to be achieved by union strength and the enthusiasm arising from class consciousness. It gradually became realized that freedom had to be founded on economic and social progress, and this could only be achieved by an integrated and healthy economy in which the economic indicators — wages and prices, capital investment, profit and technical advance — all played a part. The shape of the economy was therefore an important prerequisite not only for a socialist economy but also, at a fundamental level, for one which had a chance for survival. The Chambers therefore provided expert advice and scientific knowledge to support and direct trade union policy. For institutions intended as instruments of class struggle, by 1926 they had achieved such a position of economic and social influence through their special, technical contribution in close association with the Free Trade Unions and Social Democratic Party, that they formed a powerful political pressure group in the early years of the First Republic. After 1926, however, their influence was diminished; the legally prescribed rights of consultation became less important in a political situation dominated by the parties of the right and where, without a parliamentary majority, Free Trade Union views counted for very much less. Valuable work, however, continued in the form of the provision of certain legal and educational services as the scope, quality and quantity of their publications in the 1920s testify. Even when political compromise became impossible after 1925, the Chambers were still active in the various organs and committees of the state apparatus and bureaucracy as well as those which formed part of the 'public interest.'

As bodies with a legal foundation, what were the Chambers supposed to do in the First Republic? Section 1 of the 1920 Chambers of Labour Act outlines the general objective as being 'to represent the economic interests of employees and to advance and raise their economic and social status according to their aspirations'. It is clear that this indicates the counterpart to those of employers affiliated to the then Chambers of Commerce, which would be consistent with the Austro-Marxist view of such an institution to act as an employees' 'countervailing power' to employers' interests; to this influence between 1921 and 1933 in particular was added those of the Social Democratic Party and the Free Trade Unions to form a powerful three-pillared coalition of interests. As has been pointed out, this influence was at its peak between 1918 and 1920.

Chamber membership in the First Republic was (as now) compulsory for all employees excluding those in public service, the liberal professions and most agricultural workers. Their spheres of competence never conflicted with those of the unions. Workplace representation and collective bargaining were the unions' spheres of activity, and duplication or overlapping never became an issue in the First (or Second) Republic.

The only 'parliament' aspect of the Chambers which was evident was the electoral context of the major political parties which competed for Chamber seats and this is emphasized in the two elections for the Chambers in 1921 and 1926, in which the Socialists had a decisive majority (see Appendix F6). The depression years and unemployment tended to put the Chambers into the sidelines to a considerable extent and the rest is a matter of history: in 1933 the Dollfuss regime denied them their rights of self-administration and placed them under a government Commission, until in 1938 the National Socialists abolished them completely.

The re-establishment of the Chambers of Labour after 1945

The legal basis (the *de facto* basis was already in being at the end of the war) of the Chambers in the Second Republic is set down in the Chambers of Labour Act 1954 with the general objective to 'further the social, economic, occupational and cultural interests of employees'. As before they were reconstructed as bodies corporate in public law (*Körperschaften des öffentlichen Rechtes*) with compulsory membership, erected on a federal basis consistent with the country's geographical/provincial (*Land*) boundaries. The Vienna Chamber of Labour has a dual function; as well as being a Chamber in its own right, it also provides the secretariat for the Chambers' central organ, the Austrian Conference of the Chambers of Labour (*Österreichischer Arbeiterkammertag*). The principle of elected Councillors (*Kammerräte*), discontinued after 1933, was restored and it is they who act as the democratically elected representatives of the workers and formulate Chamber policy. This, of course, as before, follows the general lines of the electoral contest of the major political parties whose structures extend to sub-organizations reconstructed after 1945, for appropriate electoral campaigns. Appendix F7 shows the results of the Chambers of Labour elections (held every 5 years) in the Second Republic.

The changed political circumstances of the immediate post-Second World War period and the economic *dirigisme* which characterized that period brought in their train a greater degree of influence for the Chambers, compared to that which pertained in most of the First Republic. In the first place the ideas essential to political reconstruction gave the Chambers the character of an indispensable 'brains trust' (*geistige Rüstkammern*) to the newly reconstructed Socialist Party (SPÖ), an attribute which soon became more apposite to their co-operation with the trade union movement. This aspect was associated with the work of the Chamber experts in the many areas of reconstruction — economic, industrial and social — which attached the nickname GEDEHEX (*Gewerkschaft der Herrn Experten* — 'the union of experts') to them, an indication of their considerable influence and prestige.

Secondly the improved political climate from which the Chambers benefited was due to their close association to and work with the Austrian Trade Union Federation (ÖGB) which, by 1953, commanded the allegiance of about 70% of all employees. As before, the unions concentrated on collective bargaining and industrial relations, while the Chambers' spheres were the more technical aspects of economic and social policy. This was highlighted by the participation of the Chambers with the other major interest associations in the work of the Reconstruction Control Council (*Bewirtschaftigungskommission*) which in effect placed the Chambers at the centre of Austria's economic life. This was particularly relevant at a time when there was a widespread climate of co-operation, particularly before 1949 when there were no Chambers elections.

As life returned to normal social perspectives changed. There was a gradual increase in living standards as rationing was abandoned and controls were dismantled, so that the close identity of interest prevalent among most social and occupational groups faded as time went on. As government ministries now recruited sufficient experts of their own, Chamber officials now reverted to providing for employee needs, so that by 1966 the character of the present day Chambers was established.

The Chambers' influence as well as its activities are to a considerable extent prescribed by law. Many laws specify the Chambers' right to co-determination (participation). The law on essential issues is changed only gradually and this entails democratic political activity: the Chambers' attempt to achieve a monopoly in opinion-forming and consensus among members. This is particularly true of their efforts to extend and strengthen the influence of the Labour Movement which is instanced by the special provision they make for trade union officers and in particular the work of its special college, the Social Academy (*Sozialakademie*) of the Chambers of Labour, a 'cadres' type training institution which prepares men and women for service in the Austrian labour movement.

The practical expression of the Chambers' philosophy is expressed by the following functions:

a) reacting to initiatives, for example, by commenting on draft laws or by giving their opinion on various matters ('Chamber conforming' functions);

b) taking initiatives on their own or with associated interest groups, for example with the Austrian Trade Union Federation or parliamentary Socialist Group ('Chamber specific' functions);
c) the provision of services to Chamber members such as legal advice, educational grants, holidays and rehabilitation amenities, educational courses etc. ('Chamber conforming' and 'Chamber specific' functions).

The structure and operation of the Chambers of Labour

We have given consideration to the purpose and tasks of the Chambers of Labour. We must now turn to look at the organizational shape and form.

Two million of the country's 2,700,000 employees are members of the Chambers, of which there is one in each federal province, each with its own administration and whose councillors are elected for 5 years. At the head of the structure is the Conference of the Austrian Chambers of Labour which in turn elects the Presidium and Executive. (The structure is explained in Appendices F8 and F9.) The delegates and councillors are elected on a proportional basis depending on numbers of employees in each province. The Conference of the Austrian Chamber of Labour must meet at least twice yearly; its meetings are public and its decisions are taken on the basis of a simple majority.

The management of each Chamber is divided between the Executive Committee, responsible for implementing policy and the Chief Executive (*Direktor*), who is responsible for the day-to-day running of the institution.

Who are the Chambers' electorate and how are elections organized? This question is answered in the first instance more easily by saying who is not entitled to be a member or to vote. This, as with the other items of Chambers' competences, is set down in the Chambers of Labour Act 1954. Civil servants, local government officers, the liberal professions (e.g. doctors, lawyers) and managers with important decision-making powers in private industry are not eligible for membership. Agricultural and forestry workers too are generally excluded, with some exceptions which will be discussed below. Otherwise all employees are deemed to be members and pay 0.5% of their annual income up to a limit of 21,600 Austrian schillings (in 1987). Most of the membership is concentrated in Vienna which has about 630,000 members. For voting purposes all national citizens above the age of 18 who are enfranchised and who work within the legally prescribed branches of industry are eligible to vote in Chambers of Labour elections. The 'classes' of voters are divided into manual workers (*Arbeiter*), non-manual workers (*Angestellte*) and transport employees (*Verkehrsbedienstete*) who vote separately in each of the provinces.

Agricultural and forestry workers except in Vorarlberg, Tyrol, Burgenland and Vienna have their own Chambers constituted along similar lines with similar powers. Differences exist for historical reasons: in Vorarlberg and Tyrol, those workers are represented in autonomous sections of the provincial Agriculture (Employers') Chambers, while in Vienna and Burgenland the Chambers of Labour in those provinces cater for their needs. Excluded categories include managers and family helpers or those working in enterprises with fewer than 5 persons.

At a functional level, the Chambers' work today includes consultation on all matters concerning the public, opinion on all draft laws, sitting on all representatives bodies prescribed by law, the provision of statistics, the monitoring of employment law and regulations, including close co-operation with the factory inspectorate, the care and protection of apprentice and youth interests and support services for works' councillors and full-time union officials (including educational provision). Over and above this, there is the central role, dating back to 1957 which the Chambers play within the nation's social partnership institutions in managing the economy.

Policy formulation and changing trends

Our brief survey has noted the development of the Chambers and their tasks within the given social and economic conditions of the times. Policy within the Chambers has traditionally been formulated along Socialist party lines, facilitated by a considerable degree of cross-organizational membership (party, union, Chamber) and the cumulation of office of the leading personalities of the labour movement.

The politicization of institutions has been a feature of Austria compared to many other western societies and this has likewise always been a central feature of the Chambers of Labour. This politicization has always (except between 1933 and 1938) taken a democratic form in the Chambers side by side with a highly professional (or 'bureaucratic' in the non-pejorative sense) one — a mix it shares with other modern Austrian institutions. As with the elections of the union movement within the Austrian Federation of the Trade Unions, the individual union or works' councils, the industrial political groupings (*Fraktionen*) likewise contest the Chambers' elections. From Appendix F7 it is clear that the Socialists in general have traditionally had a considerable commanding lead and this lead was virtually monopolistic in the First Republic. In more recent days

Table 14.1 *Total votes cast in Austrian Chambers of Labour elections 1979 and 1984 major political parties (%)*

	Socialists (FSG)	Conservatives (ÖAAB)	Liberals (FPÖ)	Communists (GLB + GE)
1979	64.3	31.0	3.2	1.5
1984	58.7	36.5	2.5	2.2

change is more apparent, and the growing influence of the conservatives is clear to see.

To examine the extent of party political influence let us turn to recent trends. The information extracted from Appendix F7 and summarized in Table 14.1 sets out the changes in overall voting patterns at the recent Chambers of Labour elections in 1979 and 1984. If we restrict the analysis to the two major parties, it shows the Socialist vote in the last two elections is in a state of decline, a fall of 5.9 per cent while a gain for the Conservatives of 5.7 per cent of the total votes cast between the dates in question is evident. The effect is all the more striking if we look at the results (Appendix F7) from 1949: this indicates an increase in the overall Conservative vote from 14.2 in 1949 to 36.5 per cent in 1984 and a corresponding decrease in the Socialist vote from 64.4 per cent (the highest point in Second Republic for the latter being the achievement of 68.6 per cent in 1954) to 58.7 per cent in the same period. The question will be asked, is this a short-term trend? If, however, we examine the results for the years in question, 1979 and 1984, by turning our attention to the electoral employee categories (status) and classes in which they vote (*Wahlkörper*) other trends can be discerned.

The Socialists have lost ground even in the category in which they are traditionally the strongest — the transport employees' section, and it is the sheer size of the manual workers' electorate which through 'averaging' underemphasizes the degree of seriousness about the trend. The Conservatives in 1984 for the first time in their history had a majority in the non-manual category, but for the Socialists there are more serious underlying factors at work. Table 14.3 outlines the occupational and sectoral changes which have occurred in the employee categories between 1949 and 1984. There is a slow long-term trend of erosion in the support of those groups traditionally loyal to the Austrian Socialist Party, and a rapid increase in the proportion of the category less favourable to it, a trend which if continued without any compensatory ideological or

Table 14.2 Percentage of total votes cast in Austrian Chambers of Labour elections by employee categories (Wahl Körper) — major political parties, 1979, 1984

	Manual Employees				Non-Manual Employees				Transport Employees			
	Socialists	Conservatives	Liberals	Communists	Socialists	Conservatives	Liberals	Communists	Socialists	Conservatives	Liberals	Communists
1979	72.4	23.7	2.3	1.6	50.9	43.2	4.7	1.3	76.1	19.9	2.3	1.7
1984	66.5	29.2	2.2	2.0	45.7	48.7	3.0	2.4	72.5	23.5	1.5	2.6

Source: Arbeit und Wirtschaft, June 1984.

Table 14.3 Occupational voting categories for Chambers of Labour Elections: % Change 1949, 1984

	1949	1984
Manual	67.5	50.4
Non-manual	19.1	41.6
Transport employees	13.4	8.0

attitudinal change or cataclysmic social event, would mean that it is only a matter of time before the Conservatives control the Chambers. Some observers point to an indication of this where already at provincial level the Tyrol Chamber of Labour was captured by the Conservatives in 1984, thus joining Vorarlberg in this respect.

It is possible that there are other underlying demographic and social changes at work — such as shifts of population from the eastern part of the country where the Socialist Party has its traditional stronghold, to the west which, though rural, is rapidly industrializing. The new 'computer classes' (yuppies?) are likely to have less in common with the Socialists than with the Conservatives and there may well still be a generational aspect where the old rather than the young tend to favour the Socialist Party.

This question has been raised not in any partisan spirit but to highlight the political factor in Chamber life at a time of change. On the other hand, Vienna is still highly influential and in the Vienna Chamber the Socialists outnumber the Conservatives by 2:1. The question remains: would a change in political power, Conservative domination of the Chambers of Labour, mean a diminution of their influence? Or perhaps their disbanding? There is very little to suggest this to be the case. Not only is the Chamber participation in the major decision-making organs of state an important check in the system but the services they provide are no less likely to be needed in the future. Changes of emphasis may ensue, but even then that is a long way off.

Evaluation and future prospects

If we evaluate the Chambers of Labour since their establishment in 1920, certain conclusions emerge. The first thing to be observed is their transformation from an instrument of class struggle to an institution for the formulation of ideas on economic policy and the protection of employees' interests. They are characterized as an organization with rather grey, behind-the-scenes, 'backroom boys' graduating from a 'brains trust' to a corps of '*apparatchiki*' or technocrats serving individual and interest-group demands as well as providing service in the national interest. The personnel of the Chambers of Labour, which have a high 'academic' content, indicate that they are composed of highly motivated, dedicated men and women.

Secondly, as an employees' institution in a country unique for its 'dual system' of employee representation, since their inception the Chambers have never been seen as competition for the trade unions: the division of functions between unions and Chambers has been such that the latter have developed into an intellectual arm and aid to the unions whose prime task has been workplace representation and collective bargaining. They have provided support services for the unions. There has never been a demarcation dispute in this regard. The Chambers' tasks are basically grounded in law and this has been a helpful feature of the division of function.

Thirdly, in approaching employee interests within the framework of the general interest (Renner would have approved of this aspect of Chamber work as an illustration of his concept of the 'general will') and by participating in national level consensus agreements of social and economic importance, Chamber officials and policies have played their part in Austrian democracy. The reader is prompted to reflect on the historical importance of the 'phase of consolidation' of 1918–20. Despite retreats after this time they continued to perform essential and valuable functions constituting a workers' instrument of self-administration (if not completely a 'workers' parliament'), and a counter to the weight of the then-powerful authoritative Chamber of Commerce (now Chambers of the Economy). Some writers also see the Chambers as a superstructure to the Works' Constitution Acts, while many have seen them particularly as a substitute for Works' Councils after the onset of the corporate state: while yet others see them, at a general abstract level, as the highest form of economic democracy.

From time to time arguments occur concerning the Chambers' special contribution to social policy which in the Austrian context means the non-economic considerations (but including employment and industrial law) of political decision-making in the round. To limit the Chambers' contribution to this sphere of activity as all-embracing would be necessarily too restrictive.

If anything, the great strengths of the Chambers of Labour emerged in periods of social stress, when social democracy was on the defensive. The Chambers' experience from those times was carried forward into forms of co-determination and co-responsibility in the Second Republic. After the re-establishment of democracy and the restoration of the Austrian nation after 1955 the Chambers became somewhat less prominent and the state bureaucracy absorbed many of their personnel. Some contemporary observers speak of their current problem being one of 'image', but then this may be another way of saying that they have a usefulness which is out of proportion to their public recognition.

Modern Austria is a welfare state country. The Chambers of Labour do still, however, make an important contribution to services for employees. They serve as a kind of mixture of citizens' advice bureaux, a social service agency for employees and their families, legal adviser, holiday provider and most importantly provide valuable educational work of a high quality.

The Austrian Chambers of Labour are now established institutions of some importance in the country; their character is unlikely to change dramatically for some considerable period of time. Many of the past political, social and intellectual differences are now merged into a national consensus (even if of an ambiguous or unstated nature) in which the existence of these unusual institutions is not in dispute. If they have a fault, it is their inability to serve as a catalyst for discussion on the burning issues of the day with which they often find themselves involved in functional and administrative terms; without this catalyst role, however, they may continue to be respected but not valued for what they are truly worth.

15 The Chambers of Agriculture in Austria

A. H. Malinsky and R. Priewasser

Legal status and membership

In the period 1922 to 1957 a Chamber of Agriculture was established in each of the nine federal states of Austria (*Länder*) of Austria on the basis of provincial (*Land*) legislation. These Chambers of Agriculture are the legal representatives of the agricultural community within each *Land*. They are legally independent in the fulfilment of their representative duties even though the respective *Land* administrations enjoy a limited right of supervision (e.g. the requirement to submit annual reports on activities and finances). The Chambers have their offices in the respective capital towns of the *Länder* but most of them have branches in individual parts of the *Land* (district branches) and often at local authority level too.

As with all other legally based representative bodies for professions or social groups (Economic Chambers, Chambers of Labour, Chamber of Medical Practitioners, etc.) there is compulsory membership. This means that every occupier of an agricultural holding (whether owner or tenant) has to join, provided that his holding conforms to the minimum size requirement. Apart from the heads of the farm units, family members and in some *Länder* even top employees in agricultural businesses are members of the Chamber and can therefore also lay claim to its services.

Further members of the Chambers are the agricultural co-operatives, which play an important part in Austrian agriculture. Created as voluntary self-help associations for farmers, they have over a period of time developed into extremely influential institutions, for instance in the areas of agricultural credit and agricultural supplies as well as the processing and marketing of agricultural products. Membership involves the payment of a generally low subscription to cover the personnel and other costs of the Chambers' organisation.

The activities of the Agricultural Chambers

In accordance with their statutory duties the Chambers of Agriculture have the following tasks:

1 The *promotion of the wishes and interests* of agriculture and forestry in all those areas which are relevant to them. These include, for example, aspects of agricultural law (e.g. quota and price regulations relating to agricultural products within the framework of the market organization laws), aspects of domestic and foreign trade (e.g. support for marketing on internal and external markets) and also questions of taxation, food and land policies.

2 Direct *advice* to those working in agriculture and forestry on legal, economic, technical and social questions. This work accounts for a large part of the resources of the individual Chambers. Its wide scope ranges from assistance relating to intended changes in the production programmes of particular businesses to advice concerning the acquisition of agricultural machinery and plant and their optimal use (e.g. collective use by several farms), help on questions of social insurance (e.g. health and accident insurance, old age provision) and on the establishment of co-operative self-help organizations (e.g. deployment of mobile relief workers in the case of illness, stock-breeding co-operatives, equipment rings).

Recently there has been increased use of the advisory service for farming businesses which as a sideline operate as 'holiday farms'. The 'farm holiday' has established itself as a distinct type of holiday in recent years and thus made new demands on the specialist knowledge and investment activity of such farms.

3 The professional *training and further education* of the agricultural and forestry community. Quite apart from the training of specialist agricultural personnel in state agricultural colleges, the Chambers of Agriculture offer specialist courses of their own for further education in professional, technical and cultural subjects. Included in this area of further education is the regular information service for the farming community concerning recent developments in agriculture, using the organization's own newspapers and special brochures on particular topics.

4 *Representing* the agricultural community's legal and economic interests in relation to the state authorities.

5 The *appraisal* of draft legislation at federal level (*Bund* legislation) and at provincial level (*Land* legislation). The Chambers of Agriculture have the right to submit their views relating to laws even at the draft stage, if these laws affect the interests of agriculture and forestry. Through this arrangement any differences of opinion between the state and the interest group can be detected early on and in many cases can also be partially or completely resolved. This right to assess laws in the development stage (which other interest groups also enjoy in relation to their area

of concern) is an important instrument for achieving a broad political consensus and thus for securing social peace in Austria.

The organization of the Chambers of Agriculture

The activities of the individual Chambers of Agriculture are conducted by several elected bodies with differing tasks. These bodies are:

— the General Assembly
— specialist sub-groups (committees)
— the Presidium.

The tasks of the General Assembly are the supervision and control of overall Chamber activities and basic decision making. This includes the election of the members of the Presidium and the Committees, the setting of the subscription rate for members of the Chamber and matters relating to the legal status and the remuneration of Chamber employees.

The respective Committees are charged by the General Assembly with particular tasks. Those committees which are concerned with special areas of development in agriculture and forestry (animal husbandry, plant cultivation, hill farming, forestry) play a particularly important role.

Lastly, the Presidium is the highest executive body of the Chamber. It consists of a president and normally several vice-presidents and represents the Chamber externally and heads up its negotiations and its business affairs.

The personal composition of the bodies is determined by elections which take place every 5 years (in some *Land* Chambers every 6 years). All the members of the Chamber are entitled to elect the delegates for the General Assembly. The election of the members of the various committees and of the Presidium is in turn carried out by the delegates of the General Assembly.

The preparation and implementation of the decisions of the above bodies and the general discharge of relevant tasks are dealt with by the Chambers' own administrative apparatus with specialist departments.

The Conference of the Presidents of the Agricultural Chambers

In order to represent the interests of agriculture and forestry at central state level in a co-ordinated and unified fashion, it was necessary to establish an umbrella organization for the various *Land* Chambers. For this purpose an association was formed in 1953 made up of the individual *Land* Chambers as corporate members with their presidents as representatives — hence the name 'Conference of Presidents'. This Conference of Presidents can present proposals and assessments on all questions relating to agriculture; it can examine draft legislation and make representations to the appropriate authorities. In the practice of everyday politics the Conference of Presidents frequently commands greater influence than the individual *Land* Chambers, since these have transferred significant rights of political participation to their umbrella organization (e.g. negotiations on agricultural prices, support for exports and new areas of agricultural production). The structure of the Conference of Presidents is very similar to that of the *Land* Chambers (with a Presidium, a directorate, a General Assembly and an administrative apparatus, divided up into specialist departments).

The Chambers of Agricultural Workers

The Chambers of Agricultural Workers are the legal representatives of the interests of the employed section of the agricultural community, i.e. the workers and white-collar staff in agricultural and forestry businesses. Their task is to represent the economic, social and cultural interests of this group in relation to the individual employers and state bodies. There are independent Chambers of Agricultural Workers in only 5 of Austria's 9 *Länder*. In those *Länder* without Chambers of Agricultural Workers their tasks are carried out in some instances by the Chambers of Agriculture and in others — because of the very low numbers of employed workers — there is no separate representation. As with the Chambers of Agriculture, the Chambers of Agricultural Workers have a national umbrella organization, the 'Austrian Assembly of the Chambers of Agricultural Workers'.

16 Retail Co-operatives

Anton E. Rauter

The Austrian retail co-operative movement began in the 1850s, the oldest documented retail co-operative in Austria being founded in 1856 under the title of the 'Mutual Support Association of the Factory Workers in Teesdorf'. Then in the 1860s a series of co-operatives was established.

The retail co-operative movement developed rapidly in the period which followed: in 1872 the first co-operative federation in Austria was created, the 'General Federation of Self-Help German Commercial and Economic Cooperatives in Austria', which most of the existing retail associations joined. The Federation justified its existence in part by the influence it was able to exert in the creation of the cornerstone law, the Austrian Co-operative Law which came into force in 1873.

On 14 July 1901 representatives of 20 co-operative societies in Vienna and Lower Austria founded the 'General Federation of Workers' Commercial and Economic Co-operatives of Austria'. When in 1903 the Audit Law was created, this Federation applied successfully for powers of audit and since then it has remained the officially acknowledged and empowered audit federation of Austria's retail co-operatives.

In the course of time the co-operative movement became stronger, and efficient enough to run its own wholesale organization. In September 1905 the Wholesale Purchasing Society of the Austrian Retail Co-operatives (*Grosseinkaufsgesellschaft österreichischer Consumvereine* or GÖC) was established as a trading company and was converted into a limited company in 1908.

At the time of the collapse of the Habsburg monarchy the retail co-operative movement was a powerful, efficient organization in all of the Crown Provinces (*Kronländer*). But during and after the First World War the co-operatives had difficulty in surviving. At a stroke the activity of the Central Federation was limited to the area of the new and far smaller Republic of Austria. Even so the retail co-operative movement was not discouraged. Its work in the interests of the consumer continued and it was successful.

As part of a process of concentration, district co-operatives developed. In 1918, for example, there were 105 retail co-operatives with 294 outlets in the whole of Austria; in 1920 there were 103 with 584 outlets; in 1922, 108 with 687 outlets and in 1924 128 with 841 outlets. These district co-operatives created their own democratic membership organization — the Members' Committees — with the aim of maintaining an appropriate level of influence for the membership even in the large co-operatives.

In the following years the railway workers' grocery stores were merged with the local retail co-operatives to form general co-operatives, after the privileges granted by the railway companies had been abolished. The same period saw the establishment of the co-operatives' own central production facilities; as a result the co-operative stores were organized on a stricter basis.

It was also soon recognized that a system of co-operative education and training was indispensable if the co-operatives were to keep up with the times and with the main developments in the economy. The first step in this direction was made with the 1927 School for Business Administration in Vienna.

However, this development was a thorn in the side of many at the time. In 1933, immediately after the dissolution of parliament by the Dollfuss government, the retail co-operatives were placed under the regulations of the Commercial Code by authoritarian decree. On the basis of subsequent blocking orders which later replaced the Law of Veto, all further extensions of the co-operative movement were made practically impossible. Even though there was some relaxation of the restrictions in the course of time, the retail co-operatives suffered considerably under the Fascist movements which prevailed before the outbreak of the Second World War, quite apart from the effects of the enormous economic crisis.

When in February 1934 powerful political forces demanded the dissolution of the retail co-operatives it was above all the Central Federation of Austrian Retail Associations which fought energetically for their survival. However, the activity of the co-operative movement came to an abrupt halt with the outbreak of the Second World War.

Immediately after the bitter war years the leading figures in the movement began the task of rebuilding it. As early as April 1945 a committee for the re-establishment of the Austrian retail co-operatives was formed. In 1946, after the co-operatives had been successfully reintroduced throughout Austria, the Central Federation was restored under the title 'Retail Federation' at the Federation Conference in Bad Ischl. At this conference other important decisions were made: one was the foundation of the General Austrian Retail Cooperative (*Allgemeine österreichische Konsumgenossenschaft* or

AÖKG). It served on the one hand as a collective body for the administration of the movement's reserve assets and on the other as an umbrella organization for the central enterprises like the GÖC and its subsidiaries. With the restoration of the movement's assets on 1 January 1948 the legal and financial basis for a favourable development of the Austrian retail co-operative movement was laid down.

The period of strong economic growth

In the years 1949/50 the boom began to touch all branches of the Austrian economy. That said, the demand for consumer goods still far exceeded supply. A seller's market prevailed which was reinforced by the huge technological lag in industry, commerce and agriculture. Once industry had invested in some modern equipment and had extended its capacity, it was able to produce more and at a more reasonable price.

The introduction of self-service in Austria by the Linz Retail Co-operative in May 1950 had a revolutionary effect on retailing and ushered in a phase of economic growth. As a result a three-year programme was agreed by the Austrian retail co-operative movement which put its main stress on the extension of the self-service system. Whereas at the beginning of the fifties the retail co-operatives concentrated almost exclusively on food retailing, their operations were diversified in the course of the post-war period to encompass a wider commercial range.

When, in the fifties, the rebuilding of the Austrian economy was completed and the dynamic phase of expansion had created quite new market conditions which were highly competitive, a well-considered exploitation of all the entrepreneurial possibilities offered by the Co-operative Law was necessary so that the retail co-operatives could recapture their previous position in the market. A modern marketing strategy was thus developed and the way successfully prepared for the introduction of modern management methods in the retail sector.

In 1960 the first signs of a phase of increased competition were seen; private retailing was strengthened by various new organizational forms, such as chain stores, co-operative purchasing societies, discount houses, etc. In 1964 the retail co-operatives responded to this competitive pressure: the Retail Co-operative of Vienna opened the first genuine supermarket in Austria, thus taking the first step towards industrial commodity distribution. The diversification of commercial forms in retailing continued with the creation of a retailing hypermarket in Vösendorf near Vienna in 1970 and again in Vienna-Floridsdorf in 1972 as well as a furnishings store in

Vösendorf. In the case of both of these major projects, which were followed by others in the rest of Austria, price competitiveness was pushed very much to the fore. One of the reasons for the resulting and continuing financial success of such ventures is the ability to minimize costs as a result of rational purchasing, of excluding internal manipulation and of rationalizing organizational structures.

With the creation of these large units came a new expansive phase of growth, which made the Austrian retail co-operatives into the largest retailers in Austria.

The gradual increase in unit size produced on the other hand increasingly divergent aims. At an early stage, therefore — on the occasion of the 1967 Federal Conference — the overall movement agreed upon a programme of optimal concentration and a functional co-operation, in order to secure the lasting efficiency of all the retail co-operative organizations.

Amendments to the Co-operative Law, passed in 1974, laid a modern foundation for the fulfilment of the co-operatives' duties towards their members, taking national economic interests into consideration. A structural reform of the retail co-operative movement was therefore initiated as the basis for successful future development. The revolution in retailing led to changes in the traditional conception of the retail co-operative: in order to fulfil their primary duty, they agreed to adapt to the changing face of competition by giving up their status as suppliers of basic goods and taking on the far greater and more comprehensive task of supplying all the needs of their members.

Konsum Österreich

The measures necessary for this development gradually made a further process of concentration unavoidable. This resulted in the foundation of the primary co-operative Konsum Österreich (KÖ) in 1978. This nationally based co-operative reflects the economic rationality of increasing size of enterprise and is made up of five regional organizations: East, comprising Vienna, Lower Austria and Burgenland; Styria; Carinthia; Upper Austria; and West, consisting of Salzburg, Tirol and Vorarlberg. Fourteen of the previous 16 district retail co-operatives are integrated in Konsum Österreich along with the newly founded co-operative 'Central Retailing' (corresponding to the previous GÖC). The Retail Federation, which up to the formation of Konsum Österreich had functioned as a central umbrella organization, now has the role primarily of an auditing body.

Before the foundation of KÖ the centrally organized production of the co-operative movement had often been unable to keep pace with the expansion of the retailing sector. The merger helped towards a better utilization of production capacity and an improved co-ordination of developments in new branches of retailing. At present, in 1986, some 1,500 quality goods are produced in the 61 co-operative movement production plants, goods which are distinguished by the symbol of the retail co-operative movement — a figure eight lying on its side. This symbol was introduced in 1977.

Through the installation of a giant new warehousing complex, the distribution centre, in Hirschstetten near Vienna in 1981 the whole of the commodity distribution of KÖ was reorganized. Purchasing is conducted centrally for the whole retail group. The transition to industrial goods distribution is becoming increasingly evident.

The retailing sphere, which is subdivided into three retailing lines, has also been extended and unified. At present, 1,022 retail outlets (customer service shops, self-service units, retail markets, retail stores, hypermarkets, forum department stores, furnishing stores, DIY centres and specialist shops) with a total floor space of 530,147 sq. metres are in operation. Business planning is at present directed towards replacing shops which have become too small with open-plan modern stores and with retail markets. These latter two groups already make up more than 80 per cent of the retail chain store network.

The success of this tight-knit structural policy can also be measured by the fact that KÖ has started up 314 new branches since its foundation in 1978 and has made local shopping more convenient for tens of thousands of customers. It was envisaged that in 1986 the existing three retailing lines would be extended by two further lines — *Co-op Diskont* and *In-Form* (household goods). Thus, with the foundation of Konsum Österreich the economic power of the retail co-operative movement has been successfully strengthened and given an important organizational role in retailing as a whole.

KÖ is, however, not just a modern business enterprise, but also an organization with a large membership built on democratic principles. Over 800,000 members' families are able to determine the policies of the organization through elected representatives. One of the organization's exclusive services to its members is the dividend system, i.e. the repayment of money on members' purchases which amounted to approximately 296 million schillings in the financial year 1985.

The idea of co-operative self-help, which began in Austria 130 years ago, is firmly anchored today in the retail co-operative movement even though the needs of its members have changed radically in the course of time. Today the nationwide Konsum Österreich has become the most modern and the largest retail enterprise in all Austria, which through the use of the most modern marketing methods on the one hand and the upholding of co-operative principles for its members on the other not only guarantees all Austrian consumers a continual improvement of service but also ensures the continuance of those elements which have stood the test of time.

There are, however, figures which speak for themselves. Since the foundation of Konsum Österreich over eight years ago, the importance of this move towards unity and the benefits it has brought to the members are unmistakable as the following developments indicate:

- the membership of KÖ has increased by about a quarter, that is, by almost 200,000 households;
- in the past eight years dividends paid to members have amounted to 2.1 billion schillings;
- total turnover of the enterprise has risen in the same period by 60 per cent to 31.6 billion schillings;
- the floor space of the outlets has increased by 179,400 square metres;
- 314 branches, 264 of which are local suppliers such as retail markets and self-service stores, have been established or extended;
- the value of goods produced by KÖ's own factories has risen by 76 per cent;
- 7.5 billion schillings have been used for investment, almost half of this amount in the chain-store sector, just under a quarter in production and a similar amount in the warehousing and transport sector;
- 2.8 billion schillings have been used for asset depreciation;
- the workforce has risen from 18,600 to 20,400.

17 Housing Associations in Austria

Franz Lettner

In 1984 there were 239 non-profit-making housing associations in Austria, 126 of which were organized in the form of co-operatives, 110 as companies (either joint-stock companies (AG) or limited companies (GmbH)) and 3 as charities. They all belong to the Austrian Federation of Non-Profit-Making Housing Associations which is both an interest group representing the housing associations and at the same time a legal watchdog. Approximately 536,000 dwellings, one-fifth of Austria's total housing stock, are administered by the associations and in 1984 the co-operatives had 236,742 members. Ownership of the associations is largely in the hands of the federal government, the provincial governments, local government authorities, some public and a few private corporations and, in a very few cases, other housing associations, and a few industrial enterprises. In the 10-year period 1971 to 1980 inclusive, a yearly average of 17,583 dwellings was completed by the associations, 58.6 per cent of which were for owner occupation and 41.4 per cent for occupation by tenants or co-operatives. During recent years there has been a decline in new house-building, only 11,620 dwellings having been erected by the associations in 1984. The few profit-making associations are of no economic significance.

The formation of housing associations in Austria goes back to the closing years of the last century. It was a reaction to conditions so appalling as to be unimaginable today and to a housing shortage which of course was felt most severely by those at the lower end of the social scale. Early industrialization had lured thousands out of farming jobs into the towns, where they were forced to endure housing conditions worse than the cattle they had left behind. Liberal economic thinking regarded housing as a commodity like anything else, the price of which depended on supply and demand. Speculation and constant rent rises were the result, and the situation was made worse by the fact that rent income was heavily taxed. Any grimy cellar was turned into a 'dwelling', sub-tenants and 'night lodgers' were taken in to help pay the rent, overcrowding was the norm, and indeed there were some places where people lived in shifts — some being there during the day and others at night. Conditions, in other words, were similar to those we occasionally find today in third world countries.

In order to overcome this situation at least partially, self-help groups were formed here and there, initially among government employees but gradually taking in other groups of workers too. These groups were largely governed by the Act of 1873 relating to 'the establishment of co-operative associations' and sought to provide their members with family dwellings on reasonable terms, special attention being paid to protection against arbitrary rent rises and eviction. The Act stated that housing was not a commodity but was a prerequisite for social and cultural development, and laid particular stress upon the health and moral well-being of children. 'A nation's expenditure on its housing needs is a measure of its social and cultural position among the nations of the world.'

Not even the country's political leadership could remain totally aloof from such endeavours. At the end of 1907 a fund for government employees was set up known as the Emperor Franz Josef's Government Jubilee Fund (*Kaiser-Franz-Josef-Regierungs-Jubiläumsfonds*) — Austria's first public scheme for the promotion of housing. By 1909 there were already 10 building charities, 2 building companies and 17 building co-operatives within the non-profit-making sector. In 1910 the restriction to government employees was abolished and the Housing Provision Act and Housing Provision Fund came into being. Only non-profit-making housing associations (*Gemeinnützige Bauvereinigungen*) were to receive support, by which were meant organizations (a) forgoing ground rent, i.e. working on the cost-covering principle; (b) accepting a limitation on the interest return on their own capital; and (c) entering into a statutory obligation to make all assets available for purposes beneficial to the public in the event of liquidation. Such associations were legally obliged to build housing and to be subject to public supervision. These principles still apply today. They were later standardized by the Act relating to 'Housing as a Public Utility' (*Deutsches Wohnungsgemeinnützigkeitsgesetz*), which remained in force right through to the Second Republic. The essential point is that ever since the early years of the present century, self-help in house building has been publicly subsidized and that the housing associations have been regarded as an extension of government house-building policy. Hence in Austria the state has been only indirectly involved in the provision of housing for the people (constitutionally a federal government responsibility); there has been no involvement either on the part of the provincial governments and only a partial one by the local authorities — instead, the housing associations have been used for this purpose. These associations, together with the private house-building sector, are still the dominant factors in the housing industry today. It is important to understand that they do not carry out the building themselves but function predominantly as organizers and administrators of house building. They mainly make use of self-employed architects for drawing up the plans, and of competitive firms for the construction work itself.

The Co-operative Associations Act required the establishment of a 'self-regulating' mechanism in the form of a *Revisionsverband*; this function was carried out by the Reich Federation of Housing Co-operatives (*Reichsverband der Baugenossenschaften*), founded in 1916, and from 1928 onwards by the Central Federation of Non-Profit-Making Housing Associations (*Zentralverband der gemeinnützigen Bauvereinigungen*) which by 1932 had as many as 142 members. The First World War had had an adverse effect on the housing industry, and after the partition of the monarchy population shifts brought fresh housing problems. The rent freeze imposed by law under the First Republic removed the incentive for private house building so it was the housing associations which, with government support, took on the main task of erecting new dwellings. In 1921 the Federal Housing and Residential Estate Fund (*Bundes-Wohn- und Siedlungsfonds*) was established with ample funds at its disposal, and originally provided low-interest house-building credits of up to 90 per cent of the building costs, being financed from budgetary sources as well as by contributions from industry. Up to 1928 this support enabled local authorities and the housing associations to erect 8,654 dwellings. In this period the associations felt obliged to take into account the trend towards residential estates which had arisen out of the 'allotment movement'. Garden suburbs came into being, many of which are still regarded as showpieces even today. The years of severe inflation, of course, created immense difficulties for the housing associations as for house building generally in Austria. The rise to governmental power of bourgeois parties had a similarly inhibiting effect. The Housing and Residential Estate Fund received inadequate finance, priority being given to private building clients. Only 'Red Vienna' continued the house-building policies of the Social Democrats, erecting estates which made building history.

Only days after the tenth anniversary celebrations of the Central Federation, which at that time had a membership of 180 associations, Austria was swallowed up by Hitler's Germany. It was rumoured that the associations were to be dissolved, and a few tried to extricate themselves from the disaster by setting up societies in line with the Imperial German law governing non-profit-making organizations (*Reichsdeutsches Gemeinnützigkeitsgesetz*). Although the Austrian system of promoting house-building had set an example to Germany, the laws of the 'Greater German Reich' now applied to Austria as well, including the *Gemeinnützigkeitsgesetz* of 1940. Immense industrialization projects mainly devoted to armament production (such as the *Reichswerke Hermann Goering* in Linz) once more attracted droves of people from the land; they needed homes, so they converged upon these centres. Right through until the early years of the Second World War, new house-building on a grand scale was carried out by societies linked with industrial companies, and the so-called Führer housing estates (*Führersiedlungen*) came into being. Many of these, however, together with thousands of dwellings previously erected by the housing associations, were destroyed in the bombing raids of 1943–5.

After the war it was once again the housing associations which gradually organized the reconstruction. The Housing Reconstruction Fund and Marshall Aid helped with long-term loans at only 1 per cent interest. Today it seems almost miraculous that such an enormous task could have been completed at all, given the vast numbers of refugees and expellees who were housed in camps of makeshift huts, and given the fact that there was a shortage of everything: building materials, energy and skilled workers. But completed it was, in collaboration with the local authorities. After a time the old, non-bureaucratic Federal Housing and Residential Estate Fund was re-activated as the source of credit, then later still, in 1954, the Housing Scheme (*Wohnbauförderung*) was introduced.

Unfortunately it proved impossible to arrive at any comprehensive policy for land development in Austria. With the country lying in such immediate proximity to the Iron Curtain this was politically impracticable, since any encroachment upon private property was likened to 'total planning' under Communism. Soon, therefore, there was speculation involving bombed sites, and then later building land which had originally been given over to agriculture on the outskirts of towns. Land prices rose, and the housing associations found themselves forced to choose between speculative investment of their reserves to purchase building land over and above their immediate requirements, and the alternative: getting caught on the treadmill of ever-increasing land prices. In many cases they lacked the capital necessary for a proper land policy, and eventually the question of capital became critical in the survival or otherwise of the associations. Those which could purchase building plots only by having recourse to credit found themselves in difficulties.

While in general it was possible to keep party politics out of the housing associations during the reconstruction period, the end of the Grand Coalition saw an intensification of ideological conflicts even within this sphere. On the right of the political spectrum there was an emphasis on promoting private ownership, while the left favoured the old ideals of rent freezing, safeguards against eviction and support in relation to social considerations. To this day, therefore, the house-building programme is bedevilled by compromises. In 1968 the traditional sources of house-building finance were replaced by a uniform scheme run by the provincial governments under the immediate administrative surveillance of the federal government. However, environmental planning in the proper sense existed in name only. A new Charities Act (*Gemeinnützigkeitsgesetz*) provided a fresh legal basis for the housing associations (many of which had become discredited in the public eye), imposed strict rules and regulations, introduced price controls for sponsored housing, and insisted upon stronger public control. The Rent Act abolished the old rent freeze system, creating in its place, however, a maximum price control to which an 'upkeep contribution' (*Erhaltungsbeitrag*) was added. This was an attempt to rectify an unsatisfactory situation, namely that fixed rents provided no incentive to maintain and improve the housing stock. So far progress in renovating older houses has been slow. It is true that the housing associations have generally kept their houses in good repair, but now there is a need for modernization, for meeting the energy-saving requirements resulting from the oil crisis, and for protective measures against emissions from industry and traffic.

Statistical forecasts — and the experience of the housing associations themselves — both indicate that, except in the great industrial conurbations, the demand for housing is on the decline. Even so, funds do not permit the building of new homes in sufficient quantities, and house prices cannot be kept low because there is no halting the rise in land prices, building costs or even overhead expenses. Certainly there are not vast numbers of empty houses, though in many cases housing costs are beyond the means of less well-to-do sections of society. Rent subsidies have become essential, though these restrict the funds available for new building. The renovation of older houses is hampered by many technical, financial and private difficulties, as the volume of building is decreasing and contractors frequently have surplus capacity. On the other hand, clients need to be offered a better service: more account than before must be taken of individuals' housing requirements. 'Customer participation' from the planning stage right through to the administrative stage is one of the needs of the moment, and is in any case consistent with the traditional concept of the co-operative. At times, understandably, the associations have reacted to all these factors by introducing moves towards rationalization. However, mergers between several associations, maximal land use and building with industrially prefabricated units have proved non-viable solutions: today there is once again a demand for the smaller, compact unit, and this applies also to the co-operative enterprise itself.

People's increased awareness of health and of the environment demands that building shall be more in tune with human needs: buildings further apart, more green belts, etc. But all this increases costs, for in addition to housing itself many environnmental protection measures have to be financed.

In 1986, on the fortieth anniversary of its foundation after the war, the Federation issued a policy statement affirming that the housing associations represent the interests of tenants and owner-occupiers in relation to the law, the local authorities, credit institutions, building firms and architects. It demanded better quality in new building, particularly in terms of the infrastructure, greater attention to the environmental impact of housing, more participation on the part of occupants, more efficient handling of resources, greater accountability to the client, and priority for urban renewal. Today more than ever Austrian housing associations regard themselves as intermediaries between the citizens and the state in all matters connected with housing, and that in the widest possible sense of the term.

18 The Austrian social partnership

Jim Sweeney

The Austrian social partnership (*Sozialpartnerschaft*) has been praised by many of Austria's western neighbours in the past 30 years for everything that is desirable in a modern economy — prudent economic management, healthy economic growth, the epitome of social consensus and compromise, a relatively low incidence of societal (industrial) conflict and political stability. Is this idealized view what modern day Austria is really like? Does Austria have her share of the problems which beset other industrialized countries? Such questions are not easy to answer and to a considerable extent must be regarded as beyond any chapter such as this which attempts to explain the notion of social partnership.

In the first place there is probably no common definition of the term, even though there are various 'models' or levels of activity by which we can identify such an institution. Secondly, the enmeshing of institutions and processes associated with this phenomenon has a dynamism which is not easy to explain to the outsider, since there is no counterpart to it elsewhere and idealized pictures often exaggerate. Thirdly, the relationship between social and economic changes in Austria is not a simple one; the writer can only outline some of these changes and, where appropriate, draw tentative conclusions. Despite such difficulties an attempt will be made here to clarify and explain what the system of the social partnership involves.

Historical background and development

To understand such a system it is necessary to go back to the end of the nineteenth century and the beginning of the twentieth and the events which led to the fall of the Habsburg Monarchy and the establishment of the First Republic, and in particular to understand the tensions and divisions which occurred between the major political groupings at the time. Economic dislocation and the dire effects of the First World War produced a situation in which the survival of the new Austrian state was called into question by most competent observers of the contemporary scene. To secure stable conditions for Austria's existence some type of national consensus was necessary and this entailed the co-operation of the many divergent interests which constituted political life in the new Austria.

Among these divergent interests were those of Austrian Catholic Conservatives inspired by the doctrine expressed in the papal encyclical *Rerum Novarum* which had appeared in 1891, and the ideas of the Catholic social philosopher von Vogelsang. By the end of the nineteenth century those ideas asserted for workers the right to just wages and humane working conditions and envisaged in the long term a Christian civilization preserved by the absorption of the working class into the property-owning classes. Politically this represented a liberal, conciliatory, tolerant yet somehow Conservative anti-capitalist position. The then atheistic Marxist Social Democratic Party's view of a 'social revolution' leading to working-class power through democratic means did not at first seem entirely incompatible with the Catholic view so that the positions of the two largest popular political parties, Christian-Social and Socialist (Social Democrat), were not as polarized as might seem at first sight despite their differences over other matters. Evidence of this is seen later in the agreement between them (and indeed among all political parties and economic interest groups) on the form of nationalization (*Sozialisierung*) between 1918 and 1919. A similar development was evident also in the 'industry conferences' proposed by Karl Renner between 1918 and 1919 which had the object of bringing the major industrial interest groups to general agreement on the solution of the country's serious economic and industrial problems, particularly those related to the control of prices and pay.

In Austro-Marxist thought new institutions were necessary to 'compensate the working class' (Karl Renner) for their sacrifices in time of war and their participation in the struggle for social change and to this end the power of the state was to be invoked to 'balance class interests' (Otto Bauer). Even earlier, one can detect strands of co-operation such as the formation of the Labour Advisory Council (*Arbeitsbeirat*) as a section of the Ministry of Commerce from 1898 to World War I, on which representatives of the labour movement sat. This symbolized an attempt, despite much contemporary rhetoric to the contrary, of a pragmatic participation by the labour movement in the functions of the state as well as pointing the way to the functions of new institutions. Viktor Adler's comment that such a body should have 'a certain authority' is a clear indication of the pragmatism evident among labour movement leaders of the time. The views of the Right as well as of the Left gradually came to contain an element of compromise or, at least in terms of administering the economic, social and industrial affairs of the country, some kind of 'truce'.

The early momentum for such co-operation did not, however, last long, and as the post-war economic situation worsened the potential basis for consensus was eroded, and the old political and class antagonisms, often taking a violent turn, reasserted themselves. Finally in 1934 the influence of the two traditional large political party groupings (*Lager*) virtually disappeared as democratic institutions were abolished; one, (the Socialist Party) was made illegal, the other (the Christian-Socials) subsumed into the single-party state under the 'forced co-operation' of Dollfuss's new institutions which had now replaced the democratic bases of voluntary co-operation and organizational self-determination. Some observers later, however, characterized the Dollfuss 'corporate state' as an 'attempt at social partnership from above'.

Thus it can be argued that some of the early strands of the social partnership can be found in religion, political ideology, pragmatism and in the practical attempts of a nation to survive — a nation weakened by war and industrial dislocation, deficient in natural resources and foodstuffs and beset by inflation and unemployment as well as surrounded by hostile neighbours. It was to take the force of the later Fascist governments — of the Austrian variety as well as German — however, and another World War to transform Austria into a society which was at once fairly unified and consensual in its approach to the problems of the day, and even then not entirely without strife. A realignment of seemingly contradictory social and class forces was to bring about a different attitude first with respect to the country's reconstruction and fight for independence after 1945, and then as a result of a co-operative pragmatism on the part of the monopolists of political power — Socialists and Conservatives — and the 'economic partners' (trade unions and employers' organizations) to deal with the political exigencies of the time. The Socialists, for all practical purposes, gradually abandoned the traditional Marxism which had characterized their movement after 1925 while the Conservatives renounced the authoritarian tendencies which had temporarily held them in fief between 1927 and the German annexation (*Anschluss*) in 1938. These political features set the scene which formed the foundations of the modern social partnership.

The problems which emerged from the Second World War seemed to be as intractable as (if not more so than) those of the First World War. The 'economic partners', the trade unions and economic chambers, had the immediate task of participating in the reconstruction of industry and the economy, and of providing foodstuffs for the starving population as well as coping with unemployment and inflation. The restructuring of the trade unions under a unified, centralized, umbrella organization, the Austrian Trade Union Federation (ÖGB), was of particular importance in this regard, and its participation with the re-established Economic Chambers in the Wage-Price Agreements of 1947–51 laid down the industrial-economic parameters from which was to emerge the later social partnership. The negotiation of these agreements was not without difficulty. The Communist Party of Austria (KPÖ) which was represented in the immediate post-war coalition governments was set against the Wage-Price Agreements; on leaving the coalition government in 1947 it was so vehement in its opposition to them that it called a general strike in 1950. This, however, failed, and to some extent produced an antipathy to the Communist Party which has lasted to this day, although the Communists had never found very much favour with the Austrian electorate in general. The co-operation which typified the Wage-Price Agreements and institutional restructuring of the post-war period appeared to consign questions of political differences and ideology to the sphere of the political parties proper, while matters of economic interest, particularly economic growth, become the province of the 'partners'. Changes had occurred in the roles of the major political parties and interest associations and now there was an area of joint jurisdiction between these latter. Any differences which emerged were no longer couched in the language of class struggle but rather in the phraseology of negotiation.

From this time onwards various notions or 'models' of the social partnership can be discerned and it is to these we must now turn. Certain conditions were necessary for the emergence of such a set of co-operative ideas. First of all, this entailed the formation of strong, centralized, stable interest associations in the form of the Austrian Trade Union Federation and the Federal Chamber of the Economy evenly matched and able to carry their membership along with respect to their policies. Secondly, the emergence of a legitimacy of economic function and decision making not dependent on parliament, implied a *de-facto* basis of extra-parliamentary power separate from the rules of the parliamentary game and not characterized by conflicts of ideology which are the hallmark of parliamentary activities. Thirdly, the principle of concerted action through a voluntary consensus (*Konsens*) had to be present and one in which in the Austrian context the partners had a right of veto. Additionally, a particular political and social framework was necessary to allow for the effective working together of large groups and political parties whose objectives could no longer be seen as divisive, and from among whose ranks 'experts' emerged whose activites were designed to give them a relative autonomy *vis-a-vis* Parliament and whose common denominator was economic growth.

Models of the social partnership

The models set down here are not intended to account for all the behavioural elements or processes observed in the social partnership; they are in essence reductionist and 'ideal types' for the purpose of explanation and analysis. In practice most of them, naturally, are intertwined. Such ideal types range from those of a technocratic character to those of popular images which in everyday existence engender or portray strong popular emotional beliefs and sentiments about such an institution.

1. Probably the most accepted, most important and common model to be found, particularly favoured among the well-educated and politically conscious groups, is that which relates to the economic aspects and is thereby the successor to the Wage-Price Agreements of 1947–51. This is exemplified by 'The Parity Commission' (*Paritätische Kommission*) which was formed in 1957 and is sometimes referred to as the 'autonomous social partnership'. Figure 18.1 portrays it at the centre of economic policy decision-making in Austria, in accordance with the preconditions discussed above.

   The interaction processes of the various parts of this model produce a prices and wages policy which has been adhered to within the spheres of competence of the partners for the last 30 years, and accordingly makes it the longest-running voluntary incomes/prices policy in the world. The power-house of this structure lies in the 'expert' membership of the sub-committees for prices and wages, whose recommendations to a major extent regulate the growth aspects of the Austrian economic system. Through agreed modest increases in wages and prices, firms and government departments can plan and adjust expenditure and investment plans in the medium and long term. Such agreements have played their part in producing stability and a consistently high rate of economic growth between 1957 and 1983 even though problems began to occur after the mid-1970s (see economic growth rates from 1945 onwards in Appendices D1 and D6). The initiative for action and agreement lies primarily with the interest associations rather than with government, although the large nationalized sector of the Austrian economy has also been used as an economic regulator while the country has steadily followed a policy of *Austrokeynesianism* since the

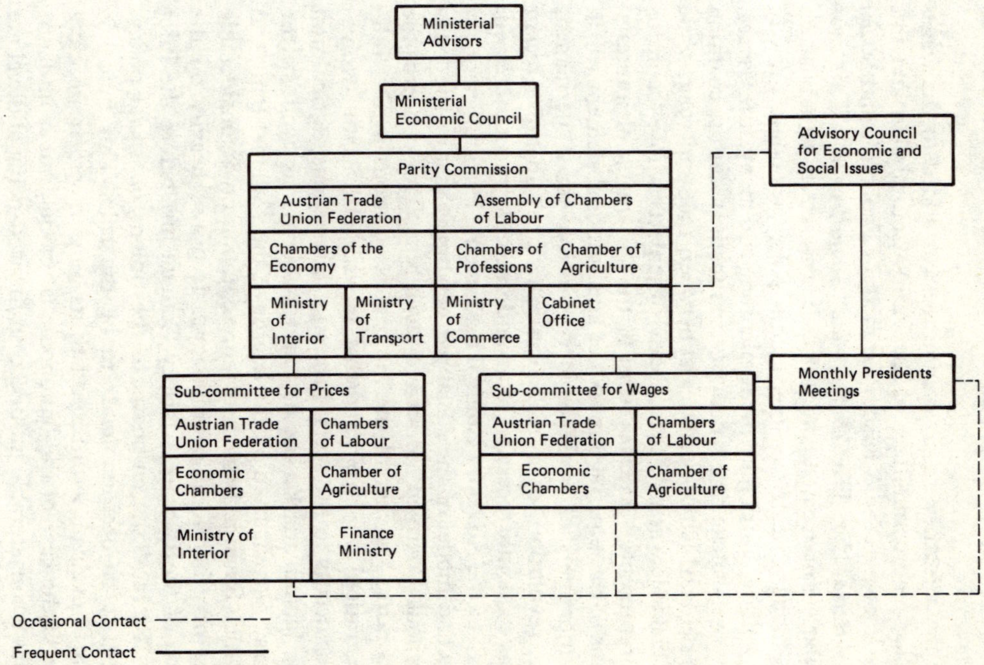

Figure 18.1 Structure of the Austrian Parity Commission

last war. The workings of the Parity Commission and its constituent parts have in no way produced a low wage or low profit economy. It has, in the main, provided a wage/cost structure which the generality of industry can afford, although in recent times external world developments have contributed to place Austrian industry at a competitive disadvantage in international trade.

In 1963 a further expert committee was added to the wages and prices sub-committees of the Parity Commission and this became known as the Advisory Council for Economic and Social Issues (*Beirat für Wirtschafts- und Sozialfragen*). This was particularly important up to 1983. It was set up to advise on the questions of principles in economic policy, economic growth, public welfare, full employment, planning and many other issues. Some writers allege that it became the substitute for the coalition governments which ceased to exist between 1966 and 1983, while others claim it was in effect a body of experts whose 'compromises' represented a newer form of the 'balancing of interests' (in terms of the experts' 'inputs') or an additional element which has a 'monopoly of truth' or is responsible for a 'permanent cultural revolution' of a 'technocratic nature'. In more recent years, as economic recession set in and unemployment increased, the work of the Advisory Council has become less important.

2. The second model of the social partnership is that of the 'non-autonomous', 'derived', or second level, type. This concerns the joint working together of the interest associations in the 'self-administration' organizations (that is with little state involvement) as occurs in the social insurance institutions, agricultural boards, labour market bodies and tribunals as well as the 'partners'' participation on the boards of the National Bank and Post Office Savings Bank and representation on a considerable number of other joint commissions. It draws heavily on the tradition of the Labour Advisory Council just before the First World War and the emphasis of the unions on social policy. Here parity co-decision tends to be the rule. This model is difficult to evaluate with respect to its outputs which are more evident in the case of the 'autonomous' model, but it undoubtedly has a considerable influence on the well-being and welfare considerations of the citizen. In short, it also forms the basis of the Austrian 'welfare state', and has its roots in the Austrian labour movement's preoccupation with social policy issues and the enormous amount of legislation in this regard enacted between 1918 and 1920.
3. Another important set of concepts is that model which

emphasizes relationships, particularly those germane to working life. This broadly equates the social partnership to a model of industrial relations. This too is a 'derived' model. In the systems approach following Dunlop and others, the inputs (from the economic, political and legal systems, for example) and their processing by the actors produces an output of rules or agreements with two tiers. The major one occurs at macro-economic decision-making level where the Parity Commission defines the parameters of national level bargaining in which the centralized aspect of the system produces voluntary agreement on broad issues (which may be legitimized by statutes). Beyond this the interest group associations of industrial trade unions and the relevant constituent sections of the Economic Chambers come together to form the 'sub-system' which negotiates on the substantive matters of pay and conditions at industry level by which settlements become legally enforceable collective agreements and which may specify adjustments at local or workplace level. The success of this system is to be seen in that leapfrogging in wages claims is not a feature and, on the contrary, wage differentials and structures tend to remain generally constant and stable between occupational groups over time, thus emphasizing the importance of centralized formal agreement.

Furthermore, disagreement or conflict behaviour (e.g. strikes) is rarely an 'output' of this system or model and it is this latter feature which many associate with the social partnership. The *status quo* of the Austrian 'mixed economy' is generally accepted and little popular resistance to it has appeared over time. To some extent this is due to the influence exerted by the major political parties (and perhaps reinforced occasionally through the formation of coalition governments). This relatively pacific salience in industrial relations (which might also be called the 'peace function' model of the social partnership) is a feature much prized by the older generation in view of the earlier violent industrial conflicts as well as by the dominant groups in social and occupational structures, but there are signs that this may be changing. (See Appendix F11 for strike figures 1951–86 and Appendix F12 for international comparisons 1966–84.)

4. A further, less easily defined, less tangible model is that in which the social partnership is characterized as a 'way of life' and something which is typically Austrian. This is one which engenders a certain spirit of co-operation and compromise in which the 'Proporz' method of allocating key jobs in accordance with the relative strengths of the political parties in parliamentary, provincial and local government is emphasized and this

arrangement is one which stresses compromise. It is probable that this or some variant of it is that which a substantial proportion of Austrians think of as the social partnership. Again, the 'success' of the Austrian economy in recent years appears to provide the justification of this type of social partnership without any regard to close scrutiny, or evaluation, of 'success'. Opinion polls of occupational groups seem to suggest that most respondents consider that the social partnership is more important than parliament, with those who work on their own account (entrepreneurs) more inclined to this view than the others.

In recent times it has become fashionable among political scientists in examining the functioning of the social partnership to designate Austria as typifying 'consociational democracy', 'liberal corporatism', 'neo-corporatism' or 'techno-corporatism', since the Austrian political system according to this view belongs to that genus of modern political taxonomy which represents a 'specific type of participation by large organized social groups in public, especially economic, policy making'. There are many reasons for such a designation but they need not concern us here. Such analyses do stress with some justification, albeit resting on selective empirical evidence, the disproportionate influence and power of interest groups *vis-à-vis* the State, and Austria, Sweden and Switzerland are often bracketed together in this regard.

Achievements of the social partnership

Comments on achievements are much more easily directed at the first model discussed above and it is this to which most analyses have been directed, and would appear most relevant and most important. There is little doubt, and indeed a great deal of evidence favouring the view, predominant among analysts at home and abroad, that the work of the Parity Commission and its constituent mechanisms has had a considerable influence in providing stability, economic growth and increases in real income for the Austrian people although there would be some dispute concerning a more equitable distribution of income resulting from it. The achievements of the Parity Commission model are nevertheless considerable and not to be lightly dismissed.

Certain aspects of nationalisation (*Verstaatlichung*) and economic planning have provided a basic foundation for the continuation of the social partnership and as an economic regulator it has served the workers' interests by providing increases in real income and low unemployment without fundamentally undermining capitalism.

At the same time it has produced a new and alternative source of responsibility by which experts administer economic policy, and this has resulted in fewer crises or problems of economic management than would have otherwise occurred. Some writers take the view that economic policy became usurped by the importance accorded to it by the drive towards an integrated social policy. This represents something of an in-argument since both aspects stress the importance of stabilization as a social value even though in times of economic recession, the emphasis tends to swing back to 'economic realities'.

Criticisms

Many of the criticisms one finds aimed at the social partnership in the popular press in Austria relate in the main to the state of the nationalized industry and the periodic illegal or unethical speculative and corrupt practices which occur from time to time but which, on careful examination, may not be a criticism of the idea of the social partnership itself. There are, however, criticisms from other directions of a social, economic and political nature which are based on a class analysis or a criticism of the social partnership from the point of view of its anti-democratic tendencies many of which, though important, are somewhat too convoluted, involved and specialized to find space here.

1 The main economic criticism at the present time is levelled at the incapacity of the social partnership to change and adjust to changing internal and external conditions, particularly those which require harsh remedies in the face of adverse market conditions or recession. It is also seen by many as a unique Austrian institutional arrangement, which for a particular period of history was instrumental in 'institutionalizing' the class struggle on the one hand, or adjusted Austrian capitalism to the new set of economic conditions after the Second World War on the other. That period has passed and a re-examination of this unique institution is now high on the agenda.

2 Another important criticism relates to the dependence of many social groups on it and this may have the effect of inhibiting or preventing change. This charge is often levelled at the stance of the unions who, it is argued, in hard times see it as a protective measure to maintain high employment or use it as a restrictive practice without which unemployment may have been much higher. For a device, once important to economic growth, it is now seen as one which now hinders it and Austrian industrialists occasionally give voice to this view in tones redolent of classical economic liberalism. Again, the source of much discontent lies

in the mismanagement of some of the resources of the nationalized industries and this has also given cause for public concern.

3 Another trenchant criticism has been that the social partnership prevents or stifles the demand for participation and does nothing for the widespread apathy about public issues which characterizes political life in Austria. The role of the experts and politicians has the effect of excluding the views of many relevant and emergent social groups thus gradually causing, unintentionally, the depoliticization of Austrian institutions. Models 1 and 3 also come under criticism from a related standpoint: this portrays the social partnership as a 'personality pact' between the leaders of the trade union movement and the Chambers of the Economy for the last 24 years — Anton Benya and Rudolf Sallinger — in which the individual is powerless against the 'fix' of the large interest groups whose views are promoted by these two powerful officials.

4 The distribution of income argument alluded to above is a much more equivocal one. Many writers over the years have made comment on the relative shares of income between profits, rent, wages and salaries, and the effects on these produced by the social partnership. The evidence is not particularly conclusive either way but irrespective of who becomes better off, the preservation and maintenance of purchasing power has been important for many groups such as the low paid, disabled and elderly, and without this mechanism greater disparities and inequalities might well have occurred. There are signs too, even though Austria has not been so adversely affected by recession as other industrialized countries, that there are strains on the welfare state and in particular the area of social security which many respected writers see as in a state of crisis.

5 Finally, there is the argument which goes to the heart of the Parity Commission model of the social partnership — the belief in economic necessity. The importance of this central type of institution is no longer so widely held as previously and, as a greater awareness of environmental issues increases, the arguments for economic growth become much more questioned than hitherto. The national referendum in 1978 which decided against the operation of the nuclear power station at Zwentendorf and the resistance to building other types subsequently, for example, is an indication that many no longer hold economic growth as a sacred cow. The rise of a Green Party and its representation in the Austrian parliament is a further indication of the existence of an alternative view of the quality of life so that the social partnership as an institution is much more under scrutiny, or

alternatively, is seen as less relevant to the important issues of the day.

Evaluation

The Austrian social partnership, particularly the Parity Commisson model, is an institution which has had a long and valuable life in increasing well-being and economic growth and, at an impressionistic level, has represented for many something which is essentially Austrian. It is, however, finite in time, or at best it may be on the brink of a metamorphosis as a result of recent strains. The sense of realism among politicians and businessmen may result in its gradual transformation into an institution of lesser importance. As a voluntary mechanism of co-operation it has always been regarded as an expedient for those who participated in it rather than a panacea for all ills; it is interesting to note the long-lasting tendency among trade unionists for example, to make reference to the 'economic partners' rather than 'social partners' and it was never seen by the unions as a permanent substitute to their own voluntary action. It is also equally interesting to note, on the other hand, that because of it the Austrian unions are less inclined to favour co-decision and worker participation on company boards; indeed the Parity Commission model has become their chief means of defining participation over the years.

As has been argued, the notion of the social partnership is an omnibus and many-sided one; and it has no equivalent elsewhere. It is the product of the peculiar economic, social and historical conditions of Austria whose continued, albeit more halting, development will be decisive in deciding how long it will last or what becomes of it. It is unlikely, however, despite the views of its more implacable and vociferous critics, that it will as a whole suddenly disappear although some of its models might well experience considerable change. The social partnership in time of recession or crisis faces different problems and requires different solutions to those which pertained during the Austrian economic miracle.

PART IV
SOCIAL AND CULTURAL ISSUES

19 Social security in Austria

Alfred Dallinger

The year 1987 may be considered significant in the history of the Austrian welfare state, being the centenary of the year in which the earliest components of one of its most important institutions — social security — were set in place. During this period trends in social policy have produced a situation where today a highly significant level of social insurance cover is provided. At the end of the nineteenth century hardly more than 1 per cent of the national income was diverted via government transfers into cover for social risks. Today the figure stands at over 25 per cent, placing Austria among the most highly developed welfare states in the world.

History of the welfare state

Under the Austro-Hungarian monarchy, prior to the 1880s there were only two instruments for dealing with social problems: marginal protection for children at work, and a repressive policy towards the poor. In 1887, following upon the social reforms introduced by Bismarck in Germany, the first steps were taken in Austro-Hungary towards the provision of a 'safety net', initially for a very small section of the labour force, i.e. workers in major industrial companies. The introduction of medical and accident insurance for this group was intended as a means of pacifying the political demands being made by the leading activists within the incipient labour movement. The vast majority of working people, i.e. those employed in agriculture and in small firms, or those in service as members of the sub-proletariat, were excluded from such social provisions until 1918.

From 1890 onwards there was a marked change in the political climate in that most of the ideas for reforms in social policy began to emanate from the labour movement. Consequently social policy lost its significance as an instrument of appeasement in the hands of the ruling classes. Arguments at company level could secure certain improvements but at government level social policy remained at a standstill, as far as the workers were concerned, until 1918. For salaried employees, however, a compulsory pension scheme was introduced in 1906; the 1907 elections were to be open for the first time to all men and the intention was to influence their voting behaviour to the detriment of the Social Democrats.

The mechanisms underlying these two pieces of legislation were to retain their significance in the further development of social policy. In subsequent years social insurance exclusively for workers remained predominant — a situation which lasted a further 70 years or thereabouts, until social and labour legislation brought workers and salaried employees much closer together.

In 1918, after the First World War and the collapse of the Austro-Hungarian monarchy, the Social Democrats became the strongest party. In view of the Revolution in Russia and the upheavals taking place in Austria's neighbouring states of Hungary and Bavaria, the Social Democrats took only two years to implement many of their ideas in the area of social policy — ideas which they had been unsuccessfully advocating for the previous 30 years. There was a further reason why, despite extremely difficult economic conditions, this programme proved to be feasible: it was supported by those social groups which now suddenly found themselves vulnerable after previously holding power; seeing the radicalization taking place among the working classes in Bavaria and Hungary, they hoped to prevent the process going any further in Austria. There were extensive reductions in daily and yearly working hours, plus a legal definition of employees' rights both individually and collectively, but in addition a significant development took place in the area of social security: for the first time there was provision for the unemployed to receive financial compensation as part of a compulsory unemployment benefit scheme. From 1920 onwards, as revolutionary fervour began to decline, bourgeois forces summoned up courage and launched a vehement campaign against the recently introduced social measures which they now condemned as 'revolutionary rubbish'. As a result unemployment insurance became more and more undermined. Up to the occupation of Austria by Nazi Germany the workers had to face a constant deterioration in other areas of social policy too. By contrast, a 'divide and rule' policy ensured that civil servants and salaried employees received greater and greater privileges. Under the First Republic the workers were the only group of employees to have no old-age or disability pension rights. The introduction of an old-age pension for workers was made contingent upon a favourable economic climate, which never materialized. When Austro-Fascism came to power in 1934 and made labour movement organizations illegal, the ideology of the corporate state meant an even stronger differentiation within the social system in terms of occupations and social groups.

Following the annexation of Austria by Nazi Germany, political repression of the labour movement reached its climax. From the standpoint of social insurance cover, however, the most significant event was the introduction of a retirement pension for workers.

After 1945 social policy was pursued under a totally new set of conditions. As a result of the nation's bitter experience of Austro-Fascism, then of Hitler's Fascism, and in view of the fact that from 1945 to 1955 four occupying powers were stationed on Austrian soil, considerable political *rapprochement* occurred between the various social forces. The most striking evidence of this was the coalition government of the two major parties, which was to last 20 years, and the development of a social partnership between the interest groups representing the self-employed, wage earners and salary earners. On both sides there was now a readiness not to carry divergent views to extremes but rather to strive for compromises, each side recognizing the socio-political convictions of the other. This meant that the principle of consensus prevailed for a long time in all important decision making, which also involved forgoing any major shifts in income distribution. As far as social security was concerned, it certainly produced steady and remarkable improvements in social benefits, although this followed the middle-class view that such benefits should be employment related and administered by the occupational and industrial interest associations. The view held by the Socialists and the Trade Union Federation was in the Beveridge tradition, namely that social security should be accessible to all and not basically tied to an individual's earning capacity or income level — but they were unable to carry the day.

In 1955, after almost 10 years of discussion, the General Social Insurance Act (*Allgemeines Sozialversicherungsgesetz*) was passed. It was a typical compromise. The various occupational groups responsible for social security continued to exist though in reduced numbers, and the right to benefits, together with the level of benefits, still depended on paid employment and income level. But now for the first time there was a single law covering both workers and salaried employees (public service employees or *Beamte* continue to have separate provision), with sickness, accident and retirement benefits for the two groups being brought more closely into line. In later years these social provisions were extended to include the self-employed and farmers while other groups such as schoolchildren and students, who hitherto had been only partially covered by social security, were given comprehensive insurance cover. Today the overwhelming majority of the population is protected by social insurance: 99 per cent are covered by the state health insurance scheme and practically all elderly people can claim the state pension.

During the first decade of single-party government by the

Socialists (1970–83) a further set of reforms was introduced in the area of social policy, bringing considerable improvements in benefits. Social legislation brought about greater equality of status between workers and salaried employees, also between women and men. Previous disadvantages suffered by socially deprived families were removed by introducing new benefits and replacing tax concessions by direct benefit payments.

From at least the beginning of the eighties, social policy in Austria as in all other European states has been in a phase of consolidation. Social policy expenditure now rises no faster than the gross domestic product. Growing levels of unemployment, stagnating incomes and growing budgetary deficits have created major policy problems for the funding of social security. Unlike many other European countries, however, Austria has succeeded in maintaining already achieved levels of social security without major reductions in benefit.

The structure of social policy expenditure

In Austria, as in most other OECD countries, the expenditure on social security expressed as a proportion of GDP has almost doubled during the last 30 years, from about 15 per cent at the beginning of the fifties to 27 per cent at the end of the seventies; since that time, as noted above, social expenditure has been rising in line with GDP. At 27 per cent the Austrian ratio of social security to GDP is just above the average for OECD states.

Social policy expenditure in general in 1985, amounting to 360 billion schillings, was divided as follows: 150 billion schillings for pensions in the private sector, 70 billion schillings for pensions to public sector employees and war victims, 60 billion schillings for health and accident insurance, 40 billion schillings for family benefits, about 20 billion schillings for unemployment benefits and about 10 billion schillings for supplementary benefits.

Hence almost two-thirds of social policy transfer payments go to pensions, one-sixth to health and accident insurance, one-tenth to family benefits, one-twentieth to unemployment benefits and one-fortieth to supplementary benefits.

Pensions

The Austrian pensions system is organized as social security. All persons in gainful employment, whether employees or self-employed, are subject to compulsory insurance. The various occupational groups have different insurers, these being, in the eyes of the law, autonomous bodies whose managerial and supervisory boards are made up of representatives of the employers, employees and government. In practice, however, their autonomy is restricted since both benefits and contributions are fixed by law. Pension insurance provides financial benefits for those reaching pensionable age, those suffering long-term incapacity for work, and for surviving dependants. The legal retirement age for men is 65 years, and for women 60 years, but in practice this affects only 10 per cent of men and less than 50 per cent of women. Ninety per cent of men retire early, either on a disability pension or on an early retirement pension payable to long-term contributors, that is those who have paid into the scheme for 35 years. The actual retirement age for men is on average less than 60 years.

The retirement pension is calculated on the basis of (a) one's level of income during the previous 10 contributory years, and (b) the length of one's contributory period. By restricting the period of calculation to the previous 10 contributory years the government aims to ensure that as a general rule a pensioner can maintain the standard of living he or she enjoyed before retirement. After a full working life, that is when a person has paid into the pension scheme for 45 years, she/he receives a pension equivalent to about 80 per cent of net income. The Austrian pension system provides for a minimum pension with other income being taken into account. If a pension is below a specified minimum amount, with the result that family income falls short of the statutory minimum, the individual concerned receives a supplementary payment to make up the difference. A widow receives 60 per cent of her late husband's pension.

Pensions are adjusted annually in line with wage trends over the previous few years. This means that recipients are not only compensated for inflation but also benefit from improvements in productivity. Pension contributions for workers and salaried employees amount to about 23 per cent of gross pay, the employee's contribution being about 10 per cent and that of the employer about 13 per cent. This covers more than two-thirds of pension expenditure; the balance is funded from the federal budget, the federal government having a statutory obligation to meet the difference between expenditure and contribution revenue.

Compared with other OECD countries Austria's pension expenditure makes up a remarkably high proportion of GDP. The OECD average is 7.7 per cent while in Austria it comes to 13 per cent. The main reason for this is the extremely early age, comparatively speaking, at which retirement pensions are taken. This results in certain problems of funding which are exacerbated by demographic factors, by the low degree of self-funding in the case of pension schemes for the self-employed (the latter pay only half the normal rate of contribution), and by various concessions for special groups which, having been granted during periods of economic prosperity, are only now becoming fully effective.

Public sector employees (*Beamte*) have their own pension scheme. They pay smaller contributions than wage and salary earners in the private sector and the basis on which their pensions are calculated is somewhat more favourable. Hence their pensions are on average 50 per cent higher than those in the private sector.

Pension reforms now awaiting discussion will aim to safeguard the funding of pension schemes for the future, and will also seek to harmonize the present benefit arrangements which do after all show considerable diversity.

Unemployment benefits

The unemployment rate in Austria, at about 5 per cent, is only half the average for OECD countries. This is the basic reason why expenditure on unemployment benefits in Austria is relatively modest as a proportion of social expenditure as a whole.

Apart from public sector employees and people merely doing small part-time jobs, all employees must be covered by an unemployment insurance scheme. Employees and employers both have to contribute between 2 and 3 per cent of total pay to an unemployment insurance fund, up to a maximum contributory level. These contributions finance unemployment benefit, assistance (similar to a pension) for unemployed elderly people, maternity benefits and lastly active job-creation measures in the labour market.

The right to draw unemployment benefit has conditions attached to it which are rather strict compared with those applying in other countries, and benefit levels are fairly modest. An unemployed person must have worked for at least a year to qualify for first-time benefit. This amounts to 40 per cent of previous gross pay plus about 50 to 70 per cent of previous net pay and is paid for a maximum of 7 months. After this period expires, social security benefit is payable in cases of real need. Unlike the person on unemployment benefit, the recipient of social security must be prepared to accept unfamiliar work if there is no immediate prospect of finding a job for which he is trained. Certain groups, though eligible for unemployment benefit, are ineligible for social security benefit, namely foreigners and married unemployed women. The exclusion of these groups and of unemployed school leavers is likely to be abolished before long.

While the flow of transfer payments to the unemployed could certainly be improved, there are two particular groups of unemployed which receive above-average cover from the unemployment scheme: nursing mothers and elderly people. Women who have previously been in work receive maternity benefit for a year to enable them to be at home with the child, and elderly employees who become unemployed but are not yet eligible for a pension, receive benefits which are similar to a pension and which amount to between two-thirds and four-fifths of their previous net pay.

Health insurance

About two-thirds of all health service expenditure in Austria is met by the statutory health and accident insurance scheme and by government grants to hospitals. Almost all Austrians are eligible for sickness benefit. Accident insurance only covers accidents connected with one's work, hence there are fewer beneficiaries included under this heading. Both these schemes are financed by income-related contributions from employees and employers. Sickness benefits — out-patient or hospital treatment, medicines and medical supplies — are generally available free of charge to insured persons. The self-employed and public sector employees have to pay a small charge as do almost all insured persons when purchasing drugs.

Out-patient treatment is almost exclusively carried out by doctors in private practice, not by out-patient departments in public hospitals. Most private doctors have a range of contracts with the various health insurance bodies and are then reimbursed by the latter for their services. The insured are free to choose their own doctor. Private doctors and their professional interest groups have considerable power since they possess a virtual right of veto against the building of public out-patient departments. One result of this is the uneven health care over the country as a whole.

While the area of out-patient treatment shows certain deficiencies in medical provision, the situation is rather the reverse in the case of in-patient treatment. In some areas and some groups of illnesses there is an excess capacity of hospital beds. The major reason for this is the way in which hospitals are funded. The finance for most of the running costs comes not from the owners (mainly the local authorities and the provincial governments) but from the fees paid on a daily basis by the social insurance bodies, the deficit being made up by an organization comprising various public corporations. In view of the decentralized manner in which the hospitals are organized it has not yet been possible to draw up a hospital plan for the whole country and to use this as a basis of financial management.

Family benefits

Employers are required to pay about 5 per cent of the total wage bill into what is known as the 'Fund for the Equalization of Family

Burdens' (*Familienlastenausgleichsfonds*) which finances all of the following: family allowances, maternity grants, marriage grants, free school travel, school books, marriage guidance centres, maintenance loans, grants to single mothers, etc. Austria leads the international field with such family benefits.

Welfare benefits

Unlike the above-mentioned social benefits which are available nationwide and to which everyone normally has a legal right without having to prove need (except in the case of social security benefit for the unemployed, and the granting of the minimum pension), welfare benefits operate essentially on the principle of self-help. Assistance is given only when the family's financial resources are insufficient and cannot be adequately supplemented by the other social services, which are the first line of defence. Social welfare benefits are the responsibility of the nine provincial governments. Some of the other social services are not obliged to observe any minimum levels of benefit, the result being that in times of economic difficulty welfare benefits are more in demand. Because of the financial problems faced by the provincial governments and the local authorities, this safety net of the social security system is now overstretched and the rules for eligibility are becoming increasingly strict. As long as the welfare system is in fact required to do no more than meet individual cases of need, the present mechanisms are adequate; but if it is increasingly expected to provide a safeguard against risks specific to entire social groups, its present system of funding will make it unable to cope. The need in the longer term is that the various social services, which are meant to come into play before the welfare system, should be restructured in favour of the lowest paid.

Concluding remarks

Despite certain deficiencies, Austria is one of the most advanced of all welfare states. More than a quarter of the proceeds of its economic growth is diverted to the area of social security.

In the case of family benefits and largely also in the case of pensions, social provision may be regarded as adequate, though this is less true as regards unemployment and welfare benefits. The need in the longer term is to ensure that all the social security systems provide the lowest paid with sufficient benefits to live on. In Austria, unlike other European countries, no attempt has been made to overcome the economic crisis of the past 10 years at the expense of the more socially deprived, which has meant that its social system has remained in good repair.

Although arguments flare up repeatedly over social security 'scrounging' and over-provision by the state, the major social forces are largely agreed that the safety net should remain largely intact. But this does not remove the need to consider reforms aimed at more efficient systems of funding and at the introduction of other criteria for calculating benefits; these should be less related to income and more relevant to social needs, less concerned with causes and more concerned with ultimate objectives.

20 The distribution of wealth and income

Walter Schwarzenbrunner

Introduction

Austria is one of the countries showing the most marked economic improvement since the end of the Second World War. Between 1950 and 1985 national output increased more than fourfold in real terms, and between 1970 and 1985 alone the real per capita gross national income rose by 53 per cent, well ahead of the OECD average of 35 per cent. The purpose of this chapter is to investigate the way in which Austria's increased wealth has been distributed among individual social groups. This, however, is by no means easy since there is a great dearth of statistical information on wealth and income distribution in Austria, data on the distribution between profit income and wage income being particularly sparse. Problems of methodology in interpreting the data are a further source of difficulty. In the first and more detailed section, some of these problems will be briefly presented and the major features of the development of functional income distribution expounded. This will be followed by a brief outline of income differences within the group of employed persons. The article ends with a brief account of the major problems of distribution policy within the context of the Austrian tax system.

Statistical data on wealth distribution in Austria are even more meagre than on income distribution. Wealth tax statistics merely yield a few clues as to the concentration of the wealth assessed for wealth tax, but the great bulk of unattributable assessed financial assets is not statistically accounted for. Nevertheless wealth tax statistics show that about 130,000 persons are liable for wealth tax, i.e. the entire amount of wealth registered for tax purposes is owned by about 1.7 per cent of the population. The richest 10 per cent of those liable for wealth tax, i.e. less than 0.2 per cent of the population, own more than half (55 per cent) of all such wealth, while the richest 1 per cent (less than 0.02 per cent of the population) owns almost a quarter of it.

The development of functional income distribution

Consideration of functional income distribution and its development resolves itself into the question of how the different types of income have developed — the difference being dependent upon the recipients' position in the economic process. In broad terms therefore it comes down to the distribution between profit income and wage income. The statistical sources for investigating functional income distribution are the National Income Accounts (*volkswirtschaftliche Gesamtrechnung*). This is the only consistent set of statistics available on the subject of national economic distribution and goes back, in its present internationally disseminated form, no further than the 'System of National Accounts' published by the UN in 1968.

Disappointment awaits anyone hoping that the complex statistics of the national accounts will yield simple and unambiguous answers to questions on functional income distribution. Nevertheless it is possible, with some difficulty, to draw certain conclusions as to the general direction which functional income distribution has been taking. The following is a brief summary covering Austria during the period 1954 to 1985. The selection of 1954 as the base year arises from the fact that a harmonized and revised set of accounts going back to that year has recently become available.

As far as income distribution is concerned, the essential quantity in the national accounts is national income which is derived from gross domestic product by deducting the depreciation of fixed capital and the balance of indirect taxes and government subsidies. It can be interpreted as the sum of all the gross incomes earned in the market place by all persons and corporate bodies. National income also includes, for example, the undistributed profits of joint-stock companies, and government income arising from the activities of state-owned companies with their own legal status. As regards functional income distribution, the first essential is to discover what proportion of national income is represented by the gross remuneration of employees received from domestic producers and how this ratio develops over a period of time. If it rises, this means that the income of employees has risen as a proportion of total national income. This is precisely what has happened in Austria as a long-term trend during recent decades, just as in all developed industrial nations (see Table 20.1). In 1954 the wage ratio in Austria stood at 60.1 per cent; it reached its highest point so far in 1981 (75.9 per cent), and the 1985 figure (71.5 per cent), although well below the peak of 1981, is still considerably higher than the mid-fifties level. This long-term trend indicates without any doubt that the relative weight of wage incomes as a whole has increased; this in itself, however, is no evidence that any redistribution has taken place in favour of

Table 20.1 Statistical indicators of functional income distribution

	Employees as a proportion of the total labour force (%)	Employee remuneration ÷ national income (%) (wage ratio)	National income per member of the labour force (1974 = 100)	Gross income per employee (1974 = 100)
1954	65.9	60.1	16.5	17.7
1964	73.5	62.9	37.4	37.7
1974	82.5	70.0	100.0	100.0
1981	85.4	75.9	168.9	176.9
1984	85.6	71.9	209.6	207.4
1985	85.9	71.5	223.0	218.7

Source: Österreichisches Statistisches Zentralamt.

wage earners and to the disadvantage of those receiving profit income, for during the same period the number of wage earners as a proportion of the total labour force has risen sharply, while both in absolute and in relative terms the self-employed category has shown a marked decline. The proportion of employees in relation to the total labour force rose from 65.9 per cent in 1954 to 85.9 per cent in 1985. So one is bound to ask how the trend shown by the wage ratio is to be assessed, bearing in mind the trend in the structure of employment, whether re-distribution has taken place, and if so in which direction.

Unfortunately this question has no clear-cut answer, for various statistical and methodological problems make it impossible to draw precise conclusions. One fundamental problem relates to the way in which global income values are assigned to different groups within the labour force. In particular, a very serious methodological problem arises from the fact that, in the definition of national accounts, profit income is assigned to the self-employed group: there are various income values which in fact cannot be assigned to any persons at all, i.e. the undistributed profits of joint-stock companies, and government income from entrepreneurial activity. Then again, profit income also includes all income deriving from the ownership of capital, such as share dividends and interest on savings accounts and securities. And such interest, it is rightly pointed out, is not earned exclusively by the self-employed. In view of the total lack of attribution prevailing in this area it is quite impossible to break the figures down so as to show classes of persons. This creates problems for all attempts to interpret distribution, for fundamental to such interpretation is making a personal classification of the income values contained in the national accounts.

Even the process of breaking down the aggregate of gross wages in relation to the employees' group is not as straightforward as it might appear at first sight. In the national accounts, types of income are differentiated on a functional basis. This means that in the case of people who, though formally classed as employees, in practice have an entrepreneurial function, incomes ought to be classified as arising from entrepreneurial activity. But this does not happen, since there are not the facilities to record such information. Such wrongly classified incomes also include those of senior executives and similarly those of business owners who employ themselves in their own firms, as well as those incomes received by members of such a business owner's family who frequently assume formal employee status in order to gain tax or social welfare benefits. Such wrong classification of incomes, for lack of better recording methods, impairs any inference made regarding the *level* of different types of income so that, for example, no valid conclusions can be drawn from the national accounts as to the average income for employees compared with the average income for the self-employed.

Such problems are less serious when it comes to drawing conclusions about the *trend* of distribution since in this case they present a difficulty only insofar as their scope or relative weight may have changed. This, however, is precisely what has happened in some areas during the period under discussion. To stay with the examples already mentioned: the proportion of interest on savings and securities going not to the self-employed but to employees has most probably seen a substantial rise. The significance of formal employee status assumed by members of business owners' families has quite certainly shown a sharp increase in the years since 1973, the year when the incidence of the personal tax system was modified so that the unit became the individual rather than the household. This made it advantageous, in the light of the existing progressive income-tax scales, to spread company profit income formally between several members of the family. Even though there are clear indications that the resulting distortion of distribution figures is on the increase, it is impossible to eliminate such distortion by statistical methods.

Despite these problems of recording and classification, certain cautious interpretations, based upon the national accounts, may undoubtedly be made regarding trends in functional income distribution. To these problems must be added computational sources of error connected with the fact that all estimations of trends in distribution have to be based upon changes in the value of income in terms of an arithmetic mean. Changes in the structure of the labour force, which make such adjustments necessary in the first place, occur in such a way as to produce, once again, distorted results. Just to take the most essential point by way of illustration: the sharp decline in the number of self-employed, both in absolute and in relative terms, occurred because many people in this category who were on a fairly low income gave up their self-employed status. But the mere fact that these below-average earners ceased to be self-employed caused the average income of the remainder to rise year by year without any single individual necessarily having an effective increase in income! This could be adjusted if precise data were available as to the incomes earned during their last year as self-employed persons by those who are now no longer in this category. Since no such data are available, however, there is no alternative but to make use of those distribution values which are least affected by such problems.

These methodological questions, which have received no more than a brief mention here, were the subject of a very thorough academic discussion in Austria a few years ago. The conclusion reached was that a comparison of per capita income per employee with national income per member of the labour force was the value providing the best basis on which to estimate trends in functional income distribution.

Table 20.1 contains index numbers (1974 = 100) for these per capita incomes for selected years during the period under consideration. These data show in general a very regular progression: both national income per member of the labour force, and also gross per capita income per employee increased sixfold in nominal terms between 1954 and 1974, and rather more than doubled from 1974 to 1985. The conclusion which the Austrians draw from this is that functional distribution of the national income shows a very stable progression in the long term and that, again in the long term, there has been no marked degree of redistribution. However, the interpretations based upon this come to different conclusions, depending upon the weight attached to the distorting effects, briefly referred to above, of the various problems of methodology: employers' interest groups stress the point that employees are sharing to an ever-increasing degree in interest income, which itself has seen considerable growth, and conclude that the central finding — namely the long-term consistency of functional income distribution — in fact points to redistribution in favour of employees. From the standpoint of the latter, however, in addition to the examples already quoted there are various other aspects producing distortions in precisely the opposite direction and suggesting that, if anything, the income position of employees has worsened in comparison with the self-employed. At least there is no serious dispute that since the beginning of the 1980s the trend in functional income distribution has shown marked gains in the case of profit incomes, and this is evident in several ways from Table 20.1, for example the very fact that the global wage ratio progressively declined from 75.9 per cent in 1981 to 71.5 per cent in 1985, even though at the same time the number of employees as a proportion of the total labour force continued to rise. It is also apparent from the indices of per capita incomes that the relative position of those receiving wage incomes has markedly deteriorated.

There is one factor which does not appear at all in these figures yet which has a very adverse effect upon the income position of employees as a whole: the unemployment which has been clearly on the increase, in Austria as elsewhere, since 1981. The number of unemployed rose from an annual average of 53,000 in 1980 to 139,000 in 1985, representing a rise in unemployment rate from 1.9 per cent to 4.8 per cent. In the light of such a rise, any initial impression as to the long-term constancy of functional income distribution needs to be suitably modified. This means that, as a result of the gains made by profit incomes since 1981, there has been a very considerable shift in favour of such incomes compared with the period of full employment in the early seventies — a situation which causes increasing concern in Austrian trade union circles. The most noticeable feature of the trend in functional income distribution in the eighties is that the traditional formulation whereby distribution trends were viewed as being functionally related to cyclical fluctuations became discredited. The textbook model of a relative improvement in profits during periods of economic upturn with wages following suit during the next economic downturn was discernable in the pattern of income distribution in Austria until the end of the seventies. But the most recent large leaps in profit incomes took place in 1982 and 1983, when the Austrian economy, like that of other countries, was still in a period of persistent recession. Profit incomes continued to rise during the subsequent slight upturn in the economy.

The explanation for this untypical course of events can only be that during the recession the great majority of Austrian companies succeeded, by means of staff cuts and rationalization exercises, in shifting the burden on to the shoulders of their employees. On the other hand, the trade unions in recent years have not succeeded in fully exploiting the bargaining advantage brought about by rationalization. A large part of the reason for this is the fact that union wage policies have traditionally taken their cue from the iron and steel sector which is precisely where the rationalization-induced bargaining advantage has for many years been over-exploited when compared to the fall in market prices as a result of the worldwide steel crisis. The companies affected have therefore suffered considerable and, in some cases, increasing losses. So it is particularly in industry that profits show exceptionally wide variations. The exploitation of a bargaining advantage in the more profitable sectors of the economy will assume a special significance during the remainder of the eighties. In this connection a policy priority for the unions is achieving a job-creating reduction in working hours without a loss in pay. This hardening stance in the unions' distribution policy is seen on the one hand as an imperative in the interests of employee solidarity; on the other hand the experience of recent years has once again shown very clearly the difficulties which the unions face in getting their demands met (not merely in terms of wage policy) under rising unemployment. And the union leaders now totally accept the view that a reduction in working hours will be essential in the fight against unemployment.

The distribution of employees' income

Trends in functional income distribution are not the only issues to dominate the theory and practice of distribution policy in Austria. Increasing attention has also been paid in recent years to divergent wage levels for similar or at least comparable forms of activity, so that the principle of equal pay for equal work now actually has legal status, and a government-run Complaints Commission has been established. The immediate background to this was the obvious discrimination being practised against women in terms of pay, even though they were doing precisely the same work as men. Ultimately, however, the law covers only the most extreme and blatant cases of sex-specific pay discrimination, and has been unable to solve the more deep-seated problem of a segmented labour market. Pay discrimination against women is largely due to the continued existence of sectors in which female employment predominates, and to the existence of female-specific jobs, both of which are characterized by low pay. Investigations carried out by the Austrian Central Statistical Office provide concrete information as to the degree of pay advantage enjoyed by male employees. Table 20.2 shows that, taking male employees as a whole, their pay advantage stands at about 27 per cent. A striking feature is that sex-specific pay differentials in the case of public sector employees (*Beamte*) are comparatively small (8 per cent).

The particularly high differentials in the case of salaried employees as a whole arise from the top salaries earned by such employees in highly qualified and executive positions. In this category it was not possible to calculate income advantage over women because too few of the latter are in such positions, and in the statistical sample were too meagrely represented for any sound conclusions to be drawn. Table 20.2 also shows that there is no linear relationship between qualification levels and sex-specific income differentials.

Problems parallel to (and overlapping) those just discussed are also found in the area of sectoral-specific income differentials. Here there are concrete data for the individual sectors of industry based upon the survey of employees' remuneration carried out by the Federal Chamber of the Economy (*Bundeskammer der gewerblichen Wirtschaft*). Table 20.3 makes clear the very considerable dispersion of average values shown by workers' effective wages so that, for example, in 1985 wages in the chemical industry were 17 per cent higher than the average for industry as a whole, while in the women's sectors — the textile, leather and clothing industries — they were between 17 and 33 per cent below this average. A further analysis, on the basis of qualification levels, revealed that wage differentials

Table 20.2 Sex-specific pay differentials 1985

Occupation	Pay advantage of men (%)
Unskilled workers	17
Semi-skilled workers	41
Skilled workers	38
Workers as a whole	37
Salaried employees (lower grade)	36
Salaried employees (middle grade)	22
Salaried employeees (higher grade)	24
Salaried employees as a whole	44
Public sector employees (*Beamte*)	8
Employees as a whole	27

Source: Österreichisches Statistisches Zentralamt.

between the sectors are fairly similar at all qualification levels, i.e. from the unskilled to the skilled worker.

The problems discussed here have led to discussions in recent years as to whether a legally fixed minimum wage should be introduced in order to reduce sectoral wage differentials. For many years the trade unions representing the various sectors have been pursuing a wages policy whereby low levels of pay should either be raised by above-average amounts or actually placed in higher pay grades.

The distributive effects of the Austrian tax system

The government's taxation policy, as well as its social policy, is the real starting-point for its policy of income distribution. Taxation policy is bound to have distributive effects even if purely fiscal considerations have determined its implementation. Reference was made above to the basically progressive nature of the income tax system. But the levelling tendency of the progressive income-tax scales is seriously weakened by the numerous allowances and concessions which are used, particularly by those on higher incomes, as a tax-effective means of reducing their liability.

Companies, employers and those in the liberal professions are particularly well placed when it comes to tax avoidance measures.

Table 20.3 Effective wages of industrial workers 1985 (indices of sectoral averages)

Chemical industry	117
Vehicle industry	115
Iron and steel industry	113
Mining	112
Paper industry	109
Gas industry/district heating	107
Building	106
Machine tools	106
Foundrywork	104
Glass industry	103
Stonework and ceramics	102
Engineering	101
Food and drink	97
Electrical industry	96
Iron and metal goods	94
Woodwork	93
Sawmills	89
Paper and cardboard processing	86
Textile industry	83
Leather processing	75
Leather manufacture	70
Clothing industry	67
Industry as a whole	100

Source: Bundeskammer der gewerblichen Wirtschaft.

Some of these are expressly provided for by government policy as instruments of economic policy designed, for example, to promote investment. Others amount simply to tax avoidance without any higher objective. Table 20.4 shows the considerable effect this has had, particularly during the last ten years, in reducing the amount of profits tax paid. The national accounts show that while gross profit incomes rose by 136 per cent between 1974 and 1985, revenue from all profit taxes increased by a mere 56 per cent. The taxation of employees showed a different trend: here, against an increase in gross incomes of 127 per cent, revenue from income tax rose by 203 per cent.

A further factor contributing to the shortfall in profit taxes is that, in practice, the rapidly increasing income from capital assets

Table 20.4 Incomes and taxes (1974 = 100)

	Gross remuneration of employees	Personal income tax	Gross income from profits	Profit taxes
1954	13.5	4.7	19.6	14.8
1964	33.6	15.6	44.2	34.6
1974	100.0	100.0	100.0	100.0
1981	187.0	233.9	156.4	130.8
1984	214.7	273.0	218.4	137.4
1985	227.6	303.8	236.6	156.5

Source: Österreichisches Statistisches Zentralamt.

remains almost entirely untaxed. It is true that such income is subject to income tax but, because of the lack of attribution of most tax assessments, this tax is hardly ever paid. Also, since the only proceeds to be taxed at source are those arising from a holding in joint-stock companies but not from investments in the form of bonds or securities, by far the greater portion of income from capital ownership remains entirely untaxed! Attempts to rectify, at least partially, this unsatisfactory state of affairs came to nothing between 1983 and 1985 in the face of an extensively organized campaign by conservative political forces, the bourgeois media and the banking sector.

This issue, however, will be an important priority in the major reform of taxation contemplated by the new coalition government. It is, after all, not merely a question of the distributive aspects or of a just taxation system: it is a matter of having a rational economic policy.

Since income from the ownership of financial capital receives grossly preferential treatment from a tax point of view compared with returns on capital tied up in companies, there is reluctance to declare such company capital for assessment. It is hoped that this danger will be counteracted by the development of a firm consensus within society.

21 Education in Austria

Herbert Moritz

Austria is proud of its educational system, and arguably has every right to be so. International comparisons such as the 1979 OECD Report show that Austrian young people of both sexes are well able to cope with present-day demands and to keep pace with world-wide developments. And this is essential if Austria is to be able to make its own contribution towards the progress of mankind, and to do so into the twenty-first century. This has been the aim of the educational policy pursued by the Austrian government ever since the Socialist Party took over in 1970.

Many new ideas have emanated from the Austrian educational system and had international influence. One has only to think of the school reform movement after the First World War under the Social Democrat Minister for Education Otto Glöckel who later became President of the Municipal Educational Authority of Vienna. On the other hand Austria has always been ready to take up ideas for reform which are under discussion abroad and to implement them within the framework of its own educational system. Educational reform in Austria is therefore, seen as a whole, an ongoing process, and it follows that any treatment of what is a highly dynamic educational system can give no more than a fleeting impression.

The schools

The structure of the Austrian school system

The history of the Austrian school system is the story of progress from schools which were specific to one social class — the *Volksschule*, the *Bürgerschule* and the *Gymnasium* — to schools which are open to all sections of the population without distinction. Essentially, the 8-year *Volksschule* has become the 4-year *Grundschule* or primary school (still sometimes referred to as the *Volksschule*); the *Bürgerschule* has become the 4-year *Hauptschule* which represents the next stage and is very similar to the junior classes of the *Gymnasium* or grammar school; and the latter is now known as the *allgemeinbildende höhere Schule* (AHS), that is a secondary school providing a general education. Alongside the senior classes of the

AHS (classes 9–12), some separate schools catering for the same age group (*Oberstufenrealgymnasien*) have come into being. Priority has been given, however, to developing the vocational training aspect of the school system — as required by the demands of the contemporary world. (See Figure 21.1.)

Out of a total of about 6,700 Austrian schools, just under 10 per cent are private establishments, mainly church schools. Those private church schools which are under public law have their staffing costs (covering both teachers and non-teaching staff) entirely met by the state.

Between 1970 and 1986 the number of teachers employed in Austrian schools doubled — from 60,000 to 120,000, and this despite the fact that the number of pupils has sharply declined: since 1976/7, when the school population peaked at 1,511,634, there has been a drop of almost 19 per cent. In 1970, state expenditure on educational services amounted to almost 8 billion schillings (7.8 per cent of the federal budget), reaching its highest point in 1980 with 27.5 billion (9.1 per cent).

The legal basis of the Austrian school system

The Austrian school system has its legal basis in the School Acts (*Schulgesetze*) of 1962. At that time legislation affecting the schools was accorded constitutional status which means that any amendments to such legislation require a two-thirds majority in the National Assembly. The consequence is that the two major parties, namely the SPÖ and the ÖVP have to agree on any changes to be made. In other words a compromise has to be reached, with all the advantages and disadvantages of such an arrangement.

The federal government is responsible for legislation relating to the school system and also for its implementation. Responsibility for the building and equipping of schools which provide compulsory general and vocational education, lies with the provinces or the local authorities; the federal government has responsibility for intermediate and senior schools and also for Colleges of Education.

Schools providing compulsory general education are responsible in the first instance to the district educational authority and in the second instance to the provincial educational authority; schools providing compulsory vocational education, those providing vocational education at an intermediate or senior level, and general secondary schools, are all responsible in the first instance to the provincial educational authority and in the second instance to the Federal Ministry for Education, Art and Sport.

The School Acts of 1962 require the state-funded schools of Austria to be available to all, irrespective of birth, sex, race, status,

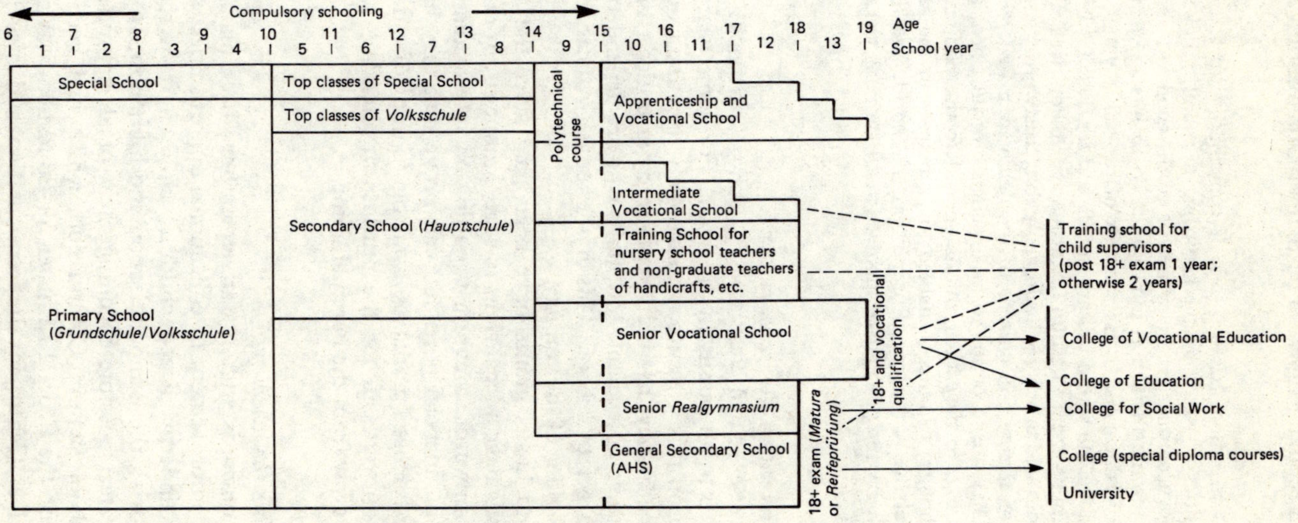

Figure 21.1 *Austria's school system*

class, language and religion. The School Organization Act of 1962 states:

> The Austrian school has the task of contributing to the development of the abilities of young people according to moral, religious and social values, and according to the values of truth, goodness and beauty, by means of teaching which is appropriate to their stage of development and type of education. It has the task of providing young people with the knowledge and skill necessary for life and for their future occupation, and of enabling them to acquire education for themselves. Young people are to be educated to become healthy, capable, trustworthy and responsible members of society and citizens of the democratic Federal Republic of Austria. They are to be led to independence of judgment and to social understanding, to have their minds opened to the political and philosophical thought of others, enabled to participate in the economic and the cultural life of Austria, Europe and the world, and, imbued with a love of liberty and peace, to be involved in the common tasks confronting mankind.

Social benefits within the school system

Ever since the school year 1972/3, school textbooks have been provided free to all pupils by the state. For some years now total expenditure on this measure, an extremely important one in terms of educational policy, has been kept steady at under 1 billion schillings. Free travel is available for pupils who are dependent on public transport to get to school. This has removed educational barriers in various regions of the country.

School and hostel grants have been paid since the school year 1971/2. Pupils have a legal right to school grants if, from their tenth school year onwards, they are attending an intermediate or senior school, are in financial need and can prove that they have a good school record. Hostel grants are available to pupils from their ninth school year onwards if, for the purpose of attending school, they have to live away from the parental home.

Reforms within the school system

From 1970 onwards attempts at reform have been mainly directed towards the improvement of educational opportunities (particularly for socially underprivileged children, children from remote rural areas, and girls), the democratization and humanization of schools, and the greatest possible encouragement of all aptitudes. To this end the School Reform Commission, which had been set up in 1969 to advise the Federal Minister for Education, was re-activated in 1970 and a 'Centre for Experimentation and Development in Schools' (*Zentrum für Schulversuche und Schulentwicklung*) was created within the Federal Ministry for Education, Art and Sport. The following is a brief summary of the results of these reforms:

- the pre-school class (providing special teaching for children who, although of school age, are not ready for school) has now been brought into the regular school system;
- a modern foreign language is now taught as early as the third and fourth year of the *Volksschule*;
- the *Hauptschule* has been changed from a two-stream organization to one with common teaching but with three sets in German, mathematics and a modern language;
- sets have been introduced in vocational schools (*Berufsschulen*), also special courses to enable pupils completing the vocational school course to take the equivalent of A levels (known variously in Austria as the *Reifeprüfung* or *Matura*) and to enter university;
- special courses have been created for school leavers from intermediate and senior schools;
- the period of training of teachers for *Volksschulen*, *Hauptschulen* and special schools has been extended from four to six semesters;
- Colleges of Vocational Education (*Berufspädagogische Akademien*) have been set up to train teachers for schools providing vocational education;
- the system has been developed whereby the senior classes of the AHS can exist as a separate institution (compare the British sixth form college);
- regulations concerning separation of the sexes in school classes have been abolished;
- curriculum reform has been carried out in all schools, giving prominence to integrated studies, environmental education, insight into the world of work, and political education (peace studies);
- school councils have been introduced within schools, also pupil representation at higher levels: there are Pupils' Advisory Councils (*Schülerbeiräte*) at both provincial and federal levels;
- collaborative bodies have been set up within schools for representatives of staff, pupils and parents: class and school forums in schools catering for pupils of compulsory school age, and joint school councils in all schools beyond the ninth school year;
- a reform to be introduced shortly involves the first year of the *Grundschule* where pupil assessments will be in words rather than in numerical grades (the traditional *Noten*).

Foreign children in Austrian schools

Not only is Vienna the seat of many international organizations but

Austria itself gives asylum to refugees from the countries of eastern Europe and is host to a considerable number of foreign workers. According to a survey carried out in 1981 there were in Austrian schools about 26,000 pupils of foreign nationality, including about 9,750 of Yugoslavian and about 6,500 of Turkish nationality. In 1986 as many as 18.5 per cent of all pupils of compulsory school age in Vienna were the children of foreign workers.

Austrian schools are open to all foreign children as a matter of principle; the child of the foreign worker has absolutely the same right to education as the Austrian child. To encourage her/his integration in the school she/he receives special instruction in the German language while teachers from the country of origin also teach the mother tongue and instruct the child in that country's affairs to prevent alienation from the native environment.

In addition there are private foreign-language schools for foreign children such as the Vienna International School, the American International School, and the Lycée Français, plus a Soviet, a Japanese, a Libyan-Arabic, an Iranian and a Czech school.

Higher education

Reform of universities and higher education in Austria

During the last two decades the situation of institutions within higher education in Austria has undergone a fundamental change. The education they provide has been extended in that new courses have been introduced, new universities have been established and existing capacity has been increased. There are currently over 600 courses available (in about 430 subject areas) at the following institutions:

- 12 Universities
  - the classical universities of Vienna, Graz, Innsbruck, Salzburg and Linz
  - Technological universities in Vienna and Graz
  - University of Agriculture in Vienna
  - University of Veterinary Medicine in Vienna
  - University of Economics in Vienna
  - University of Educational Sciences in Klagenfurt
  - University of Mining in Leoben
- 6 Kunsthochschulen
  - Academy of Fine Arts in Vienna
  - *Hochschulen* for Music and Dramatic Art in Vienna, Salzburg and Graz

–*Hochschule* for Applied Art in Vienna
–*Hochschule* for Artistic and Industrial Design in Linz

Expenditure on universities has risen accordingly: nearly 14 billion schillings during the financial year 1986 compared to 1 billion schillings in 1965.

Since 1966 a reform of full-time courses of study has been in progress at the universities, based upon the 'General Act Governing Higher Education' of that year (*Allgemeines Hochschul-Studiengesetz*). This has meant new regulations for all courses. The University Organization Act passed by Parliament in 1975 took account of the increased demands made upon modern universities by bringing in a reform of their structure and administration: the different groups involved in a university (staff, students, and administrative personnel) could now have their interests represented within its academic decision-making bodies, that is a process of democratization was introduced which ensures that all parties have a say in the university's affairs. The reform of courses at the Kunsthochschulen was initiated by an Act of 1983 (*Kunsthochschul-Studiengesetz*) and is in full progress.

Courses and degrees in Austria

Access to all Austrian universities and *Hochschulen* is open to all who meet the educational requirements (which usually means those who have passed the *Matura* exam), and they may follow any discipline they choose. (Study at *Hochschulen* is also dependent on passing an entrance examination.) Since 1972 all courses have been free. Students in financial need have a legal right to a grant provided their work is satisfactory.

Despite the constant rise in student numbers it has been possible, with considerable effort, to maintain the principle that universities are open to all comers. The number of matriculated students from within Austria was 43,122 in the academic year 1970/1, but by 1984/5 it had risen to about 133,000. There are approximately 14,000 teaching staff including 2,000 professors.

The overwhelming majority of students follow full-time courses leading to an academic degree, namely a diploma or a doctorate. Diploma courses are primarily to provide academic or artistic training for a given profession and last 8–10 semesters (up to 16 semesters at the *Kunsthochschulen*). The degree of *Magister* or *Diplomingenieur* is conferred upon those successfully completing their course. Doctoral studies serve mainly to develop the ability to pursue independent academic research. They presuppose the successful completion of a diploma course or its equivalent, and last between 2 and 4 semesters. Candidates must pass the doctoral viva (known as the *Rigorosum*) to be awarded the appropriate doctorate. The study of medicine can be undertaken only as a doctoral course.

Foreign students at Austrian universities and Hochschulen

As far as foreign students are concerned, essentially the same entrance requirements apply as for Austrian nationals, namely the possession of an Austrian *Reifeprüfung* certificate or an equivalent qualification. Failing this, the necessary supplementary examinations must be passed before matriculation can take place. An adequate knowlege of German is a basic qualification. Furthermore, a foreigner's examination certificate must give the right of direct access to the universities of the country where it was obtained.

In a number of subject areas unlimited admission of foreign students is currently not possible since large numbers of such applicants try for places in Austria, having been turned down abroad. Individual universities and *Hochschulen* therefore have to limit admissions in accordance with the number of student places available. Foreign students are required to pay course fees of 1,500 schillings per semester, though under certain conditions (for example if a student comes from a developing country) such fees are waived. In addition, the Federal Ministry for Science and Research provides scholarships to enable foreign students to follow courses at Austrian universities and *Hochschulen*, and the Republic of Austria also gives scholarships to students from non-European developing countries.

Adult education

Historical survey

The structure of adult education in Austria shows a certain lack of cohesion which arises from its historical development. Its institutions were not created by the state or by any one central organization but arose through private initiatives or were funded by various social groups, including the political parties and the Catholic Church.

The beginnings of adult education (*Volksbildung* or *Erwachsenenbildung*) in Austria go back to the nineteenth century and were given considerable impetus by the labour movement. Its modern organization by the state began with the establishment of the First Republic: it was Otto Glöckel who as Minister of Education set up an Adult Education Office (*Volksbildungsamt*) within his ministry, and this was followed by the establishment, by each provincial government, of an Adult Education Department (*Volksbildungsreferat*) which was subject to that central body.

Co-operative adult education

In the Second Republic too, it was a Socialist Minister of Education who gave fresh impetus to this educational sector: in 1980 the then Minister, Fred Sinowatz, announced plans for the development of a co-operative system of adult education. All classes of society as far as possible, particularly those with little schooling, were to have educational opportunities appropriate to their needs. The freedom, variety and independence of organizations providing adult education must be guaranteed as must voluntary participation in what they have to offer. The most important step towards improving the structure of adult education is to be closer co-operation with the schools.

A broad distinction may be made between general and vocational adult education. The backbone of the highly developed Austrian adult educational system is formed by about 350 adult education centres and 2,400 other educational training centres. There are also about 50 residential establishments and over 2,400 libraries for those pursuing adult education. Vocational education is provided by specialist organizations and the institutions of the social partnership.

It is estimated that approximately 10 per cent of all Austrians take part each year in some organized adult education activity; about a quarter of a million regularly attend courses providing, in the main, in-service training; and a few hundred working people succeed each year in passing the *Matura* exam of a general secondary school, thus making up for what they failed to achieve in their youth.

The diverse organization of adult education means that its funding is also diverse. Large contributions come not only from the state, but also from the Austrian Trade Union Federation, the Chambers and the Churches.

There seems, therefore, to be a secure future in Austria for what is surely indispensable in an ever-changing world: the type of institution which takes account of the fact that there can no longer be such a thing as a completed education, but that a person who is no longer at school must have the opportunity of constantly broadening her/his knowledge and developing intellectual agility so as to be better able to cope with the problems of society, work, family and leisure. Austrian adult education therefore takes its natural place within the overall concept of education, aiming as it does to help the individual to develop mental powers and creative abilities, so serving both individual interests and the interests of society.

22 Intellectual life and culture: the legacy of the two fascisms

Johann Dvořak

Reconstruction, Cold War and the Grand Coalition

> I remember how people in Austria were obliged to cultivate the appearance of superficiality so as not to make themselves unpopular, how they would do anything in the world to avoid giving the impression of being over-subtle. It's a game I know well, having played it myself in my youth, and nowhere so hypocritically as at the University of Vienna. Any analytical ability, any gift of penetrating insight was concealed under an air of innocence, under feeble jokes and frequent laughter, even though this was not always called for. As soon as anyone's face took on an undisguised expression of seriousness or intense thoughtfulness, he was in danger of being spurned as a Red or maybe even as a Jew.
>
> Hilde Spiel writing on the thirties

> Unlike Austria from 1945 onwards . . . there were some states in which, immediately after their liberation from Hitler's Reich, the new government, however temporary and provisional, invited all those expelled under Hitler & Co. to return as soon as possible to their liberated homeland.
>
> Viktor Matejka

> And Klemperer . . . told me that despite all the efforts of his agent in Vienna he could not get a single engagement, and the same was also true in Salzburg. This was because the Nazis (people like Herr Böhm, the chief standard bearer Karajan and others) had everything in their grip and were already exercising their influence upon the various organizations.
>
> Alfred Rosenthal in a letter to Ernst Křenek dated 1.4.1948

The military defeat of National Socialism in 1945 certainly did not mean a cultural renaissance in Austria. Austria was, after all, the only country to have suffered under two forms of fascism in direct succession: under the Austro-Fascist regime of Chancellors Dollfuss and Schuschnigg from 1933 to 1938, and then under National Socialism from 1938 to 1945.

Fascism cannot be adequately defined in terms of its characteristics, such as the mass movement, Führer cult, anti-liberal and anti-democratic thinking, its anti-Semitism and so on; the essential point is its *social function*, namely to bring about the permanent destruction of the working class, its organizations and its culture.

It is clear that working-class culture does not exsist in a collection of particular works of art or simply in a certain type of living accommodation and so on; it is not an individualistic but a collective culture and exsists in the creation of mass organizations (trade unions and workers' parties) whose purpose is to help represent the common interests of the workers; it encourages the development of a new attitude, that of solidarity, and it attempts (by means of unemployment schemes and social insurance) to take collective precautions against the social risks found in the capitalist system. Along with all these endeavours it seeks to develop an awareness of the common interests of the workers, and it embraces all their individual and collective hopes and aspirations. Fascism means the destruction of the workers' collective achievements and also of their hopes and future aspirations (all of which are inseparably bound up with the strength of their organizations): the workers, as isolated individuals with no awareness of common class-interests, are to be absorbed in the new national community or corporate system.

However, even when culture is considered merely as the sum total of particular works of art and their consumers' attitude towards them, one is still in an area of social conflict, since works of art represent prevailing ideas and life-styles as well as suggesting lines of criticism or ways in which such ideas may be overthrown. Hence conflicts over works of art and their interpretation, and also over the social status of art as such, reflect the clashes of interests between different social classes.

During the period of the First Republic, after 1918, many representatives of the intellectual *avant-garde* (in areas ranging from literature, music and architecture to psychoanalysis and the scientific world view of the 'Vienna Circle') hoped for great things from the new democratic state and from the politically and cultural ambitious working class: they looked for greater liberty and advancement of art and science, a greater openness to innovation, a public whose way of thinking and style of living would be quite different from that of the contemporary bourgeoisie who despised and opposed modern trends just as much as they did the proletariat.

The Vienna of the twenties and early thirties, under its Social Democratic leadership, broke new ground politically as well as culturally. 'Red Vienna' was a world-renowned example of new departures in school reform and adult education, social, health and economic policy, urban development and architecture — an example of policies benefiting the mass of the population whose living conditions and opportunities for shaping their own lives had been drastically improved within a very few years. The Austrian Social Democrats in Red Vienna provided an example of radical reforming politics within the framework of parliamentary democracy and the capitalist system, and in so doing presented to working-class movements in the West an alternative, as it were, to the model of revolution in the Soviet Union.

The struggle for modernism and the attempt to make full use of the intellectual *avant-garde* movement in Austria was not a discussion about aesthetics or the scientific method: it was essentially a struggle over ways of thinking and styles of living, about freedom of self-determination both for the individual and for society.

With the victory of Austro-Fascism and that of National Socialism in Germany, central Europe saw the destruction of modern art and science, of all attempts at self-determination in life style, and of all radical movements aimed at the enlightenment of the bourgeoisie — as well as the destruction of working-class organizations. Many intellectuals, such as artists, scientists and leaders of the labour movement, were expelled, arrested or killed. This not only put an end to every promising attempt at creating a better, more humane, more beautiful world but erased even the memory of such aspirations from people's minds.

In 1945 the leading functionaries of the two major parties (SPÖ and ÖVP), both now reconstituted and re-named, agreed to put the past behind them and to concentrate on reconstruction. But what was to be reconstructed? Shattered government buildings, churches, theatres and opera houses, factories, schools and so on? Social structures, or what? And if social structures, then the question still remained: which ones?

The answer given to this was often very simple and straightforward. The writer Alexander Lernet-Holenia stated in November 1945: 'All we need to do in fact is to continue from the point where we were interrupted by a madman's dreams; in fact we do not need to look forwards but only backwards.' His backward look, however, was certainly not directed at the democratic and social achievements of the First Republic!

Rudolf Henz, an important cultural official during the Dolifuss-Schuschnigg regime, expressed his conviction thus: 'As I see it, our work now (1945) ought to start where it left off in 1938.' It had left off in Austro-Fascism.

Both Austro-Fascism and National Socialism had been ended by foreign military intervention, not by successful resistance from within. Hence after 1945 there was no day of reckoning either for those who had abolished democracy and handed Austria over to the Nazis, or for those Austrians who had followed the National Socialist line in administration, the law, the police, the army and various Nazi organizations and who had been zealously involved in political persecution, war and mass murder. Their victims were dead or at any rate were living in exile (with very few people showing any desire to bring them home), and anyone attempting to reappraise Austria's past under National Socialism (to say nothing of Austro-Fascism) was immediately branded a Communist. Thus, referring to the exhibition entitled 'Never Forget!' (*Niemals Vergessen!*) which was held in the autumn of 1946 at the House of Artists in Vienna, Rudolf Henz wrote: 'Behind the motto "Never Forget!" there lurked the real call: "Forward into a People's Democracy!".'

Those who had served the Austro-Fascist corporate state had nothing to worry about, but anyone daring to be anti-Fascist or actually a Communist could expect any amount of unjust treatment. However, it must be pointed out that the Communist Party of Austria was utterly insignificant, that the mass of workers and salaried employees were organized either in the trade unions, which were dominated by the Social Democrats, or in the Socialist Party itself or in both, and that the Soviet occupation force scarcely interfered in matters of cultural policy, adopting a highly conservative stance.

The account given by Hilda Spiel of a discussion with Ernst Fischer typifies the situation in Austria in the early post-war years:

> 'No one doubts', he said, 'that the education system is the key to the future. But our schools, particularly our secondary schools and universities, are in a hopeless state. While I was in office we dismissed or pensioned off fifty Nazi professors from the University of Vienna. It wasn't enough, but it was a start. Now everything has come to a standstill. We do not have enough teachers, so there's talk of giving the old guard their jobs back. No one is recalling professors from exile. Academics went over to Hitler practically en masse, and party members are still to be found in high places. The portrait of the principal of the "Hochschule" (University) for World Trade, for example, has got a fresh dab of paint on it where someone has recently painted over his party insignia.'

Intellectuals who by fleeing abroad had escaped physical annihilation at the hand of the Nazis, were described by Hans Weigel in Austria as 'Creatures à la Arnold Zweig' (a German writer, 1887–1968, who spent most of the period 1933–48 in Palestine) — and no one raised any objections to the phrase. It was Weigel who expressed the view that anti-Fascism merely served to 'divert attention from those enemies of democracy which are much nearer to hand'.

The reconstruction of Austria after 1945 meant the removal of the visible results of war, the restoration of the economy, and the reinstatement of that 'culture' which had played no little part in the victories gained by the two Fascisms; at the same time it meant the systematic suppression of the past. The latter process was made easier by the Cold War with its attendant anti-communism, and also by the fact that it was in the interests of the leading Social Democratic functionaries not to enquire too closely into the reasons for the defeat of the labour movement at the hands of Austro-Fascism.

The absence of critical reappraisal of the past brought with it of course a widespread inability to engage in critical analysis of the present. Critical thinking and general discussion about the past and present of Austrian society were unwelcome to the ruling Grand Coalition, not least because Austria's economic reconstruction was made possible only by years, indeed decades, of self-sacrifice on the part of the mass of the population in terms of pay and consumer goods, and it was easier for people to put up with shortages if they knew nothing about the historical reasons for them and so quite simply never thought about the matter. Positive thinking and deliberately forgetting were the order of the day, rather than remembering and criticizing the *status quo*.

This was reflected in the cultural policy of both the federal and provincial governments including, to a degree, the city of Vienna. It was not the reconstruction of progressive, critical, democratic and urban traditions which received encouragement but the perpetuation of anti-progressive, anti-democratic and anti-urban schools of thought: the kind of artistic creation and historiography was promoted which kept close to the Habsburg tradition, to Catholic-Conservative ideas, and to pan-German nationalist ideologies. This was the thinking behind professional appointments in universities, the training of teachers and the financial sponsorship of artistic and scientific work. Hence artists, academics and journalists were often able to take up their activities precisely where they had left them before 1945 or 1938, and in the forties, fifties and early sixties many of the younger generation learnt to adapt and come to terms with the situation. If they did not, they ran into trouble, received no commissions, failed to get jobs, and so on.

The contribution made by Austrians to modern literature in German has been, and still is, both significant and extensive but young authors after 1945 were either successful abroad or in a hopeless situation at home. The cultivation of modern art forms by the older school (from Musil, Broch and Canetti to Schönberg, Berg, Webern, etc.) and the pursuit of science (from psychoanalysis to formulations of the scientific world view) — all this had to take place abroad.

Full employment and social reforms: the intellectual climate of the 1970s

The bourgeoisie, since the collapse of the Monarchy, has resisted anything

> connected with the political rise of the working class. In the process they have either become a prey to nationalist enthusiasm in all its bewildering forms, or they have entrusted themselves almost completely to the strong leadership offered by capitalism and clericalism. In the cultural realm, this has produced the paradoxical situation whereby the defence and propagation of free thought and humanism — a set of ideas which is bourgeois in origin — is now undertaken by the Social Democrats, frequently in face of opposition from the bourgeoisie itself.
>
> Robert Musil (after 1918)

> Vote Social Democrat! In this land of political illiteracy the politics of the Social Democrats can demonstrate what might be described as the essential ability to read and write. So anyone who votes for them is not just backing a party but backing commonsense, which alone can save this state of ours from total disintegration.
>
> Albert Paris Gütersloh/Franz Blei (1919)

It is only possible to speak of a gradual easing in the cultural climate of Austria, and a partial move to reject the cultural legacy of the two fascisms, after the end of the Cold War and the relaxation of international tension in the late fifties and early sixties and the achievement of full employment from the mid-sixties onwards. For the first time in generations, this latter achievement gave all blue- and white-collar workers (particularly school leavers) the prospect of permanent, life-long employment. There was even a shortage of labour which had to be made good by the employment of foreign workers.

The widespread job security, together with relatively advanced industrial and social legislation and a high level of trade union membership in Austria brought about a certain cultural change among workers and salaried employees (particularly the younger ones), and an enhancement of their individual and collective self-awareness and self-esteem: as material conditions improved, there was once again the opportunity to plan one's own life in the longer term, which also involved starting to ask questions about social change and how standards of living could be further improved. The party which profited politically from this new climate, but which in fact had already helped to bring it about, was the Socialist Party of Austria (SPÖ); in 1970 it won the parliamentary elections and in 1971, for the first time in its history, achieved under the leadership of Bruno Kreisky an absolute majority of votes and of seats — a success maintained until the beginning of the eighties.

The demand for the democratization of all areas of life, which involved catching up on liberalization processes (already of long standing in the western democracies) and aiming at the continual improvement of material conditions for the mass of the population, at modernization of the economy and at comprehensive reforms of education, the legal system and the health service — all these things formed part of the programme, and the reality, of socialist policies under the Kreisky government.

It is no accident that during this period, for the first time, most of the younger intelligentsia (outside the universities) — writers, composers, artists, actors, etc. — publicly supported the Socialists. And even the universities began to reform and become more democratic in the wake of the worldwide student riots: the position of dominance long held by the professors was modified through the participation of students and assistants in all university decision-making bodies. Holding critical opinions at variance with received orthodoxy no longer automatically precluded an academic career.

The enormous increase in student numbers resulted in considerably more academic staff at the universities, and the sheer numbers involved made it difficult to exercise close political control or to vet politically all applicants for academic posts. Nevertheless the majority of university lecturers, and of school teachers, remained conservative in outlook; anti-democratic attitudes and behaviour patterns were maintained, social science surveys revealing that, in the view of many university academics, the votes cast by university professors at parliamentary elections should count for more than those cast by labourers.

Even so, in the historical and social science disciplines there were the beginnings of a more critical approach to Austria's past and present — an approach encouraged by the government. Research into contemporary history produced facts and documents which helped to destroy some cherished legends and beliefs: for example, the alleged Communist coup in 1950 (which in fact was a mass strike movement against the freezing of wages and rises in the cost of living; the Communists merely tried to latch on to it); or Dollfuss having destroyed democracy only in order to save Austria from the Nazis (whereas in fact he was prepared to smash the Social Democratic Party and the free trade unions in collaboration with the Nazis; the latter were just not informed in time); or the Christian Socialists and Social Democrats having been jointly to blame for the collapse of the First Republic (in fact the former had been constantly trying to get rid of the democratic constitution, while the only blame attaching to the latter is that they were too democratic and were not prepared to fight the threat of fascism by means of a revolution).

Then too there were repeated scholarly attempts to provide a reconstruction of the real cultural achievements of the past. Such achievements were seen not in the long-standing traditions of 'Austrian-ness' as such but in the early attempts at the democratization of society (from the Viennese Jacobins at the time of the

French Revolution, via the Revolution of 1848, to the labour movement); in the tradition of radical enlightenment; and in the work of critical intellectuals up to and including those trends within Viennese modernism which, not content merely to promote 'spiritual uplift' in those attending artistic events, also sought to improve the material condition of the masses.

The liberal cultural climate which prevailed during the period of Social Democratic governments under the Chancellorship of Bruno Kreisky from 1970 to 1983 was largely due to the degree of material security enjoyed by the mass of the Austrian people, though it is true that this liberal outlook was overshadowed from 1973 onwards by the possible effects of the world economic crisis and by the threat of mass unemployment. Under Kreisky, government policy laid great stress on fighting both actual and possible unemployment, and as long as this was the case, neo-conservative slogans and programmes stood little chance of success. But under Kreisky's successor Sinowatz the Social Democratic Party proved quite unable to come up with any new ideas for solving existing social problems, and instead sought refuge itself in conservative and reactionary philosophies, thereby losing votes particularly among the workers and salaried employees, as well as the support of the critically-minded intelligentsia.

The return of the past: anti-semitism, a 'Grand Coalition' and the making of a 'new Austria'

> It was the country where tyranny was rewarded and anyone unable to forget was punished.
>
> Marianne Fritz, 'Dessen Sprache du nicht verstehst'.

With the accession of Fred Sinowatz to government and party leadership, a systematic attempt was made to create the impression that the seventies with their full employment, democratization, liberal outlook and various reforms belonged like Bruno Kreisky himself to a sunny past, whereas now in the eighties grim reality with its numerous problems had at last caught up with us; and more than that: the blame for our present difficulties lay in fact with Kreisky — it was his legacy that now had to be overcome. The items to be found on the current political agenda were not how to maintain the living standards of the masses, not democracy and cultural development, not ongoing social reforms, but 'belt-tightening', reorganizing the national budget, less discussion and more discipline. This new cultural climate was not the result of a policy change introduced by right-wing parties but sprang rather from the perceptions of reality entertained by the new Social Democratic leadership; one of their dreams was of a return to the 'problem-free' fifties when there was still a 'Grand Coalition', when critical thought could be easily suppressed, when nobody criticized leading politicians for simplistic thinking or lack of reasoning ability (this being all of a piece with the meagreness of life in general), and when fairly modest expectations were still the general rule.

In March 1986, during the presidential election campaign when questions and accusations were being voiced about what until then had been a closely-guarded secret, namely certain periods in the life of the then candidate and subsequent Federal President Kurt Waldheim, the Austrian People's Party (ÖVP) launched an anti-Semitic witch hunt the like of which Austria had never seen since the days of Lueger and Hitler. Jews were described by the General Secretary of the ÖVP Michael Graff as 'disreputable types', Jewish organizations were accused of having the effrontery to interfere in (supposedly) internal Austrian affairs, and the Jewish 'world conspiracy' was re-discovered. Media controlled by 'Jewish circles' (clearly a wide range extending from the *Washington Post* to *Spiegel* and *Die Zeit*) were alleged to have unleashed an international campaign against the ÖVP candidate and indeed against the whole of Austria.

Overnight, anti-Semitism had once again become socially acceptable; it was no longer the preserve of obscure right-wing extremists but was part of the official campaign strategy of the major opposition party. The Socialist Party of Austria (SPÖ) under its leader Fred Sinowatz, who was still Federal Chancellor during the presidential campaign, wished to avoid open confrontation with the ÖVP on the subject of anti-Semitism and so ducked the issue, instead of showing moral strength and putting the forces of anti-Semitism to flight. At the time of the Austrian National Assembly elections in the autumn of 1986, leading functionaries of the ÖVP including Alois Mock, the party's candidate for the Chancellorship, repeated their stereotyped attacks on Jewish groups and organizations. There was no attempt to check the truth of their allegations; Jewish groups, it was asserted, were 'seeking their own gain by the constant repetition of old lies and slanders', and 'all decent and honourable Jewish organizations' were called upon to 'dissociate themselves from the dirty tricks' of the Jewish World Congress.

In the general election of November 1986, the SPÖ, led since the summer of that year by the acting Federal Chancellor Franz Vranitzky, remained the strongest party while the ÖVP suffered losses both in terms of votes and of seats. After the elections the two parties entered into a 'Grand Coalition', with the ÖVP talking about a 're-constructive partnership' and the SPÖ speaking of 'consolidation' and 'a thrust towards modernization'.... The message is clear: there is no room for criticism of the *status quo* in the interests of possible improvements, merely acceptance of whatever comes along lest the situation deteriorate still further.

Such a return to the uncritical culture of austerity will mean a systematic reduction in mass income, higher levels of unemployment and poverty, and hence the erosion of those conditions which are essential for free cultural development and for the self-respect of workers and salaried employees.

In the face of the current tendency to revert to the days of the past, the crucial question confronting critical scholarship and progressive education is this: whether and to what extent they can preserve and transmit the cultural and social achievements of the past.

23 The media

Hans Heinz Fabris

The history of the mass media in Austria is closely connected with the political, economic, social and cultural development of the country. However, external influences have also had a decisive influence.

It is not generally realized that Austria has played a notable part in the history of modern mass communications, particularly in the areas of photography and the cinema. Austrians were also among the pioneers in television. At the same time this whole important sector has been more closely involved with, indeed dominated by, foreign interests than is the case with most other areas of social activity.

Circumstances under the monarchy did not favour the development of the mass media. The history of the press is at the same time a history of continuous struggle against censorship and political repression, and the same applies to literature and to book publishing. Nevertheless freedom of the press did receive its first legal recognition in 1867, Article 13 of the State Basic Law declaring: 'Each person has the right to express his opinions freely within the limits of the law, by word of mouth, in writing, print or by pictoral representation.'

In the early years of the First Republic important steps were taken towards liberalizing the legislation which covered the media: as early as 1918 the Provisional National Assembly introduced a ban on censorship and this was followed by the Journalists and Press Act of 1922. In the thirties, however, with the establishment of the Austro-Fascist corporate state and the annexation of Austria by Nazi Germany, this trend was halted, first of all in a piecemeal fashion then, at a later stage, completely. The Austrian media came under the control of the Nazi propaganda machine so that, for example, the Viennese film production company *Wiener Film* was assigned a particular role: to produce films as a medium for entertainment and diversion.

After the Liberation in 1945 the media were rapidly restored through the influence of the Allies within their respective occupation zones, and their present state is largely the result of decisions taken in the immediate post-war period. Since the media and the content of modern culture are generally 'western' in outlook and substance, Western Germany and the USA are seen as the main sources of inspiration. Thus, the view that Austria has an independent mass media must be subject to qualification. The influence, however, of the political parties and the major interest groups is considerable — especially those of the 'economic and social partnership'. A 'social partnership of the media' has come into being, in the form of co-operation between publishers' associations, the Union of Journalists and the Austrian Radio and Television Service or ORF (*Österreichischer Rundfunk*). In recent years this has come to play a major role in the process of formulating new laws and allocating public funds, etc.

The individual sectors of the Austrian media will now be briefly introduced and described, and finally there will be a consideration of the importance of the mass media in contemporary Austrian life.

The daily newspapers

There are at the present time eighteen different editorial units responsible for a total of thirty-one titles. The party newspapers have lost much of their influence and only survive because of government press subsidies. A characteristic of the Austrian newspaper scene is the extremely high degree of concentration in terms of circulation and readership coverage: the three major daily papers reach between them two-thirds of the entire national readership. The *Neue Kronen-Zeitung*, a popular daily selling over one million copies, probably has the highest circulation in the world when compared with total population. Certainly within Europe such a level of concentration is surpassed only by Ireland. Regionally too there are strong tendencies towards concentration. The editorial line followed by most of the daily newspapers can be described as middle-class/conservative. By international standards the Austrians are only average newspaper readers.

Periodicals and magazines

The illustrated periodical market is dominated by West German titles though in recent years a few Austrian periodicals have succeeded in regaining a substantial share. The most important Austrian news magazine is *Profil* but in addition there are more than 2,000 specialist journals and periodicals, mostly serving limited readerships.

Table 23.1 *Readership coverage of the Austrian daily press*

Newspaper title (incl. regional editions)	Readers	Readership coverage in %
Independent newspapers		
1. *Neue Kronen-Zeitung* (Vienna, incl. *Länder* editions)	2,511,000	40.7
2. *Kurier* (Vienna, incl. *Länder* editions)	957,000	15.5
3. *Kleine Zeitung* (Graz and Klagenfurt)	635,000	10.3
4. *Oberösterreichische Nachrichten* (Linz)	283,000	4.6
5. *Tiroler Tageszeitung* (Innsbruck)	259,000	4.2
6. *Salzburger Nachrichten* (Salzburg)	178,000	2.9
7. *Die Presse* (Vienna)	160,000	2.6
8. *Vorarlberger Nachrichten* (Bregenz)	165,000	2.7
9. *Wiener Zeitung* (Vienna)	(no figures)	–
10. *Neue Vorarlberger Tageszeitung* (Bregenz)	97,000	1.6
Party newspapers		
SPÖ dailies		
11. *Neue Zeit* (Graz)	106,000	1.7
12. *Arbeiter-Zeitung* (Vienna, incl. *Länder* editions and *Salzburger Tagblatt*	136,000	2.2
13. *Kärntner Tageszeitung* (Klagenfurt)	138,000	2.2
14. *Oberösterreichisches Tagblatt* (Linz)	58,000	0.9
ÖVP dailies		
15. *Neue Volkszeitung* (Klagenfurt, incl. *Salzburger Volkszeitung* and *Neue Tiroler Zeitung*)	84,000*	1.4*
16. *Südost-Tagespost* (Graz)	116,000	1.9
17. *Neues Volksblatt* (Linz)	73,000	1.2
KPÖ daily		
18. *Volksstimme* (Vienna, incl. *Warhheit*, *Volkswille*, *Neue Zeit*)	(no figures)	–

*Figures do not include *Neue Tiroler Zeitung*.
Source: *Media-Analyse 1985*, a survey carried out in 1984 and published in part in March 1985 by the Verein Arbeitsgemeinschaft Media-Analysen, Vienna.

The Austrian Radio and Televison Service (ORF)

For many years it has been possible to receive numerous foreign programmes in Austria but the ORF still has a monopoly on programme production within the country itself. The ORF, a public corporation, broadcasts two television and three radio programmes. As part of its service *Österreich Regional*, programmes made by the nine *Land* studios are also broadcast, and these studios contribute to the third radio programme as well as to the television programme. Then there is 'Blue Danube Radio' with English-language broadcasts and international shortwave. The ORF also carries Teletext. The Broadcasting Act (*Rundfunkgesetz*) requires balance, objectivity and independence on the part of the ORF, lays down programme requirements, and specifies the composition of the various governing and controlling bodies. The supreme governing body, known as the *Kuratorium*, consists of representatives of the government, the political parties, the interest groups and viewers' and listeners' associations. The ORF is by far the largest media institution in the country, employing over 3,000 permanent staff and a large number of freelance personnel. Approximately 115 hours of radio programmes and 20 hours of television programmes are broadcast daily. Radio and television are the media with the greatest population coverage. Although there are discussions in Austria about whether the ORF's broadcasting monopoly is justified, the supporters of independent broadcasting have so far failed to make much headway. The managerial policy of the ORF seeks to counter such tendencies by extensive self-commercialization, particularly of television programmes, and by co-operation with the West German TV channel *Zweites Deutsches Fernsehen* (ZDF), for example in the use of the satellite programme *3 Sat*.

The use made of radio and television is now steady at a high level (though the average daily viewing time of around 110 minutes for adults and 75 minutes for children is somewhat below the average of many other countries), and the market is now almost totally saturated. Table 23.2 indicates changes in television viewing.

Cable broadcasting

In the mid-eighties about 8.5 per cent of the population in Austria was provided with cable television. This is the same percentage as in West Germany, far behind Belgium (81 per cent), the Netherlands (54 per cent) and Switzerland (47 per cent) but ahead of France (2.5 per cent). The Vienna network, however, is the third largest in the world after Amsterdam and San Diego. It is anticipated that by 1990 about 17 per cent of households will be cable-linked. Overall the process of installation is well behind schedule.

Film and cinema

As in other countries, cinema attendances in Austria have sharply declined, largely owing to the increasing ascendancy of television.

Table 23.2 Daily television viewing 1965–80 (in %)

Year	Persons with TV in household	'Viewed yesterday'
1965	33.2	30.1
1970	65.6	56.7
1973	82.5	66.6
1976	89.9	70.4
1978	92.1	74.3
1980	93.5	72.0

Source: Gehmacher, Ernst, *Trends der TV–Nutzung in Österreich*, Vienna 1980.

Figures dropped from over 120,000,000 in the fifties to just under 17,000,000 thirty years later, and many cinemas, particularly in rural areas, have been forced to close. Cinema audiences have become ever younger. All this has had a lasting effect upon Austrian film production: during the period 1946–69 about twenty cinema films were made each year whereas during the seventies annual productions numbered only between three and nine. Only in relatively recent years has there been any government film subsidy so that now one hears of the 'New Austrian Cinema', examples of which are winning ever greater acclaim at film festivals both at home and abroad. In the past Austria's success tended to be in areas such as the *avant-garde* film.

Of the films shown in Austrian cinemas, 80 per cent come from no more than four countries: top of the list is the USA, followed by Italy, West Germany and France. This arises largely from the distribution policy of the large international film-making companies.

Books and publishing

The dependence of the Austrian book market upon (West) Germany goes back to the nineteenth century. In the trade therefore the market is regarded as covering the whole German-speaking area (*gesamtdeutschsprachiger Markt*) which means, for example, that more than one out of every two books offered for sale in Austria is from a West German publishing house.

In Austria approximately 8,000 new titles come on to the market each year of which only about 3,500 appear in the shops — the rest being dissertations, etc. The amount of time available for book reading is much reduced and literary works in the traditional sense tend to be less popular than non-fiction books. Austrians tend to be only average book readers despite the quite sizeable subsidies provided by the government and the local authorities for libraries and literature. Reading behaviour varies mainly according to education, social background and place of residence. The publishing houses find the unfavourable economic situation exacerbated by the fact that a considerable number of books are sold through a book club known as the *Buchgemeinschaft Donauland* in which Bertelsmann, the international media giant, has a majority holding, and by cut-price suppliers, in supermarkets, etc. Very few authors, therefore, can live on their income from literary activities alone.

One remarkable area in which Austria is an example to many other countries is the government 'schoolbooks' scheme' (*Schulbuchaktion*) — a product of the period of educational reforms in the seventies — whereby pupils in approximately 7,000 schools are provided with 13,000,000 free schoolbooks each year. About 100 publishing houses are involved in the scheme.

Records and music cassettes

For two decades the music industry was dominated by a cartel of recording companies made up largely of foreign enterprises such as Amadeo, CBS, EMI, Polydor, etc., and even after the expiry of the cartel's contract the market situation has not greatly changed. In terms of turnover, Austria is about sixteenth in the recorded music market within the western world. Only in recent years have a number of small independent producers been able to get established alongside the large companies, and *Austro-Pop*, represented by numerous prominent performers, has made great strides to become an export success. The music scene in Austria, the traditional home of classical music, has been re-invigorated particularly in the area of youth culture.

The new media

In addition to cable broadcasting and Teletext (an additional service provided by the ORF), the new media include visual display text (VD text), satellite broadcasting, video and the video disc as well as a large range of equipment in the area of office and business communications. Surveys have shown that by the end of the eighties one in every two workplaces in Austria will be equipped with a VD unit. The use of micro-electronics and the new information and communication technologies are likely to have a considerable impact in terms of rationalization, although developments in Austria have hitherto lagged behind those in many other countries, and are slower than expected (or desired) by the industry. This may, on the one hand, be due to the fact that because of the economic situation the demand potential from private households is too low and that there is widespread scepticism about the new technology among large sections of the population. On the other hand it may arise from the agreement arrived at by the social partnership to adopt a fairly cautious approach within companies (an example being the collective 'new technology' agreement between unions and publishers regarding the introduction of new newspaper and printing technologies), or from the deficiencies of equipment and systems which seem to be far behind the degree of reliability claimed for them by the manufacturers.

The postal service has so far had little success with its VD text service known as BTX (*Bildschirmtext-Service*). On the other hand there has been a (largely unexpected) boom in sales of video recorders. At the present time, however, it looks as if the new media will prevail not so much in the private and recreational sphere as in the world of work, particularly in the office and administration sector. Even so, as far as overall economic production and the proportion of total employment are concerned, Austria like other countries is seeing the early stages of what has been called 'the information society'.

The Austrian Press Agency (APA)

It is of major importance for any national media system today that the nation concerned should have its own news agency which is also able to make its voice heard in the international news market, dominated as it is by a very few worldwide agencies. The *Austria Presse-Agentur* (APA) is a national news agency inasmuch as its main function is to gather news from Austria itself. Special correspondents are sent to cover events abroad which are of special interest to Austria, though for many years the vast majority of all foreign reports (about 94 per cent) have come from no more than four agencies: AFP, AP, DPA and Reuters. The East European agencies and those of the Third World, with their news pool, have certainly been making rather more of an impact in recent years though so far this has scarcely been reflected in the news statistics.

The APA, a co-operative owned by Austrian media companies, has considerably expanded its services during the past few years. It plays a major role as a news trading centre between East and West, the same being true generally of Vienna and Austria as a whole because of the large number of foreign correspondents who are based there. The International Press Centre (IPZ) in Vienna similarly houses numerous national and international news agencies as well as providing offices for correspondents of the foreign media.

Media and communications policy

During the immediate post-1945 period all major decisions relating to the media were taken by the Allies. However, in the years that followed, media legislation was largely a matter for government, the political parties and the interest groups representing employers and staff in the various media. Unlike many other countries, Austria has no single Ministry of Information with overall governmental responsibility for the media, but rather this responsibility is divided between many ministries. The government nevertheless has a widespread involvement in the media: in the broadcasting sector as the owner of *Wien-Film* (though this closed down its production workshop in 1986); in the area of the press as the owner of the *Wiener Zeitung* and the State Printing Office; and particularly through its control of Posts and Telecommunications which plays a leading role in the introduction of new media technologies. The political parties, which during the seventies were formulating media policy, have in recent years been increasingly replaced by the 'social partners' whose word carries considerable weight in the allocation of public funds and the drawing up of legislation. Thus for example the Austrian Trade Union Federation produced a detailed media policy, one of its results being that industrial disputes (such as printers' strikes) which in other countries were the order of the day, were practically unknown in Austria. On the other hand the fact that the social partners have taken over this whole area in the life of society means that critical public discussion is faced with immense difficulties. In recent years media and communications policy has remained by and large the province of a few experts and interested parties and apart from ongoing arguments about the ORF there has been scarcely any broader public discussion of related issues. The same applies not only to national affairs but also to issues in the area of international media policy such as the discussions concerning a new world-wide information system.

The media in the daily life of the Austrian people

It is clear from examining the media consumption of the Austrian people that making use of the various means of communication — listening to the radio, watching television and using the new media — accounts in total for a very considerable portion of people's leisure activities. (See Appendix G1.) In particular watching television is the major pursuit of socially under-privileged classes while it is mainly children and older people whose media consumption has increased as a wider range of options has become available.

This situation has far-reaching effects: it creates a new set of conditions within which young people grow up and become socialized; it raises the issue of the extent to which the media provide orientation or merely escapism, also to what extent they inform or manipulate; and it may even affect the nation's political culture. The trend towards a 'telecracy' was already very clear under the 'journalist Chancellor' Bruno Kreisky, and these tendencies, collectively referred to as 'show-business politics' (*Politik als Showgeschäft*), have meanwhile become even stronger.

Summary

The overall power and decision-making structures which obtain in Austrian society are reflected in the realm of the media. So, speaking in very broad terms, one may say that influence upon the country's media system is shared more or less equally between the state, private enterprise and foreign interests.

Because of Austria's long history as an authoritarian state, a liberal press was relatively late in developing while critical journalism has come into being only in very recent years. This process of democratic 'normalization' — particularly by western European standards — has historically been subject to repeated interruptions.

At the present time the major problems faced by the Austrian media spring from a domestic market which, being relatively small, is heavily dependent on other countries and particularly on the technological developments of an increasingly international media world, dominated by the USA, Japan and western Europe. However, as Austria has grown economically stronger and acquired a greater national and cultural identity, so the Austrian media as a whole have been invigorated. Whether this trend will continue almost certainly depends on overall political and economic developments and also on the state of international relations.

24 The churches and politics

Gerhard Steger

Statistics of Austria's confessional structure

According to the 1981 census, no less than 84 per cent of Austria's 7.5 million population belong to the Roman Catholic Church, an indication in itself of this church's dominance in the country. Admittedly the number of Catholics has slightly decreased since 1971 (when the figure was over 87 per cent), but the same applies also to those Christian denominations which are numerically strongest after the Roman Catholic Church. Among the Protestants, the proportion of Lutherans (i.e. those subscribing to the Augsburg Confession) fell from 5.7 to 5.4 per cent between 1971 and 1981, and that of Calvinists (i.e. those subscribing to the Helvetic Confession) from 0.3 to 0.2 per cent. The Old Catholics (see below) declined from 0.4 to 0.3 per cent. Adherents of the Jewish faith remain constant at 0.1 per cent, while followers of Islam increased from 0.3 per cent to 1.0 per cent mainly as a result of the influx of Turkish immigrant workers.

Those with no religious affiliation have increased by 41 per cent since 1971 and now account for 6 per cent of the population, i.e. after the Roman Catholic Church these form the largest group. The lowest proportions of Catholics are found in the provinces of Vienna (71.5 per cent), Carinthia (83 per cent) and Burgenland (84.4 per cent), the latter two having the largest proportions of Protestants (11 and 14 per cent respectively). Vienna has the highest proportion of those with no religious affiliation (13.5 per cent).

The Roman Catholic Church

From the Counter-Reformation onwards a close alliance existed between the House of Habsburg and the Roman Catholic Church. After the collapse of the Austro-Hungarian Empire in 1918, the so-called 'marriage of throne and altar' was replaced by a far-reaching, strongly anti-socialist collaboration between the Christian-Social Party and the Catholic Church — the movement known as Political Catholicism.

The Christian-Social Party was able to rely on the large number of inter-connected Catholic clubs and societies as its auxiliary organizations, as well as upon the close network of Catholic presbyteries most of which were in the service of Christian-Social Party propaganda. The Church for its part could be certain of the party's support in seeking to maintain a strong Catholic influence upon legislation in the areas of education, marriage and abortion as well as in such matters as state funding for the Church.

In the First Republic political Catholicism was personified in the figure of Ignaz Seipel, a prelate who was also a Christian-Social Party leader and Federal Chancellor, and whose strongly anti-socialist policies greatly exacerbated political conflict within Austria. The Austrian bishops repeatedly issued pastoral letters at election times in support of the Christian-Social Party; the letter of 1925 was the most scathing of all, putting social democracy on a par with the devil! This attitude on the part of the Church provoked a growing anti-clericalism among Austrian Social Democrats, while within the labour movement there was an exodus from the Catholic Church. A social democratic organization known as the Alliance of Religious Socialists, together with a handful of moderate clergy, failed to end the confrontation between the Church and the labour movement.

In 1933 the Federal Chancellor Engelbert Dollfuss introduced his authoritarian style of government and declared his intention to implement the lessons of the social encyclical *Quadragesimo anno*, issued by Pope Pius XI in 1931. Not only did the Roman Catholic hierarchy fail to protest at this attempt by Dollfuss to legitimize his anti-democratic policies by the use of ecclesiastical documents but also, after the bloody suppression of the Austrian labour movement in February 1934, it explicitly came out in support of Dollfuss.

With the end of the period of Nazi barbarism which had made Christians, Socialists and Communists alike the objects of persecution, the Catholic Church in Austria adopted a new policy. It withdrew from party politics and the liberal-minded Archbishop of Vienna, Cardinal Franz König, made a great contribution to dialogue with the labour movement as well as rendering sterling service to the 'science and religion' debate, the Ecumenical Movement, and so forth.

Political pluralism within the Catholic Church of Austria began to manifest itself particularly after the Second Vatican Council when there developed something which had previously been an impossibility: a school of thought within certain church organizations which was markedly open in its attitude towards democratic socialism. This body of opinion has some weighty exponents, particularly in the Catholic Young Workers' Movement (*Katholische Arbeiterjugend*), the Catholic Social Academy in Vienna and the industrial chaplaincy movement. It has found itself in conflict with conservative circles within the Church, including some bishops, but so far has managed to survive. The positions common to the movement may be stated as follows: advocacy of a thorough-going redistribution of wealth in order to favour the socially deprived, support for freedom movements in the Third World, opposition to the arms race, and commitment to the environmental protection debate. These church groups frequently subject the Austrian labour movement (particularly the Trade Union Federation) and the social democratic movement to criticism from a left-wing position — a phenomenon which is entirely new in Austria.

On the other hand, conservative trends have also been gaining ground within the Roman Catholic Church of Austria, as in the Church throughout the world. This is seen, for example, in the areas of the hierarchy, the Church's use of the media and the still extensive network of Catholic clubs and societies. These trends also find expression in party politics: in recent years some members of parliament belonging to the Austrian People's Party (ÖVP), which still has more supporters among practising Catholics than any other party, have attempted to restore closer links between the Church and the ÖVP.

The chances of success for a new right-wing Political Catholicism, however, are extremely remote. The Austrian people have shown in opinion polls that they wish that the Church to be above party politics; moreover they are exposed to secularizing tendencies which do not favour right-wing Catholicism, and lastly, despite the neo-Conservative trends which are present, political pluralism within the Church is so far advanced as to make a new right-wing Catholicism impossible to realize without involving the Church in some extremely bitter conflicts.

While the Catholic Church has a traditionally good relationship with the ÖVP and has largely normalized its relations with the Austrian Social Democrats, its links with the third parliamentary party, the national-liberal Freedom Party of Austria (FPÖ) are extremely tenuous; this party's supporters, as is shown by the opinion polls, are less sympathetic to the church than are the Social Democrats.

Overall, the Roman Catholic Church in Austria still has a wide range of means at its disposal for exercising social and political influence. Through its services, its organizations, its numerous publications (some with a very high circulation), its radio and television broadcasting times, through religious instruction in the schools, etc., it has at its command many instruments for shaping public opinion. These, however, by no means guarantee that the Church's viewpoint will prevail. This was very apparent during the 1970s when despite tremendous effort the Church failed to prevent reform of abortion legislation in Austria: interruption of pregnancy during the first three months was made no longer a punishable offence.

The Austrian state grants financial assistance to the churches, the amount being dependent on the size of the membership. Hence the Catholic Church receives by far the largest amount of money whether in the form of an annual lump sum of 128 million schillings, state funds to meet all the staffing costs of Catholic private schools or to ensure the upkeep of church buildings which are classified as being historical monuments. The legal basis for the considerable financial benefits paid by the state to the Catholic Church is the Concordat of 1933 between Austria and the Vatican, amended by the supplementary treaties of 1960 and 1962. The fact that the Austrian Social Democrats gave their approval to these legal provisions under the Second Republic, and indeed actually increased the state's financial support when they alone were in power, shows once again the process of re-orientation towards finding a political consensus which so markedly differentiates the Second Republic from the First.

Protestant and Old Catholic Churches

Austrian Protestants were obliged to operate in secret from the time of the Counter-Reformation until toleration was granted in 1791, after which they were gradually able to achieve equality of rights with the Roman Catholic Church.

At the turn of the twentieth century a movement demanding severance of Austria's close links with Rome (*die 'Los von Rom' — Bewegung*) caused many to leave the Roman Catholic Church for political (mainly nationalistic) reasons and to join the 'Old Protestants', a movement dating from the early days of toleration. In 1921 the transference of Burgenland from Hungary to Austria significantly increased the number of Austrian Protestants and later, during the Dollfuss regime, when membership of a church was frequently a requirement for getting a job, many people with no religious affiliation joined up with the Protestants.

During the First Republic, Austrian Protestants were strongly nationalistic and often markedly anti-socialist in outlook. The strong religious socialism found, for example, in Germany and Switzerland had no counterpart among Austrian Protestants, one probable reason being found in the sociological composition of the Protestant population: the majority were farmers or members of the middle classes, industrial workers being somewhat sparsely represented. Under the

Second Republic there developed within the Protestant churches, as in the Roman Catholic Church, a broad political spectrum.

The Old Catholic Church, which came into being in protest at the promulgation of the dogma of Papal infallibility by the First Vatican Council in 1870, was able to establish itself in Austria only after prolonged difficulties with the authorities. Even in the First Republic the political orientation of the Old Catholic Church was diverse: one wing stood for pan-German nationalism while another — the stronger of the two — had a social democratic outlook. Like the Protestants, the Old Catholics also received a considerable increase in membership in 1934, with the influx of many who had previously had no religious affiliation. Political pluralism has remained a feature of the Old Catholic Church under the Second Republic.

25 National minorities in Austria

Wilhelm Filla

Austria is generally regarded, not least by its own population, as a German-speaking and therefore a monolingual country. What is all too often overlooked, both at home and abroad, is the multilingualism arising from the fact that Austria also has various national minorities living within its borders: Croatians, Slovenes, Czechs, Slovaks and Hungarians. The Roma and Sinti groups, found mainly in Burgenland and numbering an estimated 4,000 individuals, are a special case scarcely comparable to the other national minorities and are therefore generally left out of account even in the relevant literature.

The Slovenes live for the most part in the southern area of Carinthia; the Croatians and Hungarians are mostly in Burgenland though a considerable number of Croatians are also to be found in Vienna where they formed their own *Verein* or association even before the Second World War. The capital is similarly the home of the Czechs and Slovaks, an immigrant minority most of whose ancestors and old people came to the metropolis during the period of the Austro-Hungarian empire to work as ordinary craftsmen, factory hands and domestic servants. In Lower Austria the Croatians and Slovaks have become almost totally assimilated, the same being true of the Slovenes in Styria.

The Croatians, Slovenes, Czechs, Slovaks and Hungarians are known as the 'Austrian ethnic groups' (*Österreichische Volksgruppen*). In their own eyes, and also in the eyes of the population at large, they are to be distinguished from those men and women of Austrian origin whose mother tongue was not German and who came into the country as immigrant workers after 1945, eventually taking Austrian nationality. This distinction is also recognized in the specialist literature and in the eyes of the law.

The one-time *Gastarbeiter*, foreign workers who came (and still come) to Austria largely from the southern parts of Yugoslavia and from Turkey, will probably give rise to further minorities which, in view of their (currently) low social status, will scarcely be able to merge with the traditional minorities — particularly the Croatians

— within the foreseeable future. Owing to lack of space, the present article leaves the *Gastarbeiter* out of account and similarly the various refugee groups which have come to Austria during recent decades.

The Croatians — mainly peasants — settled in present-day Burgenland and Lower Austria in several waves of immigration during the sixteenth century. Traders and craftsmen, who might have formed the nucleus of a bourgeoisie, hardly emigrated at all during that period and right up to the present day such a bourgeoisie has been almost entirely absent. Hungarians came to present-day Burgenland as frontier guards and 'legionnaires' of the Hungarian ruling princes. After the Turkish wars Hungarians lived a segregated existence in leasehold settlements or *Meierhofsiedlungen*.

The Slovenes in Carinthia are descendants of the Alpine Slavs who populated large areas of present-day Austria from the early seventh century AD onwards and who until the middle of the eighth century constituted an independent Karantanian princedom.

Today the Burgenland Croatians live in several linguistic enclaves. They are rather more likely than the German-speaking *Burgenländer* to work on the land (usually as smallholders), though the proportion of industrial workers is growing. Many Croatians commute to work and thus show a strong tendency towards assimilation within working life. There is a small group of Burgenland-Croatian intellectuals which is on the increase.

The social structure of the small Hungarian minority is more diverse than that of the Croatians. A few belong to the aristocracy and its successors. A comparatively large number are employed in the services sector. A high proportion are pensioners. Whereas the Croatians are Catholic, the Hungarians are divided between three confessional groups: Catholic, Calvinist and Lutheran (subscribing to the Augsburg Confession).

The Slovenes in southern Carinthia live nowadays in far less self-contained groups than do the Croatians in Burgenland. They too are predominantly Catholic, and a higher proportion of them work in agriculture than do the German-speaking population. A numerically increasing stratum of Slovene intellectuals is gaining in significance. To a far greater extent than the minorities in Burgenland, the Slovenes own their own businesses. The minorities in Austria show an imbalance of social structure compared with the population at large: the almost total absence of a bourgeoisie and also of a working class which can be said to be minority conscious.

The most striking trend among all the national minorities in Austria is their numerical decline since the beginning of the Second Republic in 1945. This raises the major problem with which they are confronted: that of assimilation. This again is closely linked with

Table 25.1 Numerical trends of national minorities in Austria

	Croatians	Slovenes	Czechs (+ Slovaks)	Hungarians
1910 census	44,243	74,210	119,447	26,570
1951 census	34,427	42,095	4,118	5,566
1971 census	28,084	23,579	7,967	14,815
	(24,332)[1]	(20,972)[2]	(6,528)[3]	(5,447)[1]
1981 census	22,371	18,371	5,168	12,415
	(18,567)[1]	(16,175)[2]	(4,067)[3]	(c.4,000)[1]

Notes: 1 = Burgenland only; 2 = Carinthia only; 3 = Vienna only

the belated but ongoing modernization of those largely peripheral areas (other than the large cities) in which the minorities tend to settle. The fact that their numerical decline is nothing less than dramatic is demonstrated by Table 25.1. It should be noted that no account is taken here of the particular problems connected with the recording of minorities in the Austrian national censuses. Some responsible estimates give higher figures than those in Table 25.1

During the decade 1971–81 the Carinthian Slovenes declined in number by 23 per cent, the Burgenland Croatians by 24 per cent, the Burgenland Hungarians by 27 per cent, and the Vienna Czechs (and Slovaks) by as much as 38 per cent. The minorities are distinguished not only by language and numerical size but also by legal provisions guaranteeing their existence and development. The State Treaty of 1955 'concerning the restoration of an independent and democratic Austria' specifies, in its much-quoted Article 7, the 'rights of the Slovene and Croatian minorities', but mentions as the home of these minorities only Burgenland, Carinthia and Styria though there are scarcely any Slovenes or Croatians still living in Styria today. On the other hand it fails to mention the Croatians in Vienna, and also the Hungarians, Czechs and Slovaks. The Roma and Sinti, many of whom were killed by the National Socialists and who received no reparation payments after the war, are not recognized as minorities in any legal sense.

Article 7 is of considerable political significance as far as Austrian minority groups are concerned in that the rights which it enumerates have for decades been a matter of dispute between the minorities and sections of the German-speaking majority together with the latter's political representatives. Burgenland is a special case in that here the dispute has been within the ranks of the Croatian minority itself.

The following are the detailed provisions of Article 7:

— the right of minorities to have their own organizations and meetings, and to have newspapers, etc. in their own language;
— their right to elementary education in their own language, and also to a proportionate number of their own secondary schools;
— in administrative and judicial districts with a mixed-language population, the admission of Croatian and Slovenian as an official language, and the provision of bilingual signs to indicate place-names, etc.

The Article forbids any organization to act with a view to depriving the Croatian and Slovenian population of their distinctive character or rights as a minority. For such rights to be implemented or claimed, Article 7 does not require minorities to be of any minimum size within their respective settlement areas.

Whether the minority rights enshrined in Article 7 have been implemented as intended by the State Treaty is a matter of dispute. The official position, particularly in Burgenland and Carinthia, is that the Treaty has been largely fulfilled though there may possibly be some differences of interpretation, whereby the two large minorities, through their representatives, draw attention to a series of unsolved problems and unsatisfied demands.

This fundamental discontent, which has lasted now for decades, was not substantially relieved by the Ethnic Groups Act (*Volksgruppengesetz*) of 1976. One of the contentious issues — but by no means the only one — was the Act's stipulation that the provision of bilingual place-name signs was dependent upon one quarter of the population in a given area belonging to a minority group. Furthermore, the requirements relating to ethnic group development were not formulated in such a way as to make them compulsory. Hence the minorities were extremely hesitant to send representatives to the Ethnic Groups Advisory Councils which, as required by the Act, were set up in the Federal Chancellery, and in fact the Slovenes sent no representatives at all.

In view of what the national minorities regard as an unsatisfactory situation where, judging by the action taken so far, it seems impossible to ensure the ethnic groups' continuance and development, a conference held on 19 and 20 April 1985 agreed upon an 'Ethnic Groups' Charter' which was signed by the representatives of the major organizations concerned and addressed to the federal government and the relevant provincial governments. The signatories of the Charter were the Council of Carinthian Slovenes, the Central

Association of Slovene Organizations in Carinthia, the Burgenland-Croatian Cultural Association in Vienna, the Burgenland-Hungarian Cultural Association and the Minority Council for the Czech and Slovakian Ethnic Group in Austria. In addition to these, there are various other organizations and institutions which declare their solidarity with the minorities and support their cause.

From a sociological standpoint there is a considerable difference between the situations of the two large minorities, i.e. the Slovenes in Carinthia and the Croatians in Burgenland. Whereas in Carinthia there is latent conflict, occasionally flaring up, between the Slovene minority and the large majority population whose attitude to the minority and its development varies from indifference to hostility, in Burgenland the line of conflict lies mainly within the Croatian group itself — between those who are willing to assimilate and those who wish to see the ethnic group maintained and strengthened. This latter conflict, furthermore, has party-political overtones. There is hardly any conflict involving the small minorities, nor do these attract much public attention.

The development of the minorities will depend in future not only upon government policy; a crucial factor will be the extent to which they succeed in bringing their own influence to bear upon the social processes of modernization and change in the areas where they live, so shaping such processes in their own interests.

26 Research and research policy

Heinz Fischer

The importance of research and development was greatly underestimated in Austria until the late 1960s. Industry depended largely on imitative procedures while academics and technologists moved away to work for foreign companies and foreign research establishments. In 1970, expenditure purely on R and D amounted to only 0.6 per cent of Gross Domestic Product, far below the European average.

Clear signs of a change of thinking came with the decision to introduce the Research Promotion Act (*Forschungsförderungsgesetz*) in 1967 and the establishment of a Federal Ministry of Science and Research in 1970. Since that time government spending on R and D, and also the amount spent on it by industry, have considerably increased and during the decade 1970–81, within the OECD area, Austria was one of the nations that led the field with respect to rates of increase in R and D expenditure. The proportion of such expenditure in relation to GDP has more than doubled and currently stands at about 1.3 per cent, placing Austria in a median position among the OECD nations, level with, say, Norway, Finland, Denmark, Italy or Canada. It should be pointed out that in Austria research for military purposes is practically non-existent. This can be seen by comparing Austrian government expenditure with that of various EEC states: in terms of government expenditure on civil research, calculated in European common currency units of account per head of population, Austria in 1984 was ahead of Belgium, Italy and the UK.

The funding of research and experimental development in Austria has for years been shared more or less equally between government and industry. Most (about 88 per cent) of federal expenditure on research and its promotion is administered by the Ministry of Science and Research; this includes research-promotion funds earmarked for construction work in connection with higher education and for university hospitals. If socio-economic criteria are applied, federal expenditure on research and its promotion can be seen to be allocated as follows: almost 29 per cent is devoted to the furtherance and general dissemination of knowledge, a similar percentage to the promotion of the nation's health (particularly through research in the university hospitals), about 16 per cent to industry-related research, and 7 per cent to the promotion of social and socio-economic development.

The Federal Ministry of Science and Research not only administers most of the federal expenditure on research, it is also responsible for research co-ordination. It has responsibility for matters connected with academic teaching and research, in particular therefore for the universities, the Austrian Academy of Sciences and the other scientific and research establishments, for matters connected with museums and historic monuments, and also for scientific foundations and funds.

Two Acts — the Research Promotion Act of 1967 (amended in 1982) and the Research Organization Act (*Forschungsorganisationsgesetz*) of 1981 — form the legal basis for all government-sponsored research activity. The Research Organization Act contains guiding principles and objectives for government promotion of science and research, creates a system of consultation on scientific matters, also a comprehensive system for disseminating research information, and regulates not only government research promotion and government research contracts, but also the research undertaken at universities and other institutions of higher education. The Research Promotion Act is the legal basis of the two research promotion funds which, since being set up in 1967, have proved to be valuable instruments for promoting research on a self-help basis: the Fund for the Promotion of Scientific Research is mainly concerned with furthering pure research at universities, while the Research Promotion Fund for Trade and Industry provides companies with loans and grants for applied research projects and experimental developments. Taking the average over several years, this covers about 5–6 per cent of all R and D costs in trade and industry.

Austria has 12 universities covering various subject areas which includes two technological universities plus one university each for the following disciplines: Economics, Agriculture, Veterinary Medicine, Mining and Educational Sciences. There are also two institutes specializing in the Fine Arts.

The universities form the backbone, so to speak, of Austrian research. The unity of teaching and research is considered to be a fundamental organizational principle of Austrian universities. Approximately two-fifths of the universities' total budget is for promoting research and of this just under half is for pure research. The plan for university staffing levels (1986) envisaged more than 11,000 posts of scientific and non-scientific personnel in research institutes; this gives a full-time equivalent of about 4,650 people employed in R and D. Just over a quarter of these are engaged in the natural sciences, a further quarter in human medicine, just over 14 per cent in the humanities and technical sciences respectively, 12 per cent in the social sciences and the remainder in agriculture, forestry and veterinary medicine.

Two important institutions in the area of non-university scientific research are the Academy of Sciences and the *Ludwig Boltzmann-Gesellschaft*. The latter is an organization which provides support to research institutes (currently 70 in number) operating between university and non-university research. It functions mainly in areas relevant to social policy, acting as a link and a service agency between scientific research and its practical application.

In the area of applied research the Austrian Research Centre Seibersdorf acts as an intermediary between pure university research and pure industrial application and development. Its activities, which aim to foster industrial co-operation, cover the areas of energy and safety, materials research, isotope and radiation technology, measurement and information technology, environmental protection, health and nutrition, and not least industrial and company consultancy.

Other institutions operating in the area of applied research are: the Federal Experimental and Research Institute Arsenal which is the largest non-university technical research establishment in the country; the Research Society Joanneum in Styria, which consists of 26 research units working in separate fields, the main emphases being space research, information technology, sensor and measurement technology, and environmental research; finally there is the Association of Co-operative Research Institutes of Austrian Trade and Industry which comprises no less than 54 independent units, all regularly engaged in R and D projects for clients in trade and industry. Research policy has the task, on the one hand, of ensuring that research resources are available — by means of grass-roots subsidies to research establishments, the issuing of research contracts and the granting of research funds, as well as indirectly through tax concessions — and, on the other hand, of ensuring the best possible overall conditions for research and development and for fostering efficient co-operation between state and industry. This co-operation begins already in the process of deciding where the emphases and priorities in research ought to lie — a process which forms part of the mandatory system of consultation. In the relevant committees, representatives of the state, the scientific world and industry have equal status and are therefore able to co-operate fully in arriving at decisions relating to research and scientific policy. This in turn ensures that the steps which need to be taken receive the support of all interested parties.

Similarly, the research strategy document known as the Austrian Research Guidelines 80, which spells out the tasks and objectives to be faced by research policy in the 1980s, was drawn up as a result of co-operation between representatives of the social interest groups, the research establishments and the government. The document delineates what may be called the infrastructure of science and research and the steps needed to improve it, particular importance being attached to co-ordination, consultation and assessment; research planning; information and documentation; training and further education; and not least the transfer of knowledge from the universities to industry. A considerable section is devoted to central areas of research promotion whereby the selection from the various promising areas of research is made on the basis of the scope and limitations of Austrian research potential, and also the likelihood of success. The areas stressed are multi-disciplinary in character; they are of practical application, and divide into two major groups: those relating to man and society, and those relevant to industry and technology. The first group contains in particular: the environment, transport and environmental planning, medicine and the biological sciences, social development, cultural development, peace and conflict, education, and science and technology for the Third World. The second group, in addition to the whole area of innovation in industrial technology, covers in particular micro-electronics and information technology, materials and raw materials, energy, biotechnology and genetic engineering, space and agricultural, forestry and water management.

Integral parts of the document are those dealing with ways of promoting direct and indirect funding of R and D and also of encouraging international co-operation, which especially for a small country like Austria is of crucial importance in view of the ever-increasing globalization of science and technology.

In accordance with the programmatic guidelines of this strategy document, particular research and technology programmes have been developed in recent years. Research funds made available by the Federal Ministry of Science and Research have been used to strengthen the scientific infrastructure of the universities in particular with a view to carrying out given research projects, while funds provided by the Ministry of Public Services and Transport are being used to promote the economic application of such university-based research by turning it into marketable products or processes. The pilot programme in micro-electronics and information technology was initiated at the beginning of 1985 and shortly afterwards a similarly structured programme in biotechnology and genetic engineering was developed; preparations were also made for a programme concentrating on the technology of new materials with special reference to metallurgy, ceramics, plastics, laminates, and the production of high-performance magnetic materials. Two further programmes in the areas of software and environmental technology are currently at the planning stage.

The strongly increasing trend towards the internationalization of science and research, and also of economic development, brings great challenges to small nations in particular. For years therefore, Austria has sought to participate more and more in international research co-operation and to promote the international aspect of Austrian science. Especially for a small country like Austria, and for her scientists, international contacts and co-operation are necessary, indeed indispensable. It is for this reason that Austria, an associate member since 1981 of the European Space Organization, has sought full membership which became effective from January 1987. A great advantage of this is that it permits participation in all decision making and gives unrestricted access to the two major programmes to which the organization is committed. In the same way, Austria has been involved from the outset in the European technology initiative EUREKA which aims at boosting the productivity and competitiveness of European industries on the world market by means of increased co-operation between companies and research institutes in the areas of high technology. Particularly for Austria and the non-EEC states, EUREKA provides a highly attractive opportunity for co-operation.

Austria is currently involved in 12 projects under the auspices of the EEC Committee on Science and Technology (COST) which encourages co-operation in scientific and technological research. However, international co-operation occurs not only in the area of high technology but also in other areas. So, for example, Austria participates in UNESCO's large-scale programmes 'Man and Biosphere', in the 'International Geological Correlation Programme' and in the 'International Hydrological Programme'. Co-operation in international organizations is supplemented by bilateral agreements with various countries while Austria is the home of international research establishments such as the Institute for Applied Systems Analysis and the European Centre for Training and Research in Social Welfare.

The foreign scholarship scheme created in 1984 and known as the *Erwin-Schrödinger-Auslandsstipendienaktion* has the object of enabling young, eminently qualified Austrian researchers to spend 1–2 years working at those research centres which are considered the best in the world for their particular research purposes. The research carried out during this period is intended to relate to scientific sub-disciplines or methods which are insufficiently covered at Austrian research centres, and to enable the know-how so acquired to be put to use at home. Because demand for these scholarships has been so great, the funds to provide them were doubled in 1986.

Research policy has the further task of laying the foundations for decision making as to the future shape of technology by submitting it to comprehensive and timely appraisal in order to take account of such aspects of safety, social acceptability, environmental protection, and health. A newly created Advisory Council for the Evaluation of Technology (*Beirat für Technologiebewertung*) coordinates such appraisal and evaluation within Austria; its task is to provide both the political decision-makers and the public at large with information well in advance regarding trends and developments in technology, and to indicate their possible consequences. As a scientific institution it is able to make use of the Institute for Socio-Economic Development Research belonging to the Austrian Academy of Sciences.

A successful research policy enabling efficient research and development to be carried out will still be the essential prerequisite for a successful technology policy even in the 1990s. Co-operation between science and industry, with a view to the efficient transfer of knowledge and technology, will need to be greatly strengthened. International co-operation must be further developed, the foundations for which need to be laid early, i.e. in the courses offered by universities. Not least, the importance of a policy on technology will need to be so firmly implanted in the public mind that it comes to be widely accepted in Austria as a matter of national concern. This will happen only if there is a further quantitative rise in research expenditure. The aim is to increase the total expenditure on research and development to 1.5 per cent of Gross Domestic Product by 1990, and to 2 per cent by the year 2000. This is an objective which it will not be easy to attain and which will require considerable effort from both state and industry, but it is seen as the only possible way to maintain and secure the nation's standard of living.

PART V

EPILOGUE

27 The Austrian way — perspectives and problems from the past to the future

Jim Sweeney and Joe Weidenholzer

I

The foregoing contributions represent an attempt to answer the questions 'What is modern Austria' and 'Why is it as it is?' In this epilogue we shall bring together some of these themes and refer to some of the problems to which solutions have yet to be found as part of the process of social evolution. This latter aspect to some readers may be the most unsatisfactory of the project: to some extent we can only ask the questions; the reader must fall back on his or her own devices to find the answers.

It is remarkable that within the space of seventy years, within a virtual avalanche of events, there should have been so much that has been catastrophic from which has emerged two beginnings. Each new beginning has had many similarities: defeat in war, the trauma of economic and territorial readjustments, deprivation and scarcity, and a deep pessimism concerning survival. These features were not only economic and political: they were also deeply psychological and this is an aspect of human behaviour which has become more significant for Austria. Each new beginning contained some differences, however. The 'shock of reduction' from a multi-ethnical, multinational empire to a small fairly homogeneous ethnic country and the birth trauma in the establishment of the First Republic with little basis to survive, to the later eager desire for independence in the Second Republic, is a marked contrast. So too were the imposition of the stringent financial conditions and the hostility of the 'successor states' during the First Republic compared to the conditions of the post-Second World War and the assistance given by the victors (at least some of them) firmly to establish the Second Republic. To these must be added those essential differences which are the distinguishing characteristics of both Republics.

The First Republic, the 'state no-one wanted' has to be sharply contrasted with the Second — the 'state everyone wants'. Why was this? The answer lies to some extent of course in the changed international conditions of the Second World War compared to those which prevailed at the end of the First. In the period after 1918 Austria was almost completely stripped of territory under the banner of the self-determination and independence of others. She thereby suffered in a depressed world economy which followed the prevailing economic dictum 'beggar my neighbour' and placed her at the mercy of the international money lenders. After 1945 Austria pursued the goal of her own self-determination and independence economically and financially aided by the Allied Powers who had by now become aware of the vital importance of those factors of economic deprivation in Europe which had contributed to the Second World War and its attendant disasters.

Something had also happened to the Austrian people. First of all the Nazi occupation had kindled a new spirit of rising national consciousness; secondly, particularly in those parts of Austria under post-war Russian occupation, there developed a desire for complete independence from foreign occupation. This latter aspect is particularly interesting when one recalls that in the First Republic, certainly till the early 1930s, there was an overwhelming view among the populace that Austria could only survive in some form of association (ranging from many forms of federal to unitary solutions) with Germany.

The negative feelings and attitudes about being 'Austrian' were gradually replaced by those of a positive nature. To a great extent internal events brought about such a change. First of all the withdrawal of the Catholic Church directly from the political arena, the end of Political Catholicism, and the abandonment on the part of the Socialists of their active (rather than philosophical) Austro-Marxism and the class struggle brought to an end the traditional *Lager* mentality which had prevailed among the two major political groupings since the 1880s. These two factors ushered in a greater readiness for co-operation and consensus. The Socialist gains and their euphoria in the early 1920s to some extent contributed to the fears of proletarian dictatorship which in turn gave rise to the violent conflicts of the late 1920s and early 30s, as well as to Austrian and German Fascism between 1934 and 1945 which many came to hold as responsible for the country's plight. Socialist thinking abandoned its Marxist inevitability and analysis of class conflict and after 1945 advocated political and social change within a democratic framework. Co-operation became necessary for independence and it was in this spirit that the post-war coalition governments continued well beyond the life span (twenty years compared to two) of those of the First Republic.

This thrust for independence, as we have seen, provided the

impulse for the development of an Austrian national consciousness which above all sharply distinguishes the Second Republic from the First and to which the Austrian State Treaty with the Allied Powers of 1955 and the subsequent neutrality of Austria gave practical expression as well as formal recognition. By this time all the major traumatic circumstances which had transpired since 1918 had now passed: the doubts over economic viability, the German annexation, the Russian occupation and forced reparations and threats, the civil war mentality of the early period, the class antagonisms and violent conflicts and, more importantly, the widespread attitudes about the structural defects of the post-Habsburg Austrian state. Independence and neutrality brought about a new self-confidence. A revamped economic system, itself a compromise containing capitalist and socialist philosophies — private enterprise with a powerful concentration of public ownership — played a part in rapidly producing an affluent society which, with an enlightened welfare state, ensured a social security system which became the envy of others.

National consciousness is of course closely related to the question of national identity. This had previously been a preoccupation of Austrian literature and philosophy where German forms had been dominant in the eighteenth and nineteenth centuries and which to some extent had been reasserted with the establishment of 'German-Austria' in 1918. Evidence for this dominant German position is to be seen during the era of 'enlightened absolution' of the reigns of Maria Theresa and Joseph II during which nothing of any significance was produced in Austrian literature or philosophy. Indeed attempts at 'philosophizing' (which meant 'systematizing' or 'ideologizing') were regarded as dangerous by a monarchy which, on the face of it, while 'Germanicizing' many of the institutions in its domains, was more intent on furthering efficient administration, the natural sciences and social welfare.

The early search for the Austrian identity became part of a language and literature problem which had been accentuated in the German direction by the educational system, dominated by pan-German intellectual, petit bourgeois school teachers and educational officials from the end of the nineteenth century. There were of course similar related difficulties bound up with concepts of 'state' and 'nation' (which persist to the present day) but it was not until after 1945, in Austrian literature at least when the new crop of Austrian writers became distinctive, that such doubts about 'Austria' ceased. Identity, too, was bound up with the impediment to consciousness: alienation. So long as the citizen could not unequivocally identify with the Austrian state, then national consciousness could never become an established fact or state of mind. Only the right conditions and positive attitudes about being Austrian, and identifying things specifically Austrian, could bring this about. To a considerable extent, and perhaps in areas not sufficiently researched, Austro-Marxism by its distinctive form and alternative culture contributed to this 'Austro-consciousness' at an early stage, although it must be admitted that the Austrian phoenix which rose from the *Ostmark* ashes after 1945, the economic miracle with its social partnership and Austria's place on the international scene, is more readily identifiable with this phenomenon and contributed greatly to this transformation.

In the process of transition to the development of national consciousness, there were many obstacles to be encountered. Some of these obstacles were related to the adverse historical experience in which low economic growth and economic dependency contributed to feelings of inferiority. But the social learning processes of Austrian society were also either relatively undeveloped or incapable of being reinforced; there was therefore no proper foundation to effect the more enduring behaviour patterns associated with a strong national consciousness.

The 'German experience' has always loomed large in Austrian history. Admittedly the area is a problematic one given the nature of history and the struggles and alliances between nations. At a more basic level countries with the same language will more easily tend to view each other sympathetically, identify or conjure up affinities and kinships. Many opinion surveys in recent years in Austria portray such images of Germany. The matter is, however, much more complex and national identity is by no means related to language only or even to other common cultural aspects of social life. Responses concerning identity with Germany are by no means uniform or total even if we include those surveys or studies concerned with national character which emphasize emotional responses or traits (as appear in literature, psychology or psycho-analysis).

The German connection has recently been revived in controversial political circumstances. The Reder case and the Waldheim affair have both been the subject of heated and bitter reactions inside and outside Austria. Many of these reactions have been of a defensive nature, that is, supportive of the actions and activities of Austrians in the service of the Third Reich. How does one explain these reactions while maintaining the idea of the 'Austrian national consciousness?' Not without difficulty, it must be asserted, and here we must base our explanation on the processes of learning and socialization related to Austrian citizenship in post-war Austria. The incorporation of Austria into the German (Nazi) Reich in 1938 is as much as an historical fact as is the 'German-ness' of Austria. The ambivalence of many Austrians towards these attributes has been once again aroused and has raised once more the issue of Austrian identity. How does one explain in the Reder case the act of a young minister (Dr Frischenschlager), with no memory or experience of the events of 1938–45, welcoming home a Nazi war criminal as 'an old soldier' (which is paralleled with Waldheim's statement about 'doing his duty')?

Such attitudes surely portray a deficient 'cancelling-out' of National Socialist attitudes in Austria, so that presumably certain prevalent attitudes of being Austrian are equated with being German (or Nazi?). Alternatively expressed, the process of de-Nazification in Austria at the end of the war was not sufficiently prosecuted to allow for a distinction to be made. The eagerness to restore Austria to independence overlooked the reflection and introspection necessary to embark on such a course. To that end insufficient debate and discussion took place on the resistance to, and defence of, Hitlerian Germany, but sufficient to leave a large gap in Austrian political and social education. Following this argument many would assert that, contrary to the argument in these pages, although apparently a highly politicized society, Austria in fact possesses no real political consciousness or political maturity or, as many would put it, no sense of responsibility about its past.

The unease produced by these recent events relate to the course of Austrian history mentioned above. Out of the violence and discord of the First Republic which were a concomitant of the struggle for the Austrian State, has emerged a series of creative modern institutions within the framework of a stable, liberal-corporative (or pluralistic) social and political system. Recent events, however, prompt the question: are the structures of such institutions so wafer-thin that the powerful emotions unleashed by the Reder and Waldheim controversies can destroy the social fabric? Professor Dahrendorf, on the other hand, postulates that the spectacular achievements of the Second Republic give rise to a quite different problem. Success in his view leads to the danger of a 'crisis of legitimacy' in which social structures harden through a surfeit of stability, making adjustment and change less easy to accomplish. Such contrary observations must give pause for reflection about the direction of Austrian society.

Economic well-being and success have brought in their train that which some describe as 'growth fetishism'. The strong post-war Austrian economy has spawned a materialism manifested in a self-assurance of consumers and producers which reflects an affluent society. Quite often political party membership and privilege too plays a role in reward distribution and even though one might understand how this has developed, it has nevertheless given rise to a deep ethical disquiet concerning such a practice. This demonstrates that Austrian society is like any other advanced one: that side by side with positive attributes about nationality can exist those of a negative character which may detract from the worth and integrity of the great achievements and the contribution made by Austria to western civilization.

From national consciousness has come a pride which many opinion surveys highlight in answering the question: What is Austria? By contrast to the First Republic (albeit without public opinion surveys) Austrians are now reconciled to the fact of a small state; at the same time one finds a collective expression that 'Austria' is conceived as a continuous process in which the Second Republic is part of the same historical evolution as Habsburg Austria. In the popular mind the First Republic is a hiccup in this evolution and is regarded as something of an aberration. Modern 'Austria' is also seen by many as strong, neutral and federalistic, features which some observers see as a tendency leading to the 'Swissification' (*Verschweizerung*) of the country.

In contrast to the ill-fated First Republic, the Second has succeeded internally in most aspects of national success. It is a state where interest groups — business élites and organized workers — are strong and balanced and have replaced large political groupings as the determining forces in a modern, open society with changing technology and social structures, one in which there is no 'historical mission' or 'eternal character' but in which arguments abound about the direction and future of 'homo Austriacus'.

II

The far-reaching and contradictory developments on which Austria embarked in this century to which the way of life of her citizens can testify was evidenced also by a regular improvement in living conditions, certainly when one compares these to those of her eastern neighbours. Such an observation leads unswervingly to a conclusion that Austria is in some way a special case.

The course of events — not automatically identifiable with the establishment of the Austrian national consciousness — which occurred in the 1970s was the result of internal and external causes. As a consequence there was a tendency to view Austria as something distinctive and exemplary although this was in no way limited to her territory and her citizens, since foreigners also became preoccupied with the country's achievements.

It was a Pope who elevated this fact to a formula when in 1979 he greeted the then Austrian Federal President, Franz Jonas, with the now legendary phrase: 'Austria is an island of the blessed' (*Österreich ist eine Insel der Seligen*). From this time on, this phrase was to characterize the self-esteem as well as the foreign estimation in which Austria was held. By the beginning of the 1970s the Social Democrats had produced the best election result in their history, fighting the election under the slogan 'The Austrian Way'. This seemed to encapsulate much that was novel about the new Austria. She seemed to have successfully carved her way through the deep rifts of the East-West conflict and to have overcome the contradictions of the capitalist trade cycles. Moreover, while many other countries were dismantling their welfare states Austria was taking active steps to build hers up. It would be incorrect merely to attribute this latter action as being due to the relative backwardness in the manner of a quasi time lag from the point of view of historical trends. Much more to the point: not only was this promotion of the welfare state pursued by vote-catching politicians; it was also mirrored in public opinion encompassing the entire people who held that Austria in many respects, therefore, could present a model to the world. In particular this set of convictions served to combat the inferiority complex Austrians had about their Federal German neighbours, a disposition not only deeply influenced by the recent German 'economic miracle' but which also had, as we have seen, deep historical roots.

Of what do the special elements of the 'Austrian Way' consist? What impresses the Austrians and their friends abroad which makes it an object worthy of imitation? For a more complete answer to such questions we have to turn to Austria's role in international relations. Although the Austrian people to an overwhelming degree feel in tune with the ideals of the Western democracies, in foreign relations they attempt to keep out of East-West conflicts. This policy is a result of the obligations of the State Treaty of 1955 and the concomitant Law of Neutrality.

The 1970s, however, brought a change to an active neutrality policy. Austria became engaged as a mediator in difficult situations, seeming to represent at the same time the perfect expression of détente. At about the time the world was faced with a renewal of the Cold War in the form of the Afghan crisis, Austria celebrated 25 years of the State Treaty. For the occasion the four Foreign Ministers of the signatory states were invited to Vienna. Austria had put into effect that which was not thought possible. Above all, in the Middle East, Austria's foreign policy was to take the initiative, not least capitalizing on the personality of the then Federal Chancellor, Bruno Kreisky, who engraved this policy with a permanent character. Personal factors notwithstanding, the credo of Austrian Middle-East policy centred around the notion that by disarming the opposing forces which threatened world peace an essential contribution could be made. The limits of the influence of very small states in international relations had become all too clear, however.

But small states, 'blessed' or not, whose counsel and foreign policies might be respected in the international community, also pay the price in the modern world. As terrorism increased and developed as a threat to national governments, many believed that terrorism could only be countered in the last resort by force. The Austrian view has been that detestable as terrorism is, it is of no avail to employ force to overcome it. A considerable part of the problem was solved without additional and unnecessary victims. Nevertheless the country has not been spared from the activities of international terrorism.

There is another sphere in which one can clearly observe the phenomenon of the 'Austrian Way'. At the domestic level this particular approach may well have much more to recommend it. Full employment and budgetary deficit policies have served to maintain a growing economy and it is only very recently that some adjustment has been deemed necessary to preserve this situation. The Austrian model consists of a capitalist framework of society in which many economic agencies can be seen to eschew the logic of the market. One immediate consequence of this has produced the possibility of controlled development which calls for the thorough elimination of social conflict. It is undeniable that a high rate of economic growth and a favourable employment situation are influenced by the corporate character of the Austrian economy. On the other hand there are also negative effects — such as those manifested by a scarcity of innovative potential.

In conclusion, to look for a linear connection in Austria's development may not be useful; in the eighteenth century Johann von Justi, a noted political economist of the day, described Austria as belonging to that genus of countries which displayed 'no special genius for commerce or manufacture'. Who would seriously assert that today?

PART VI

APPENDICES

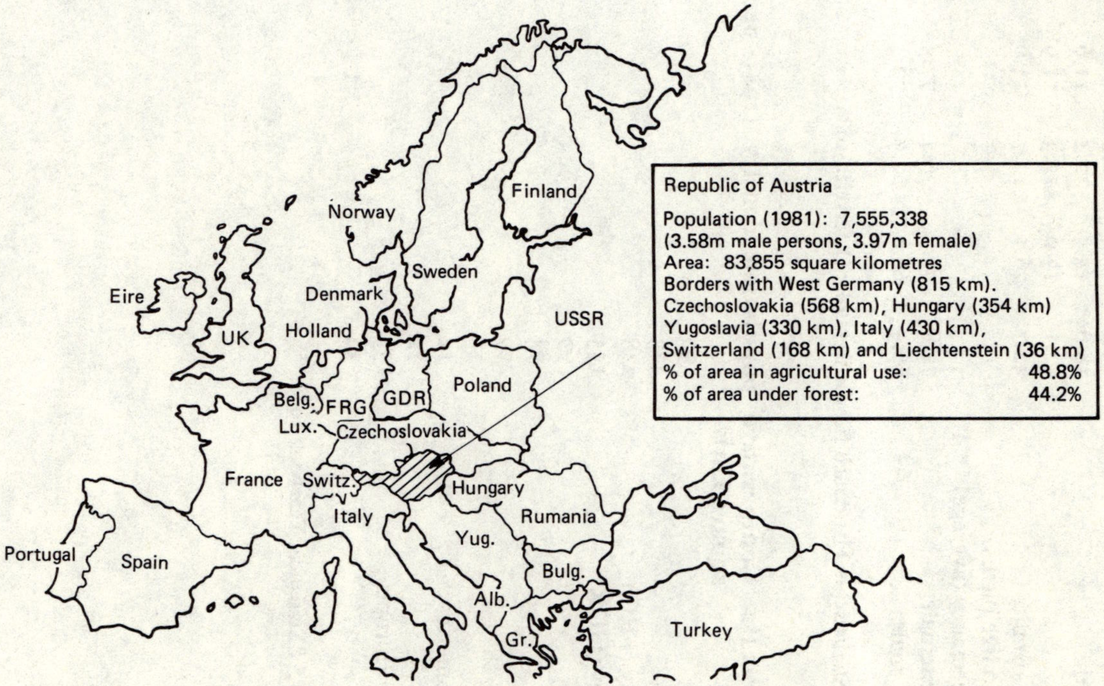

Appendix A1 Map of Europe

Appendix B1 Population development in Austria 1961–85

Per 1000 inhabitants	1961	1971	1981	1985
Marriages	8.5	6.4	6.3	5.9
Live births	18.6	14.5	12.4	11.6
Deaths	12.1	13.0	12.3	11.9
Infant mortality (per 1000 live births)	32.7	26.1	12.7	11.0
Life expectancy (average)				
in years: female	72.8	73.7	76.4	77.3
male	66.5	66.6	69.3	70.4

Source: Statistisches Handbuch für die Republik Österreich 1986.

Appendix B2 Comparative population density (1985 per square km)

Austria	90
Belgium	323
Germany (FRG)	248
Germany (GDR)	155
France	99
Greece	74
Britain	229
Sweden	18
North America	12
USSR	12
Western Europe	153
World	34

Source: UN Statistical Yearbook 1986.

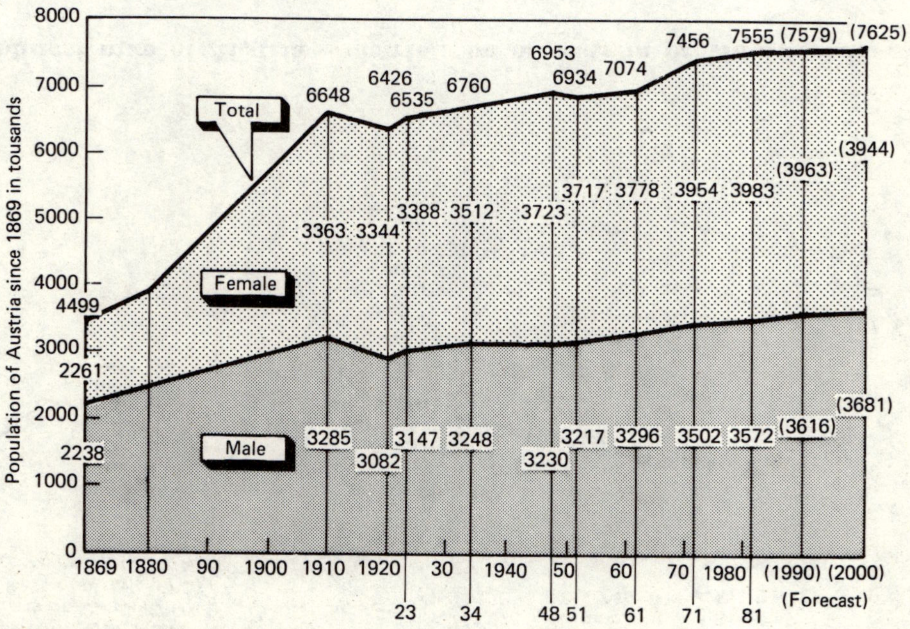

* Habsburg Austria (Cisleithania) till 1918

Source: Wirtschaftsstudio des Österreichischen Gesellschafts- und Wirtschaftsmuseums, Vienna 1985/86.

Appendix B3 Population growth in Austria* since 1869 (in thousands)

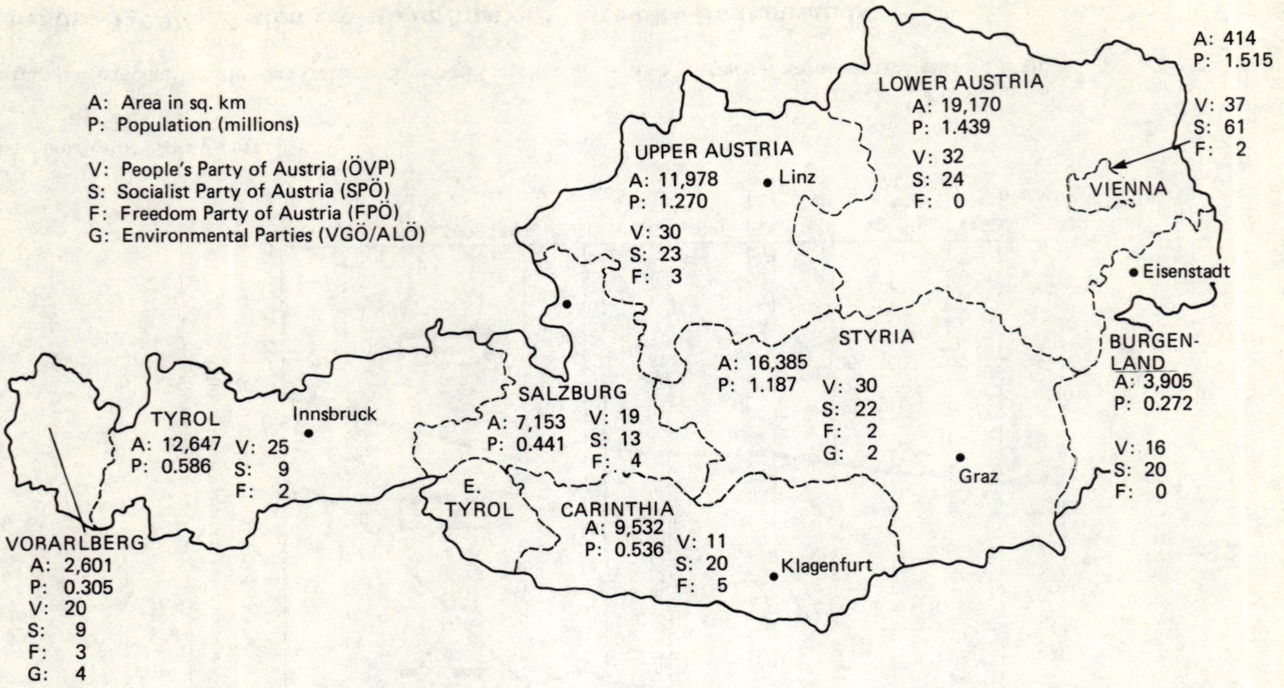

Appendix C1 Political map of Austria – distribution of seats in provincial parliaments (as at end of 1986)

Appendix C2 Presidents of Austria 1945–87

Karl Renner (SPÖ) 1945–50
Theodor Körner (SPÖ) 1951–57
Adolf Schärf (SPÖ) 1957–65
Franz Jonas (SPÖ) 1965–74
Rudolf Kirchschläger (SPÖ) 1974–86
Kurt Waldheim (SPÖ) 1986–

Appendix C3 Composition of the National Assembly 1945–87

	ÖVP	SPÖ	KPÖ	VdU > FPÖ	Greens
1945–49	85	76	4	–	–
1949–53	77	67	5	16	–
1953–56	74	73	4	14	–
1956–59	82	74	3	6	–
1959–62	79	78	–	8	–
1962–66	81	76	–	8	–
1966–70	85	74	–	6	–
1970–71	78	81	–	6	–
1971–75	80	93	–	10	–
1975–79	80	93	–	10	–
1979–83	77	95	–	11	–
1983–86	81	90	–	12	–
1986–	77	80	–	18	8

Erratum

Please note that in Appendix C2, the final line should read:

'Kurt Waldheim (0VP) 1986--'

Appendix C4 Federal Governments (Cabinet Ministers) of Austria 1945–87

	April 1945–December 1945	December 1945–November 1949	November 1949–February 1953
Chancellor	K. Renner (SPÖ)	L. Figl (ÖVP)	L. Figl (ÖVP)
Vice-Chancellor		A. Schärf (SPÖ)	A. Schärf (SPÖ)
Foreign Affairs	K. Renner (SPÖ)	K. Gruber (ÖVP)	K. Gruber (ÖVP)
Defence	K. Renner (SPÖ)		
Interior	F. Honner (KPÖ)	O. Helmer (SPÖ)	O. Helmer (SPÖ)
Finance	G. Zimmermann (Ind.)	G. Zimmermann (Ind.)	E. Margaretha (ÖVP) > R. Kamitz (ÖVP)
Industry, Trade Transport	E. Heinl (ÖVP)	–	–
Trade and Reconstruction	–	E. Fleischacker E. Heinl > K. Kolb (all ÖVP)	E. Kolb > J. Böck-Greissau (ÖVP)
Education	E. Fischer (KPÖ)	F. Hurdes (ÖVP)	F. Hurdes (ÖVP)
Agriculture	R. Buchinger (ÖVP) > J. Kraus (ÖVP)	J. Kraus (ÖVP)	J. Kraus > F. Thoma (ÖVP)
Justice	J. Gerö (Ind.)	J. Gerö (Ind)	O. Tschadek (SPÖ) > J. Gerö
Transport	–	V. übeleis (SPÖ)	–
Transport and Nationalized Industries	–	–	K. Waldbrunner (SPÖ)
Social Affairs	J. Böhm (SPÖ)	K. Maisel (SPÖ)	K. Maisel (SPÖ)

	April 1953–June 1956	June 1956–July 1959	July 1959–April 1961	April 1961 April 1964
Chancellor	J. Raab (ÖVP)	J. Raab (ÖVP)	J. Raab (ÖVP)	A. Gorbach (ÖVP)
Vice-Chancellor	A. Schärf (SPÖ)	A. Schärf > > B. Pittermann (SPÖ)	B. Pittermann (SPÖ)	B. Pittermann (SPÖ)
Foreign Affairs	K. Gruber (ÖVP) > L. Figl (ÖVP)	L. Figl (ÖVP) > J. Raab (ÖVP)	B. Kreisky (SPÖ)	B. Kreisky (SPÖ)
Defence	–	F. Graf (ÖVP)	F. Graf (ÖVP)	K. Schleinzer (ÖVP)
Interior	O. Helmer (SPÖ)	O. Helmer (SPÖ)	J. Afritsch (SPÖ)	J. Afritsch (SPÖ) > F. Olah (SPÖ)
Finance	R. Kamitz (ÖVP)	R. Kamitz (ÖVP)	R. Kamitz (ÖVP) > E. Heilingsetzer (ÖVP)	J. Klaus (ÖVP) > F. Korinek (ÖVP)
Trade and Reconstruction	J. Böck-Greissau (ÖVP) > V. Illig (ÖVP)	V. Illig (ÖVP) > F. Bock (ÖVP)	F. Bock (ÖVP)	F. Bock (ÖVP)
Education	E. Kolb (ÖVP) > H. Drimmel (ÖVP)	H. Drimmel (ÖVP)	H. Drimmel (ÖVP)	H. Drimmel (ÖVP)
Agriculture	F. Thoma (ÖVP)	F. Thoma (ÖVP)	E. Hartmann (ÖVP)	E. Hartmann (ÖVP)
Justice	J. Gerö (Ind.) > H. Kapfer (Ind.)	O.Tschadek (SPÖ)	O. Tschadek (SPÖ) > C. Broda (SPÖ)	C. Broda (SPÖ)P
Transport	K. Waldbrunner (SPÖ)	K. Waldbrunner (SPÖ)	K. Waldbrunner (SPÖ)	K. Waldbrunner (SPÖ) > O. Probst (SPÖ)
Social Affairs	K. Maisel (SPÖ) > A. Proksch (SPÖ)	A. Proksch (SPÖ)	A. Proksch (SPÖ)	

	April 1964–April 1966	April 1966–April 1970	April 1970–April 1983
Chancellor	J. Klaus (ÖVP)	J. Klaus (ÖVP)	B. Kreisky (SPÖ)
Vice-Chancellor	B. Pittermann (SPÖ)	F. Böck (ÖVP) > H. Withalm (ÖVP)	R. Häuser (SPÖ) > H. Androsch (SPÖ) > F. Sinowatz (SPÖ) > O. Rösch (SPÖ) > Erwin Lanc (SPÖ)
Foreign Affairs	B. Kreisky (SPÖ)	L. Toncic-Sorinj (ÖVP) > K. Waldheim (Ind.)	R. Kirchschläger (Ind.) > E. Bielka (Ind.) > W. Pahr (Ind.)
Defence	G. Prader (ÖVP)	G. Prader (ÖVP)	H. Freihsler (SPÖ) > K. Lütgendorf (Ind.) > O. Rösch (SPÖ) > C. Broda (SPÖ)
Interior	F. Olah (SPÖ) H. Czettel (SPÖ)	F. Hetzenauer (ÖVP) > F. Soronics (ÖVP)	O. Rösch (SPÖ) > E. Lanc (SPÖ)
Finance	W. Schmitz (ÖVP)	W. Schmitz (ÖVP) > S. Koren (ÖVP)	H. Androsch (SPÖ) > H. Salcher (SPÖ)
Trade	F. Bock (ÖVP)	F. Bock (ÖVP) > D. Mitterer (ÖVP)	J. Staribacher (SPÖ)
Education	T. Piffl-Percevic (ÖVP)	T. Piffl-Percevic (ÖVP) > A. Mock (ÖVP)	L. Gratz (SPÖ) > F. Sinowatz (SPÖ)
Agriculture	K. Schleinzer (ÖVP)	K. Schleinzer (ÖVP)	H. Öllinger (SPÖ) > O. Weihs (SPÖ) G. Haiden (SPÖ)
Justice	C. Broda (SPÖ)	H. Klecatzky (ÖVP)	C. Broda (SPÖ)
Transport	O. Probst (SPÖ)	L. Weiss (ÖVP)	E. Frühbauer (SPÖ) > E. Lanc (SPÖ) > K. Lausecker (SPÖ)
Science	–	–	H. Firnberg (SPÖ)
Social Affairs	A. Proksch (SPÖ)	G. Rehor (ÖVP)	R. Häusser (SPÖ) > G. Weissenberg (SPÖ) > A. Dallinger (SPO)

	May 1983–September 1986	January 1987
Chancellor	F. Sinowatz (SPÖ) > F. Vranitzky (SPÖ) (June 86)	F. Vranitzky (SPÖ)
Vice-Chancellor	N. Steger (FPÖ)	A. Mock (ÖVP)
Foreign Affairs	E. Lanc (SPÖ) > L. Gratz (SPÖ) > P. Jankowitsch (SPÖ)	A. Mock (ÖVP)
Defence	F. Frischenschlager (FPÖ)	P. Lichal (ÖVP)
Interior	K. Blecha (SPÖ)	K. Blecha (SPÖ)
Finance	H. Salcher (SPÖ) > F. Vranitzky (SPÖ) > F. Lacina (SPÖ)	F. Lacina (SPÖ)
Trade	N. Steger (FPÖ)	–
Trade and Economic Affairs	–	R. Graf (ÖVP)
Education	H. Zilk (SPÖ) > H. Moritz (SPÖ)	H. Hawlicek (SPÖ)
Agriculture	G. Haiden (SPÖ)	J. Riegler (ÖVP)
Justice	H. Ofner (FPÖ)	E. Foregger (Ind.)
Science	H. Fischer (SPÖ)	H. Tuppy (ÖVP)
Transport and Public Works	K. Lausecker (SPÖ) > F. Lacina (SPÖ)	–
Nationalized Industries and Transport	–	R. Streicher (SPÖ)
Social Affairs	A. Dallinger (SPÖ)	A. Dallinger (SPÖ)

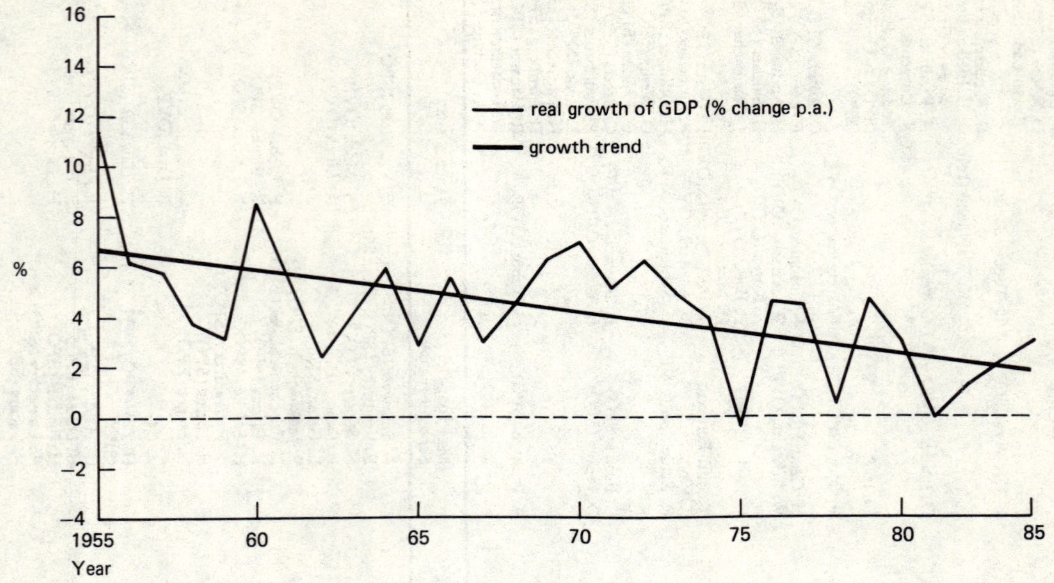

Sources: Österreich. Statistik in Zahlen, and Statistisches Handbuch für die Republik Österreich 1986.

Appendix D1 Economic growth in Austria 1954–85 (real GDP)

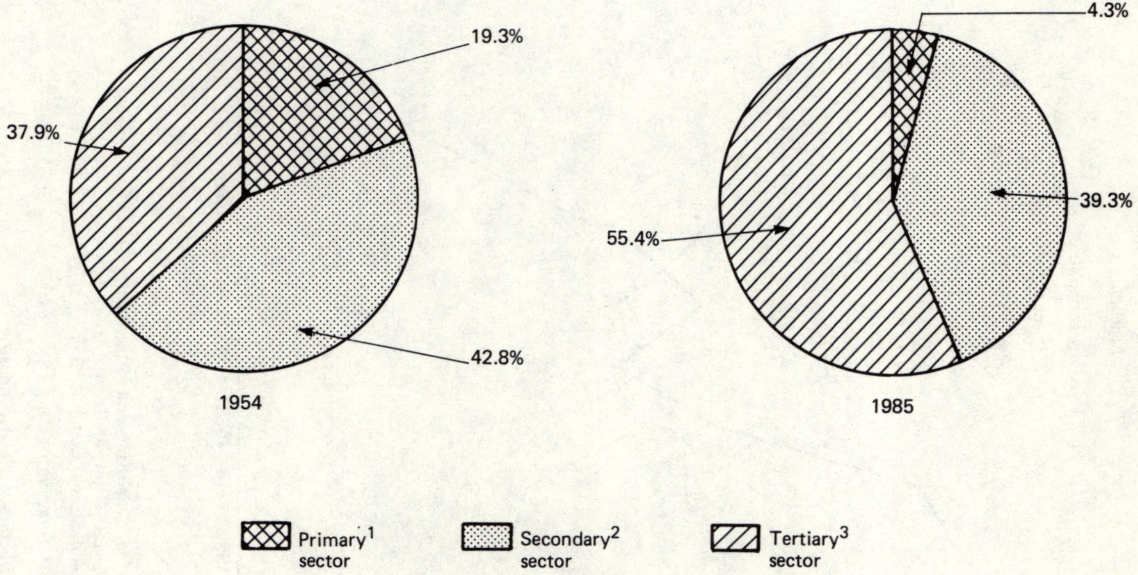

1. Agriculture, forestry and mining
2. Manufacturing, energy, water and construction
3. Private and State services

Sources: Österreich. Statistik in Zahlen, and Statisstiches Handbuch für die Republik Österreich 1986.

Appendix D2 Sectoral distribution of GDP 1954 and 1985 (at factor costs)

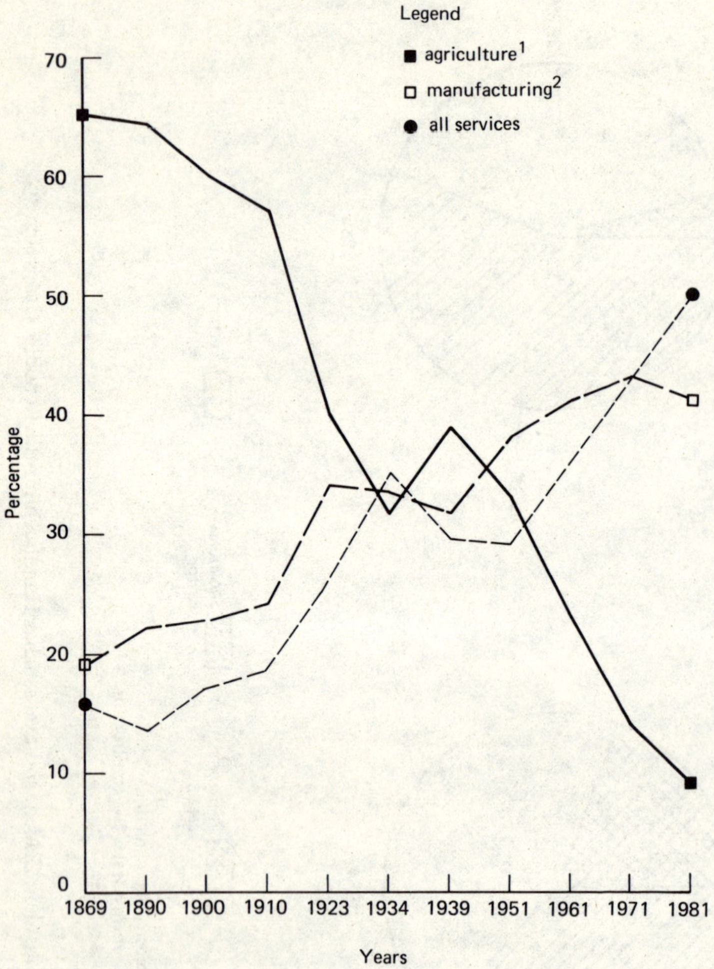

* Habsburg Austria (Cisleithania) till 1918; First Republic 1918–38; Ostmark (German Third Reich) 1938–45; Second Republic 1945–

1 Includes fishing, forestry

2 Includes construction, extractive industries

Appendix D3 Working population of Austria* (by sector 1869–1981 (%)

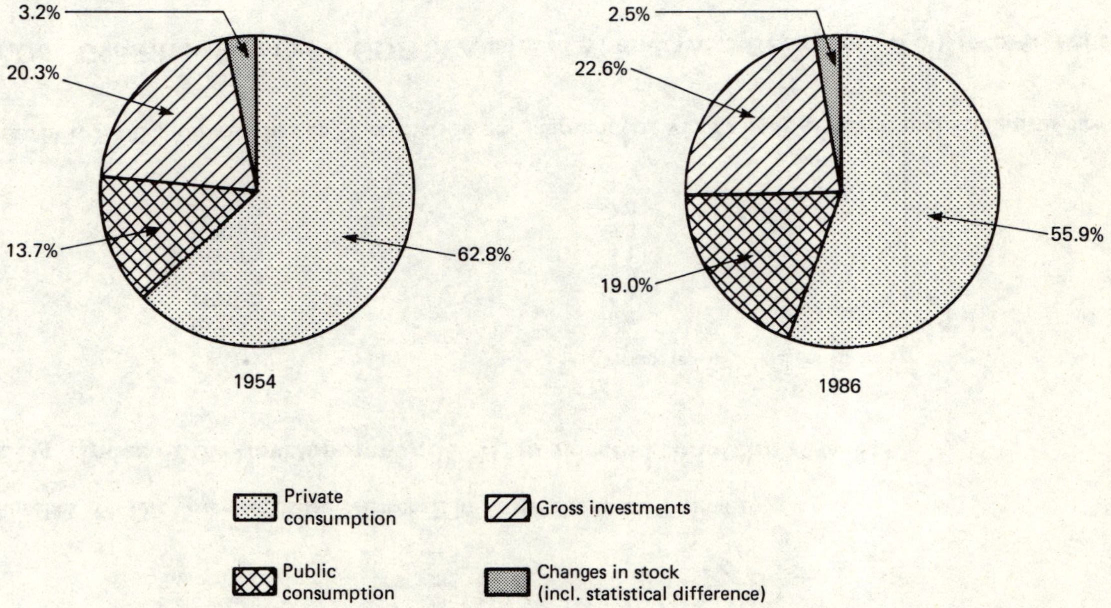

Sources: Österreich. Statistik in Zahlen, Österreichisches Statistisches Zentralamt 1986.

Appendix D4 Employment of disposable national wealth 1954 and 1986 (in current prices)

	1984		1970	1984
		1950 = 100		1970 = 100
West Germany	457		337	136
Austria	419		277	151
France	412		269	137
Italy	400		300	149
USA	298		201	148
Switzerland	288		249	116
Sweden	282		221	128
GB	224		176	127

Source: Butschek, F.: Die Österreichische Wirtschaft in 20. Jahrhundert, Vienna 1985.

Appendix D5 Index of the development of GDP in selected countries 1954–84

	A	WG
	(average rate of annual growth in %)	
1950/54	+6.8	+8.8
1955/59	+6.1	+7.2
1960/64	+5.3	+5.6
1965/69	+4.1	+4.5
1970/74	+5.3	+3.6
1975/79	+2.8	+2.7
1980/85	+1.9	+1.5

Source: Butschek, F.: Die österreichische Wirtschaft in 20. Jahrhundert, Vienna 1985 Österreichisches Statistisches Zentalamt 1986

Appendix D6 Growth rates of real GDP in Austria (A) and West Germany (WG) 1950–86 (in five-year periods)

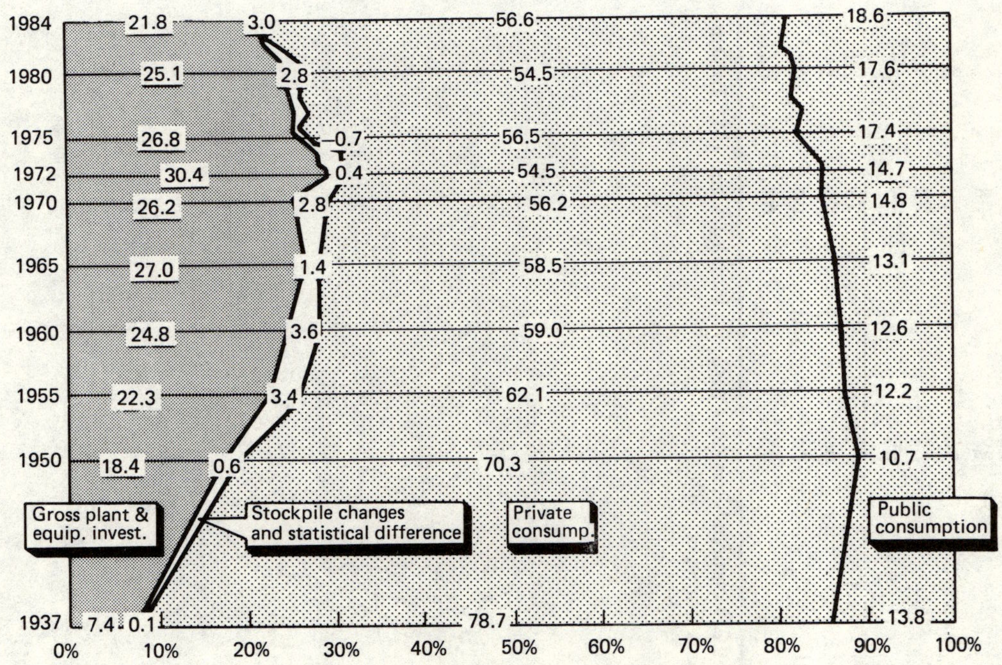

Source: Wirtschaftsstudio des österreichischen Gesellschafts- und Wirtschaftsmuseums, Vienna 1985/86.

Appendix D7 Employment of disposable national wealth Austria 1937–84 (share of investments and consumption in goods and service volume)

Appendix D8 Comparison of investment ratios in selected European countries 1965–86

Austria = 100	1965/70	1971/73	1974/76	1985/86
West Germany	93	90	78	99
France	88	83	88	84
Italy	76	75	79	81
Belgium	83	75	82	70
Holland	98	85	77	82
Great Britain	71	67	74	76
Sweden	90	77	79	85
Switzerland	102	104	90	105
USA	68	64	62	82

Sources: OECD National Accounts 1952–77, Paris 1979 and IMF International Financial Statistics, 1986.

Appendix D9 Austria's trading partners

	in Percentage of Total Imports		in Percentage of Total Exports	
	1983	1984	1983	1984
Fed. Rep. Ger.	41.5	39.9	30.8	29.6
Italy	8.9	8.6	8.9	9.4
Switzerland	4.8	4.4	6.8	6.9
Great Britain	2.2	2.1	4.1	4.4
France	4.1	3.7	3.8	3.9
USSR	4.3	5.0	3.9	4.5
USA	3.4	3.5	3.0	4.1
Jugoslavia	1.0	1.1	2.6	2.4
Netherlands	2.8	2.6	2.4	2.4
Hungary	1.7	2.1	2.2	2.2
Sweden	1.8	1.8	1.9	1.9
Czechoslovakia	2.1	2.0	1.3	1.1
Belgium	2.1	2.1	1.9	1.8
GDR	0.8	0.7	2.3	2.2
Denmark	0.7	0.7	1.0	1.1
Norway	0.4	0.7	0.9	0.9
Japan	3.5	3.3	1.0	1.0
Poland	1.0	1.3	1.1	1.1
Bulgaria	0.1	0.2	0.9	0.7
Romania	0.5	0.4	0.4	0.4
Portugal	0.3	0.4	0.3	0.3
Remainder	12.0	13.4	18.5	17.7
By Regions				
Total OECD	78.7	76.7	71.6	72.8
OECD Europe	71.3	69.3	66.7	66.4
EFTA	7.8	7.9	10.7	10.8
EC	62.7	60.4	53.7	53.3
East Europ. Countries (without Jugoslavia)	10.5	11.6	12.1	12.1
OPEC	3.8	4.8	7.4	6.4
Foreign Trade in bill. S	348.3	392.1	277.1	314.5

Source: Wirtschaftsstudio des Österreichischen Gesellschafts- und Wirtschaftsmuseums, Vienna 1985/86.

Appendix D10 The 35 largest industrial enterprises in Austria (1983)

	Industry	Branch	Turnover in Mill S.	Export ratio %	Workforce
1	VÖEST-Alpine	Steel	104,000	74.0	72,288
	VÖEST-Alpine AG	Steel	48,000	72.0	39,179
	ÖMV–AG	Oil	47,189	5.3	7,621
2	Austria Tabak	Tobacco	17,226	–	1,556
3	Chemie Linz	Chemicals	15,607	–	8,230
4	Steyr-Daimler-Puch	Vehicles	15,143	56.0	15,515
5	VEW Concern	Special Steels	14,149	–	15,557
	Chemie Linz AG	Chemicals	13,928	70.0	7,121
6	Siemens Group	Electrical	13,093	26.0	13,648
7	Philips Austria	Electrical	12,200	63.0	10,100
	Siemens AG Austria	Electrical	10,414	20.0	9,948
8	Semperit Group	Chemicals	9,897	70.0	9,121
9	Elin Union Concern	Electrical	9,481	–	
	VEW AG	Special Steels	9,009	77.0	13,817
	Elin AG	Electrical	7,793	38.5	7,450
10	Schärdinger	Foodstuffs	7,635	14.5	1,238
11	VMW Ranshofen	Metals	7,355	54.0	4,962
12	Unilever Austria	Food/Detergents	6,729	3.6	4,446
13	Hoechst Austria	Chemicals	5,498	31.6	1,827
14	Leykam-Mürztaler	Paper	4,842	61.0	2,918
15	Universale	Construction	4,210	20.0	3,650
16	Chemie Faser Lenzing	Chemicals	3,878	78.1	3,692
17	Porr AG	Construction	3,704	5.8	3,594
18	Swarovski	Optics/Abrasives	3,666	76.5	5,500
19	Andritz Treibacher	Engineering	3,662	91.0	2,647
	Chemiewerke AG	Chemicals	3,599	84.0	1,434
20	Liebherr Austria	Engineering	3,459	80.0	2,334
21	Österr. Brau AG	Drinks	3,352	2.0	3,049
22	Alpi	Foodstuffs	3,293	41.0	318
23	II Bau AG	Construction	3,220	28.0	1,920
	Öst. Brau AG	Drinks	2,996	2.0	2,554
24	Simmering-Graz-Pauker	Engineering	2,849	16.5	4,528
25	AEG-Telef. Austria	Electricals	2,712	32.0	2,357
26	Molkereiverband	Foodstuffs	2,646	–	266
27	Waagner-Biro AG	Engineer./Steel	2,571	15.4	2,985
28	Ing. Mayreder-Kraus	Construction	2,510	6.5	2,730
	Hoechst Austria AG	Chemicals	2,495	2.4	537
29	Dichand	Publish./Print	2,483	–	2,356
30	Wienerberger Conc.	Build.Materials	2,384	–	1,997
31	Hallein-Papier	Paper	2,348	82.3	1,344
32	Frantschach	Paper	2,257	64.5	1,642
33	Austr. Amer. Magnesit	Mining	2,234	76.6	2,173
34	Stuag AG	Construction	2,224	3.0	2,080
35	Brown Boveri Austr.	Electricals	2,170	27.0	2,236

Source: Wirtschaftsstudio des österreichischen Gesellschafts- und Wirtschaftsmuseums, Vienna 1985/86.

Appendix E1 Revenue and expenditure of all State Authorities (without State Enterprises) 1970–83

Bill. Schillings

	1970	1971	1972	1973	1974	1975	1976	1977	1978	1979	1980	1981	1982	1983
Revenue from sales	4,45	5,50	5,22	5,51	6,72	8,65	10,20	10,25	12,21	13,23	16,75	19,47	19,50	19,00
Indirect Taxation	61,68	70,00	82,49	97,23	106,92	111,53	119,55	135,87	139,30	151,20	162,83	173,95	183,60	194,60
Direct Taxation	41,11	46,39	55,16	61,78	75,40	76,24	82,76	93,67	110,72	118,08	128,40	143,86	148,60	160,70
Social Insurance Contrib.	41,12	47,18	53,35	61,98	72,28	83,04	92,73	105,38	123,87	134,78	148,25	160,24	172,70	186,40
Other recurrent transfers	0,71	0,82	0,93	1,02	1,19	1,31	1,57	2,48	2,61	2,67	2,84	3,26	3,50	3,60
Total Revenue	149,07	169,89	197,15	227,52	262,51	280,77	306,81	347,65	388,71	419,96	459,07	500,78	527,90	564,30
State Consumption/ Deprec.	52,62	58,96	66,71	78,12	92,93	108,10	122,47	132,94	147,88	159,19	170,87	186,84	202,60	217,70
Gross Investments	19,36	22,70	27,03	28,86	34,22	36,74	36,52	39,68	41,73	43,38	44,07	44,30	43,20	45,40
Interest Payments	4,05	4,39	4,79	5,35	6,44	8,56	12,17	14,80	18,68	21,31	24,50	28,78	36,00	40,50
Other recurrent transfers	64,43	73,05	81,97	92,69	109,01	129,99	149,28	165,96	189,90	205,71	221,78	239,24	252,60	269,80
Net Capital transfers	3,72	4,01	6,38	14,84	11,12	12,63	12,31	11,58	12,00	11,64	15,39	18,53	16,50	17,50
Total Expenditure	144,81	163,11	186,88	219,86	253,72	296,02	332,75	364,96	410,19	441,23	476,61	517,69	550,90	590,90
Balance of Inc. + Exp.	4,89	6,78	10,27	7,66	8,79	−15,25	−25,94	−17,31	−21,48	−21,27	−17,54	−16,91	−23,00	−26,60
Gross National Product (current prices)	373,91	417,71	476,84	540,08	615,59	652,52	719,71	789,31	833,95	910,91	990,63	1049,56	1134,26	1196,93

Source: Deutsches Institut für Wirtschaftsforschung, Berlin 1983.

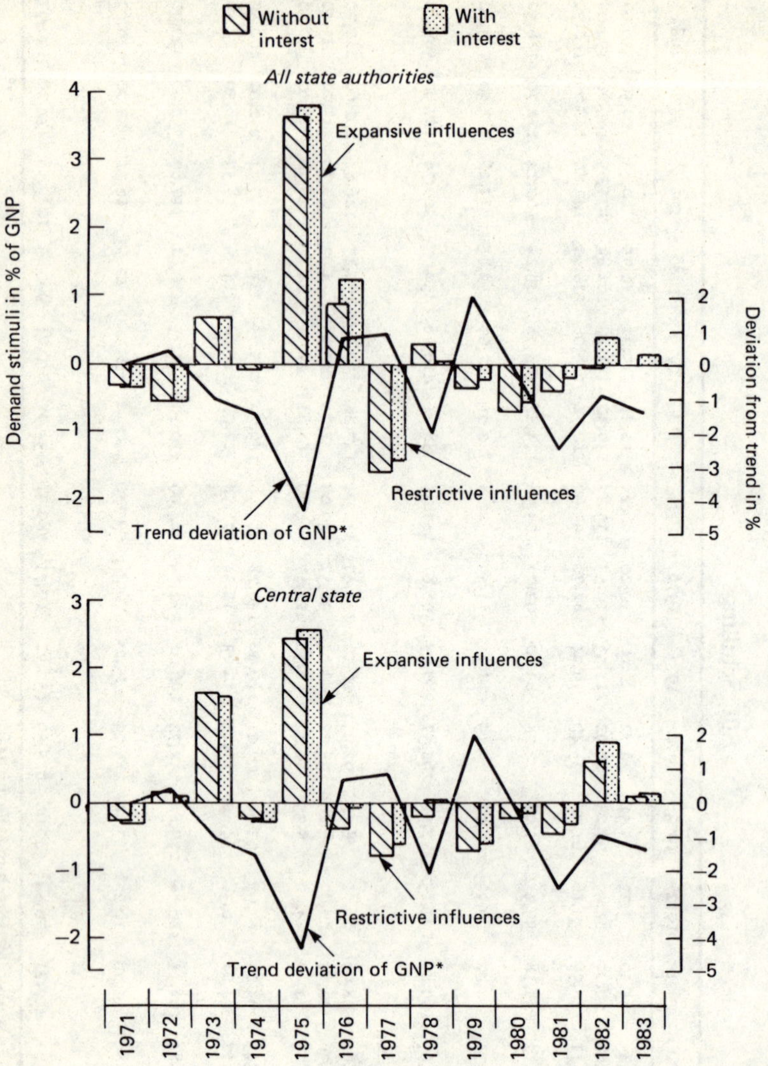

* Deviations of real GNP from the trend of %; the zero line represents the trend of GNP
Source: Deutsches Institut für Wirtschaftsforschung, Berlin 1983.

Appendix E2 State demand management and growth cycles in Austria 1971–83

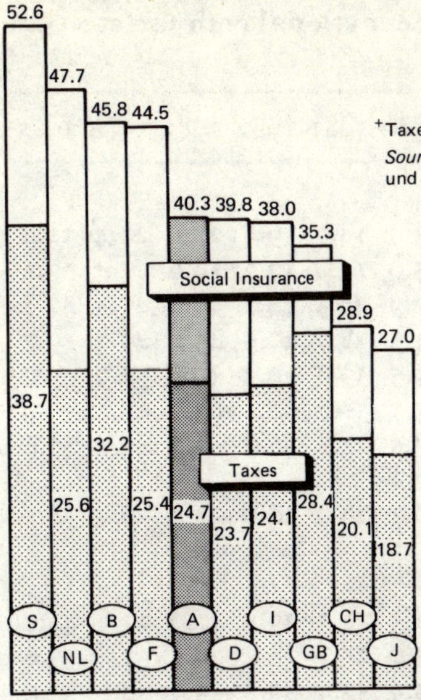

[+]Taxes plus Social Insurance

Source: Wirtschaftsstudio des Österreichischen Gesellschafts– und Wirtschaftsmuseums, Vienna 1985/86

Appendix E3 International comparison of taxation burdens[†] 1983 (as % of GDP)

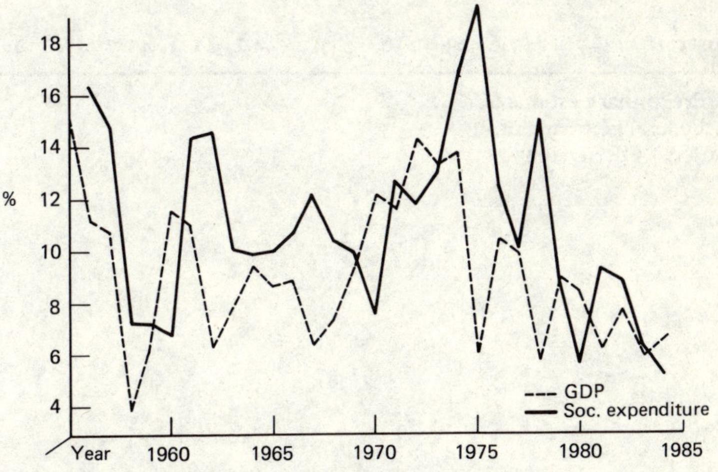

Source: Butschek, F.: Die österreichische Wirtschaft in 20. Jahrhundert, Vienna 1985

Appendix E4 The Social State in Austria — growth rates of social expenditure and GDP 1954–84

Appendix E5 Public debt: an international comparison (per cent of GDP/GNP)

	1974	1975	1979	1980	1981	1982	1983	1984	1985[1]
Central government									
Germany[2]	7.3	10.5	14.9	15.9	18.0	19.6	20.8	21.4	21.8
France	15.7	16.1	15.1	15.0	15.9	17.2	19.6	21.4	23.2
United Kingdom	49.2	44.1	43.7	40.9	44.3	44.1	44.4	47.3	47.8
Japan	11.7	15.4	30.2	34.5	38.6	40.5	45.2	49.7	49.7
Netherlands	25.5	25.6	27.2	29.5	33.6	39.3	46.4	51.9	–
Sweden	27.2	27.4	37.9	43.7	51.6	60.1	65.3	68.2	–
United States[2]	35.2	36.8	35.4	35.5	34.8	37.7	43.0	44.1	47.6
Austria[2]	10.0	15.3	25.1	26.3	28.0	30.0	34.5	36.4	38.5
General government									
Germany	19.6	25.0	30.7	32.5	36.3	39.4	41.0	41.9	42.0
France	24.7	25.8	26.2	25.0	25.9	28.3	29.8	31.8	33.6
United Kingdom	69.5	65.2	55.6	54.9	54.9	53.5	53.9	54.8	54.2
Japan	18.0	22.5	47.6	52.9	58.1	62.7	68.7	69.4	69.3
Netherlands	41.3	41.3	42.7	45.9	50.3	55.6	62.3	66.3	66.8
Sweden	30.5	29.6	39.6	44.8	52.9	62.6	65.9	67.1	68.6
United States	40.1	43.3	37.8	38.0	37.1	41.0	43.7	44.4	46.5
Austria	17.6	23.9	36.0	37.2	39.2	41.3	45.7	45.1	44.7

1 Preliminary estimates.
2 Federal government.
Source: OECD 1985

Appendix F1 Affiliated membership of trade union centres by political orientation in Austria (selected years 1900–31)[1]

Central organisation	1900	1910	1913	1918	1921	1925	1928	1931
Trade Union Council/ Federation of Free Trade Unions	98,898 (67.0)	400,565	415,195	412,910	1,079,777 (85.1)	807,515 (72.1)	766,168 (75.2)	582,687 (72.2)
Independent Free Trade Unions						20,000 (1.9)	40,100 (3.9)	24,500 (3.0)
Central Council of Christian Trade Unions	7,913 (5.3)	46,533	37,237	20,556	78,737 (6.2)	77,200 (7.4)	100,987 (9.9)	108,420 (13.4)
Independent Christian Trade Unions	–	–	–	–	70,000 (5.5)	50,000 (4.8)	15,000 (1.5)	
German National Trade Unions	4,998 (3.4)	–	–	–	40,163 (3.2)	47,019 (4.3)	51,247 (5.0)	49,645 (6.2)
Others (Neutral 'Yellow' etc.)	36,206 (24.3)	–	–	–	–	45,000 (4.3)	45,000 (4.5)	42,000 (5.2)
Totals	148,015	–	–	–	1,268,677	1,046,734	1,018,502	807,252
Proportion of Total Union Members to Total of Employed Persons (Approx.)	2%	–	–	21%	57%	40%	38%	32%

[1]Figures up to and including 1918 are for Cisleithanian Austria, thereafter for First Republic. Figures are omitted for smaller centres 1910–1918 since they are either unreliable or not available. Numbers in brackets are percentages of each centre of total for year in question (incomplete 1910–1918).

Sources: Klenner, F.: *Die Österreichischen Gewerkschaften*, Vols 1 and 2, Vienna 1951, 1953 and Gulick, C.: *Austria from Habsburg to Hitler* (German Edition), Vol. 1, Vienna 1948.

Appendix F2 Membership trends: Trade Union Central Council/Federation of Free Trade Unions 1872–1932*

Year	Totals of affiliated membership	Year	Totals of affiliated membership
1872	31 265	1918	412 910
1892	46 606	1919	772 146
1896	98 669	1920	900 820
1899	119 334	1921	1 079 777
1900	98 898	1922	1 049 949
1901	119 050	1923	896 763
1902	135 178	1924	828 088
1903	154 665	1925	807 515
1904	189 121	1926	756 392
1905	323 099	1927	772 762
1906	488 270	1928	766 168
1907	501 094	1929	737 277
1908	482 279	1930	655 204
1909	415 256	1931	582 657
1910	400 565	1932	520 162
1911	421 905		
1912	428 363		
1913	415 195		

*Numbers are for Cisleithanian Austria till 1918, thereafter for First Republic; series incomplete 1873 to 1891 and 1914 to 1917.

Source: Klenner, F.: *Die Österreichischen Gewerkschaften*, vols 1 and 2, Vienna 1951, 1953.

Appendix F3 Membership trends: Austrian Trade Union Federation (ÖGB) 1945–86

Year	Membership at year end	Density† (percentage)	Percentage of women members
1945	298 417		
1946	924 274	53.9	24.7
1947	1 238 088	67.0	26.5
1948	1 278 686	68.2	26.7
1949	1 279 520	68.0	26.3
1950	1 290 581	66.5	25.9
1951	1 310 200	66.0	26.0
1952	1 318 327	68.0	25.5
1953	1 320 343	68.9	25.7
1954	1 347 639	68.3	26.2
1955	1 398 446	67.5	26.5
1956	1 427 301	66.8	26.8
1957	1 438 755	65.8	26.9
1958	1 458 310	66.2	27.6
1959	1 474 929	66.0	27.8
1960	1 501 047	65.8	28.1
1961	1 518 004	65.4	28.5
1962	1 518 096	64.9	28.5
1963	1 531 695	65.4	28.3
1964	1 539 586	65.1	28.2
1965	1 542 813	64.8	28.1
1966	1 542 979	64.7	27.9
1967	1 512 405	64.1	27.7
1968	1 514 016	64.7	27.8
1969	1 517 124	64.4	27.9
1970	1 520 259	63.6	27.5
1971	1 526 364	62.2	27.7
1972	1 542 042	61.4	27.8
1973	1 559 513	59.8	27.9
1974	1 580 257	59.8	27.9
1975	1 587 500	59.8	28.4
1976	1 604 668	59.7	29.0
1977	1 619 103	59.2	29.3
1978	1 628 803	59.1	29.5
1979	1 641 475	59.2	29.8
1980	1 660 895	59.1	30.0
1981	1 677 265	59.9	30.2
1982	1 672 509	60.5	30.3
1983	1 660 453	60.7	30.5
1984	1 672 820	60.6	30.8
1985	1 671 381	60.6	30.8
1986	1 671 217	60.1	30.8

†Proportion of total membership to employed persons

Sources: Arbeit und Wirtschaft 1946–1986; Wirtschaftsstatistisches Handbuch, Austrian Chambers of Labour 1946–1985.

Appendix F4 Unions affiliated to the Austrian Trade Union Federation (ÖGB) — total membership 1986

Designation by Number	Union	Members	Ranking by Size of Membership
1	Union of Private White Collar Employees	348 117	1
2	Public Services Union	226 328	3
3	Municipal Employees Union	169 128	5
4	Union of Arts, Media Employees and Professions	17 761	15
5	Construction and Woodworkers Union	184 361	4
6	Union of Chemical Workers	58 272	8
7	Union of Railway Workers	117 021	6
8	Union of Print and Drapery Workers	23 476	13
9	Union of Commerce, Transport and Traffic Workers	38 160	12
10	Union of Catering, Domestic and Personal Service Employees	51 793	9
11	Union of Agricultural Workers	19 148	14
12	Food and Beverages Workers Union	42 899	11
13	Union of Mine, Metal and Energy Workers	251 112	2
14	Textile, Garment and Leather Workers Union	46 860	10
15	Union of Postal and Telecommunications Workers	76 781	7
	Total Membership	1 671 217	

Source: ÖGB Tätigkeitsbericht, Vienna 1986; Arbeit und Wirtschaft 6/1987

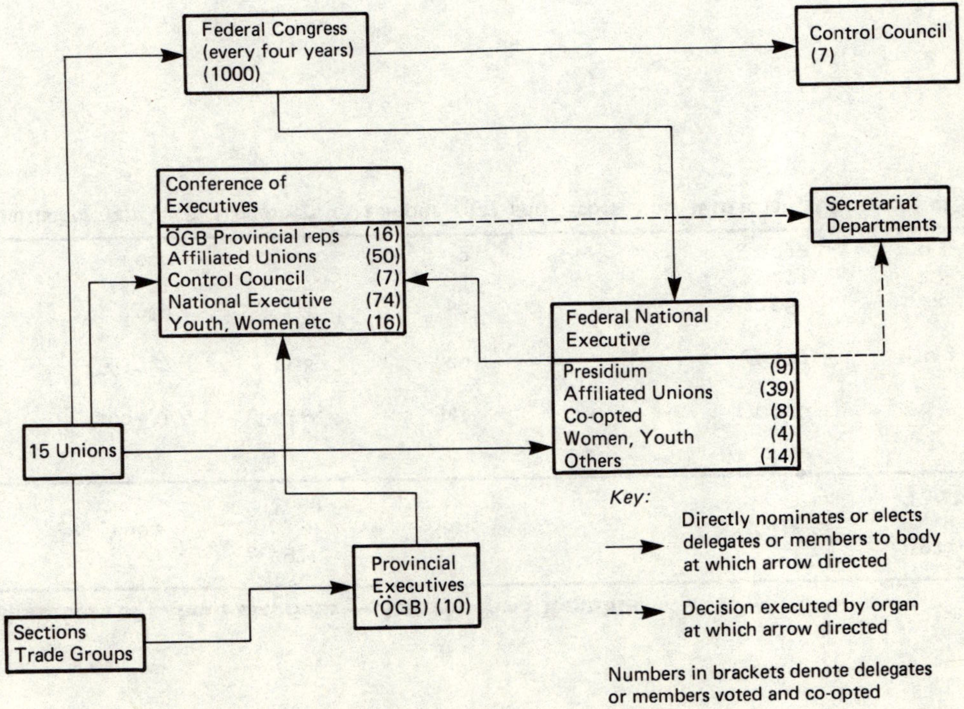

Appendix F5 The structure of the Austrian Trade Union Federation (ÖGB)

Appendix F6 Chambers of Labour elections — Austria: First Republic

	1921 Votes	1921 % of Total	1921 Seats	1926 Votes	1926 % of Total	1926 Seats
Socialist (SDAP)/ Free Trade Unions	466 831	83.9	341	430 920	78.8	322
Conservative (Christian-Social)	65 747	11.8	20	56 837	10.4	50
National (Greater-German, etc.)	7 969	1.4	56	42 960	7.8	42
Communist (KPÖ)	15 133	2.7	4	15,272	2.8	7
Others	1 096	0.2	0	1 049	0.2	0

Sources: Wirtschaftliches Jahrbuch, Chambers of Labour 1927 and Arbeit und Wirtschaft, Chambers of Labour, for years in question.

Appendix F7 Chambers of Labour elections† — Austria: Second Republic

	1949			1954			1959			1964			1969			1974			1979			1984		
	Votes	% of Seats	Total	Votes	% of Seats	Total	Votes	% of Seats	Total	Votes	% of Seats	Total	Votes	% of Seats	Total	Votes	% of Seats	Total	Votes	% of Seats	Total	Votes	% of Seats	Total
Socialist (FSG = SPÖ)	583,544	64.4	504	652,269	68.6	569	669,070	68.4	563	698,746	66.4	555	704,892	68.0	560	781,575	63.4	531	773,669	64.3	534	746,127	58.7	502
Conservative (ÖAAB = ÖVP)	128,873	14.2	120	151,929	16.0	139	182,214	18.6	161	224,520	21.4	180	243,716	23.5	196	359,269	29.1	239	372,447	31.0	252	464,751	36.5	317
Liberal (Wd. U; FPÖ)	105,565	11.7	117	23,810	2.5	19	36,011	3.7	31	37,994	3.6	27	51,479	5.0	39	57,291	4.6	29	38,852	3.2	20	31,412	2.5	13
Trade Union/‡ Left Bloc (GLB = KPÖ)	87,754	9.7	56	94,045	9.9	58	64,264	6.6	40	69,963	6.7	37	26,360	2.6	21	29,281	2.4	10	13,898	1.2	4	17,281	1.4	5
Trade Union Unity (GE)																3,382	0.3	1	3,716	0.3	0	10,555	1.0	3
Green Party (VGÖ/ALÖ)	–	–	–	–	–	–	–	–	–	–	–	–	–	–	–	869	0.1	–	294	–	–	913	0.1	0
Carinthian Solidarity (KS = Slovenien)	–	–	–	–	–	–	–	–	–	–	–	–	–	–	–							808	0.1	0
Others. Independents, etc.	–	–	–	–	–	–	–	–	–	20,223	1.9	11	9,637	0.9	4	–	–	–	–	–	–	–	–	–

† Figures relate to Chamber seats (Mandate) for Austria as a whole according to political party (grouping); the distribution is different according to Province (*Land*) : the total number of Chamber seats varies over time; in 1921 there were 421 seats for Chamber Councillors (*Kammerräte*) in Austria; in 1949 there were 797 and by 1984 there were 840.

‡ To 1974 there was no distinction among the Communist Party groupings (Trade Union Bloc, Trade Union Unity). After 1974 these groups contested the elections separately, (Trade Union Unity advocates Euro-Communist views).

Sources: Arbeit und Wirtschaft, Chambers of Labour, for years in question, and various other sources.

Appendix F8
The structure of the Austrian Chambers of Labour (AK)

The Chambers of Labour were incorporated and have been in existence as public bodies since 1920. They – in common with the Austrian Conference of Chambers of Labour ('Arbeiterkammertag') – are called upon to represent, further and promote the social, economic and cultural interests and aspirations of wage earners.

AK VIENNA*
(head office – Vienna)
has a membership of approximately 600,000 wage earners (employees) employed within the province ('Bundesland' or federal province) of Vienna: a contribution is levied from these members, and they elect 180 Chamber Councillors every five years, to represent them in the General Assembly.

General Assembly
General Assembly meets twice yearly; it designates the principal aims and main points of the Chamber's activities and decides on the use of funds. General Assembly elects the President and fourteen Chamber Councillors from among its members.

President
The Chamber President conducts the Chamber of Labour's business and acts as the Chamber's legal representative.

Executive
The Executive is responsible for carrying out the decisions of General Assembly. It discusses problems affecting the Chamber and may appoint committees to assist in its work.

Committees
The Chamber Councillors in common with the expert staff of the Chamber Administration are active in 17 committees, such as, eg. Committee for Juvenile Care and Apprenticeship Matters, Education and Culture Committee, Committee of Social Policy, Committee of Industrial Policy and General Economic Affairs.
The Committees prepare the ground for the work of the Executive and draw up statements and opinions which are submitted to the government and presented to the public by the Chamber.

Chamber Administration
A Chamber Chief Executive heads the Administration of the Vienna Chamber of Labour; under his direction a numerous staff of experienced specialists assisted by qualified office workers, deals with matters of economic, social and educational policy. Activities are structured into sections and secretariates according to various specialised fields; some of the most important of these sections are:
Social Policy – national insurance, industrial law, apprenticeship and juvenile care, working women's concerns;
Economics – economic policy, economic science, statistics;
Schools – Education – Cultural Affairs Documentation Social Sciences Library etc.

Institutions
Technical and Trades Night School
Franz Domes Apprentices' Home
Karl Weigl Training College (Social Academy)
Anna Boschek Apprentices' Home for Girls
Training and Vacation Homes
Annental and Bad Vöslau
Institute for Societal Affairs (in co-operation with the Austrian Trade Unions' Congress (ÖGB)) etc.

AK Burgenland
(head office Eisenstadt)
membership approx. 40,000 employees, 40 Chamber Councillors, 9 Executive Members.

AK Carinthia
(head office Klagenfurt)
membership approx. 130,000 employees, 70 Chamber Councillors, 11 Executive Members.

AK Lower Austria
(head office Vienna)
membership approx. 310,000 employees, 110 Chamber Councillors, 15 Executive Members.

AK Upper Austria
(head office Linz)
membership approx. 330,000 employees, 110 Chamber Councillors, 15 Executive Members.

AK Salzburg
(head office Salzburg)
membership approx. 120,000 employees, 70 Chamber Councillors, 11 Executive Members.

AK Styria
(head office Graz)
membership approx. 290,000 employees, 10 Chamber Councillors, 15 Executive Members.

AK Tyrol
(head office Innsbruck)
membership approx. 170,000 employees, 50 Chamber Councillors, 11 Executive Members.

AK Vorarlberg
(head office Feldkirch)
membership approx. 100,000 employees, 50 Chamber Councillors, 9 Executive Members.

AK Vienna
(head office Vienna)
membership approx. 600,000 employees, 180 Chamber Councillors, 15 Executive Members.

*The structure here shows Vienna as an example of a Chamber.

This is the overall or 'umbrella' organisation of all nine Chambers of Labour. It attends to all affairs falling within the orbit of Chambers of Labour, as far as they touch upon the whole territory of the Federal Republic or upon several provinces ("Bundesländer").

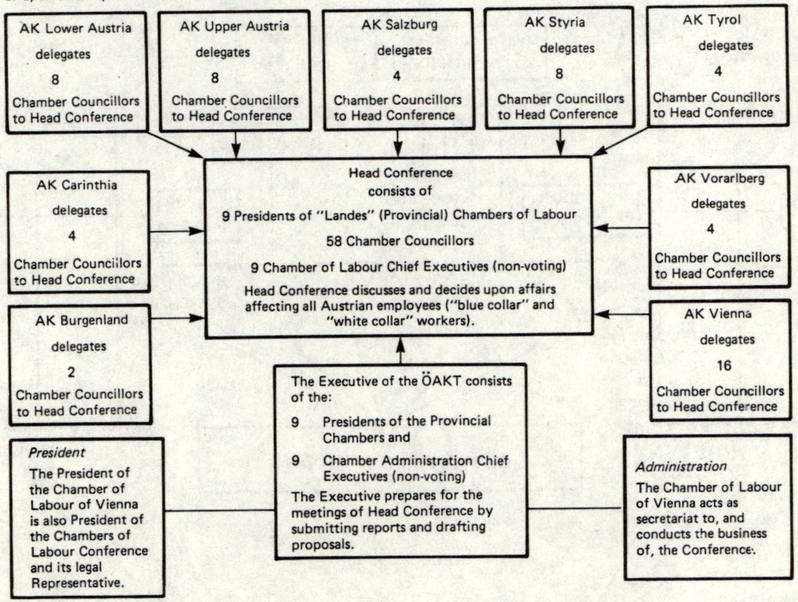

Appendix F9 The Austrian Chambers of Labour Conference

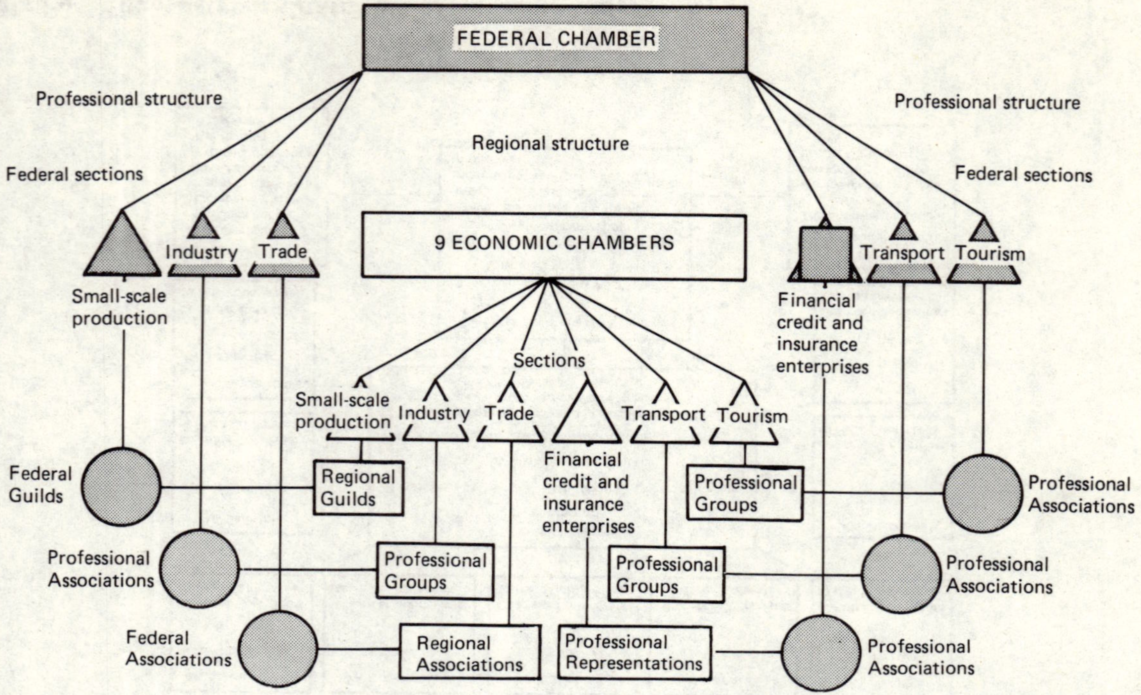

Appendix F10 The structure of the Economic Chambers

Appendix F11 Working time lost through strikes, Austria 1951–86

Year	Working days lost (000s)	Working hours lost	Employees involved	Average length of time per worker involved Hours	Minutes	Strike — minutes per employed person
1951	84	677 452	31 555	21	28	20.5
1952	75	602 758	31 942	18	52	19
1953	38	304 817	12 695	24	–	10
1954	51	410 508	21 140	19	25	12.5
1955	58	464 167	26 011	17	51	13.5
1956	153	1 227 292	43 249	28	23	36.5
1957	46	364 841	19 555	18	39	10
1958	49	349 811	28 745	12	10	9.5
1959	51	404 290	47 007	8	36	11
1960	69	550 582	30 654	17	58	14.5
1961	114	911 025	38 338	23	46	23.5
1962	648	5 181 762	207 459	24	59	133
1963	34	272 134	16 501	16	29	7
1964	35	283 588	40 843	6	56	7.5
1965	151	3 387 787	146 009	23	12	85.5
1966	71	570 846	120 922	4	43	14.5
1967	16	131 285	7 469	17	30	3.5
1968	7	53 365*	3 129	17	3	1.5
1969	19	148 139	17 449	8	29	4
1970	27	212 928	7 547	28	13	5
1971	4	29 614	2 431	12	11	0.5
1972	15	120 832	7 096	17	2	3
1973	160	794 119	78 251	10	9	33.5
1974	7	57 948	7 295	7	56	1.5
1975	6	44 098	3 783	11	39	1
1976	0.6	4 711	2 352	2	–	0
1977	0	86	43	2	–	0
1978	10	81 778	699	117	–	2
1979	0.8	6 111	786	7	46	0
1980	17	135 684	24 181	5	37	3
1981	4	32 188	17 115	1	52	0.5
1982	0.3	2 755	91	30	16	0
1983	0.5	4 115	208	19	47	0
1984	0.5	4 349	268	16	14	0
1985	23	182 019	35 531	5	7	4
1986	3	26 023	3 222	8	5	0.5

*Includes 4,590 hours in lock-outs.

Sources: I.L.O. Yearbook of Labour Statistics 1971–86; Jahrbuch des Österreichischen Arbeiterkammertages 1953–86.

Appendix F12 Strike-minutes per employed person — selected countries 1951–85

Year	Austria	Canada	Federal Republic of Germany	France	Great Britain	Ireland	Italy	Japan	USA
1966	14.5	407.5	0.5	82	48.5	536	579.5	44	190.5
1967	3.5	300.5	9	135	57.5	123.5	336	28.5	307
1968	1.5	376	0.5	–	97.5	269.5	358.5	43.5	346.5
1969	4	553.5	5.5	68	142.5	578	14445.5	54.5	293
1970	5	460	2	54	230	612	679	57.5	451
1971	0.5	195.5	98.5	130.5	294	180	555.5	85	123.5
1972	3	509	1.5	110	519	137.5	731.5	71.5	176.5
1973	33.5	357	12.5	112	152	135.5	861.5	61.5	174.5
1974	1.5	538	23	95	311	356	689.5	128.5	294.5
1975	1	625	1.5	110	127	193	949	105.5	195
1976	0	652	12.5	141	70	516.5	876.5	42	229
1977	0	183	0.5	102	215	291	562	19.5	208.5
1978	2	397	97.5	60.5	199	403	343	17	205
1979	0	404	11	100.5	620	843	910	11.5	186.5
1980	3	390	3	45	250	228	545	12	178
1981	0.5	429	1	40.5	94	242	349	6.5	130.5
1982	0	290	0.5	63	119	243	615.5	6	48
1983	0	221.5	1	40	86	183	468	6	92
1984	0	189	125	37	615.5	221	293	4	45
1985	4	151	1	20	143	243	127.5	3	37

Sources: I.L.O. Yearbook of Labour Statistics 1971–86; O.E.C.D.: Labour Force Statistics 1967–85.

Appendix G1 Leisure activities of Viennese employees 1970–80 (monthly averages)

	Total		Variation		Manual Workers		Salaried Employees	
	1970	1980	1970	1980	1970	1980	1970	1980
Reading daily newspaper	25.54	24.99	-0.55		24.88	24.65	26.33	25.26
Listening to radio	22.34	24.21	+1.87		22.04	23.24	22.73	24.59
Watching television	19.16	20.74	+1.58		20.74	21.79	18.07	20.24
Reading books	6.98	8.29	+1.31		5.26	5.32	8.60	9.91
Hobbies	5.20	7.06	+1.86		4.78	6.91	5.89	6.99
Reading magazines	5.88	6.32	+0.44		5.49	4.93	6.57	6.87
Relaxing with family	3.60	4.23	+0.63		3.75	4.88	3.72	3.99
Visiting swimming baths	2.74	2.62	-0.12		2.55	2.58	2.94	2.70
Going out in the evening	2.00	2.57	+0.57		1.75	2.28	2.24	2.74
Active sport	1.38	2.14	+0.76		0.75	1.90	1.55	2.10
Visiting public house	1.59	2.10	+0.51		1.76	2.12	1.56	2.10
Walks, excursions	2.11	2.03	-0.08		1.93	2.00	2.22	2.10
Further education	0.98	1.09	+0.09		0.57	0.45	1.38	1.29
Visiting cinema	0.79	0.50	-0.29		0.78	0.45	0.76	0.50
Attending sporting events	0.51	0.47	-0.04		0.52	0.60	0.42	0.35
Theatre, opera, operetta	0.42	0.36	-0.06		0.23	0.11	0.61	0.55
Exhibitions, museums trade fairs	0.23	0.29	+0.06		0.17	0.17	0.30	0.32
Attending concerts	0.10	0.12	+0.02		0.04	0.03	0.14	0.19

The above figures are to be interpreted on the basis that each month provides 30 potential contacts (i.e. 1 per day); in the case of "reading daily newspapers", for example, the monthly average of actual contacts was 25.54 in 1970 and 24.99 in 1980.

Source: IFES: Freizeit der Wiener Arbeitnehmer, Vienna 1981.

Glossary

Anschluss. This German term is in common usage in English denoting the annexation or absorption of Austria by Nazi Germany on 12/13 March 1938. The German term is less drastic than the English word annexation, implying the conjoining of willing, independent partners and thus belongs to the currency of German nationalism. The issue of Austrian willingness to be absorbed 'back into the Reich' is still a contentious one. Hitler's pre-emptive action to prevent the plebiscite on Austria's independence (planned for 13 March 1938) robbed historians of the chance to assess the strength of German nationalism in Austria at the time, but strengthened the (not unchallenged) view of Austria as victim of fascism.

Cisleithania (German: Cisleithanien) This term denotes the largely German-speaking territories of the Habsburg empire 'this side of' (cis-) the Leitha river (but also included Galizia and Bukovina) which today marks the north-west boundary between Burgenland, the most easterly *Land* of the Second Republic, and the rest of Austria. It thus contrasted with the other non-German-speaking territories of *Transleithania*, dominated by Hungary. Cisleithania and Transleithania therefore were the designations given to Austria and Hungary respectively after the 'Compromise' of 1867 which established the 'Dual Monarchy' (Austria-Hungary) and which survived till 1918.

Grand Coalition (German: *Grosse Koalition*). The coalition between the major parties in Austrian post-war politics, the Austrian People's Party (*Österreichische Volkspartei*) and the Socialist Party of Austria (*Sozialistische Partei Österreichs*), which ruled in Austria continuously from December 1945 to April 1966. It was reformed in 1987 under the SPÖ Chancellor Vranitzky after a 16 year dominance of the SPÖ under Kreisky and Sinowatz, the latter heading a Small Coalition (*Kleine Koalition*) with the Liberals (FPÖ) between 1983 and 1986.

Kleindeutsch/Kleindeutschland. The use of the term *Kleindeutschland* in the context of German nationalism is strongly ambivalent. The original proposals for a 'small German' solution to the national question in the constitutional debates of the 1848 revolution specifically excluded all of Austria from a future German empire. Georg Ritter von Schönerer, the Austrian pan-Germanist who was largely responsible for the Linz Programme of 1882, defined the 'small German' solution as the union of German-speaking Austria with the German Reich after the dissolution of the Habsburg Empire, and it is in this sense that the term is used in this book. (In 1848 this was promoted as the *grossdeutsche Lösung* — the solution involving a 'greater Germany'!)

Lager. This term, which is left untranslated in parts of the text, is not to be confused with customary English usage which derives from the defensive corral into which the original Boer settlers in South Africa withdrew in order to resist native African opposition and which now denotes a position of irrational resistance to impending social changes. The Austrian *Lager* concept is less pejorative in its associations, denoting purely the dominance in Austrian political culture of political groupings or 'camps' which are evident in other social spheres outside the simple parliamentary political arena. Thus political allegiance within the so-called Social Partnership, the civil service, education and state quangos is an acknowledged feature of public life in Austria. The *Lager* is thus a more clearly defined ideological home which informs social life both positively, in terms of open political commitment, and negatively in terms of the value placed on a party badge for advancing individual careers.

Land. The use of the term *Land* (plural: *Länder*) in much of the text conforms to common usage in texts on the German-speaking world. It denotes the regional subdivision in Austria's federal political structure immediately below the central level of the *Bund*. Each *Land* (region/province) has its own parliament, ministries, civil service and extensive powers of administrative competence. The English word 'province' is the apposite translation for this term in the Austrian context and is predominately employed in this book.
Nationalization/Socialization (German: *Verstaatlichung/Sozialisierung*). Both these terms are used in the text to denote the transfer of private (productive) property into public ownership.

Further reading

Chapter 1

Bauer, O. (1923), *Die österreichische Revolution*, Vienna. Benedikt, H. (1977), *Geschichte der Republik Österreich*, Vienna.

Goldinger, W. (1982), *Geschichte der Republik Österreich*, Vienna.

Paul Lazarsfeld Gesellschaft (1980), *Das österreichische Nationalbewusstsein*, Vienna.

Schausberger, N. (1980), *Österreich: Der Weg der Republik 1918–1980*, Vienna.

Stadler, K. (1968), *Hypothek auf die Zukunft. Die Entstehung der österreichischen Republik*, Vienna.

Talos, E. and Neugebauer, W. (eds) (1984), *Austrofaschismus: Beiträge über Politik, Ökonomie und Kultur 1934–1938*, Vienna.

Weinzierl, E. and Skalnik, K. (eds) (1975), *Das neue Österreich. Geschichte der neuen Republik*, Vienna.

Chapter 2

Bodzenta, E. (1980), *Die österreichische Gesellschaft. Entwicklung–Struktur–Probleme*, Vienna.

Botz, G. (1976) *Die Eingliederung Österreichs in das Deutsche Reich*, Vienna.

Bruckmann, G. (ed.) (1984), *Die Zukunft Österreichs. Das Leben im Jahr 2019*, Vienna.

Foucault, M. (1973), *Archäologie des Wissens*, Frankfurt/Main.

Gerschenkron, A. (1968), *Continuity in History and Other Essays*, Cambridge, Mass.

Heer, F. (1981), *Der Kampf um die österreichische Identität*, Vienna.

Hobsbawm, E. and Ranger, T. (1983), *The Invention of Tradition*, Cambridge.

Katzenstein, P. J. (1976), *Disjoined Partners. Austria and Germany Since 1815*, Berkeley.

Kreissler, F. (1984), *Der Österreicher und seine Nation. Ein Lernprozess mit Hindernissen*, Vienna.

Langer, E. (1966), *Die Verstaatlichung in Österreich*, Vienna.

Luža, R. (1977), *Österreich und die grossdeutsche Idee in der NS–Zeit*, Vienna.

Rauchensteiner, M. (1984), *Krieg in Österreich* (2nd ed.), Graz.

Rosenmayr, L. (ed.) (1980), *Politische Beteiligung und Wertwandel in Österreich*, Vienna.

Rothschild, K. W. (1961), 'Wurzeln und Triebkräfte der Entwicklung der österreichischen Wirtschaftsstruktur', in W. Weber (ed.), *Österreichs Wirtschaftsstruktur gestern-heute-morgen, Vol. 1*, Berlin.

Schmitter, P. C. and Lehmbruch, G. (eds) (1979), *Trends Toward Corporatist Intermediation*, London.

Schumpeter, J. A. (1961), *Konjunkturzyklen. Eine theoretische, historische und statistische Analyse des kapitalistischen Prozesses*, Vol. 1, Göttingen.

Steiner, K. (ed.) (1981), *Tradition and Innovation in Contemporary Austria*, Paolo Alto.

Stiefel, D. (1981), *Entnazifizierung in Österreich*, Vienna.

Weidenholzer, J. and Botz, G. (eds) (1984), *Mündliche Geschichte und Arbeiterbewegung*, Vienna.

Weinzierl, E. and Skalnik, K. (eds) (1972), *Österreich: Die Zweite Republik, Vol. 1*, Graz.

Chapter 3

Ausch, K. (1965), *Licht und Irrlicht des österreichischen Wirtschaftswunders*, Vienna.

Beirat für Wirtschafts- und Sozialfragen (1968), *Die Landwirtschaft in der Industriegesellschaft*, Vienna.

Butschek, F. (1978), *Die österreichische Wirtschaft 1938–1945*, Vienna.

Butschek, F. (1985), *Die österreichische Wirtschaft im 20. Jahrhundert*, Vienna.

Haberler, G. (1980), *Austria's Economic Development: A Mirror Picture of the World Economy*, Washington D.C.

Hertz, F. (1917), *Die Produktionsgrundlagen der österreichischen Industrie*, Vienna.

Hertz, F. (1947), *The Economic Problem of the Danubian States*, London.

Kausel, A. *et al.* (1965), *Österreichs Volkseinkommen 1913–1963*, Vienna.

Otruba, G. (1968), *Die österreichische Wirtschaft im 20. Jahrhundert*, Vienna.

Rothschild, K. (1947), *Austria's Economic Development Between the Wars*, London.

Seidel, H. (1978), *Struktur und Entwicklung der österreichischen Industrie*, Vienna.

Weber, W., Koren, S. and Socher, K. (1964), *Die Verstaatlichung in Österreich*, Berlin.

Chapter 4

Bluhm, W. T. (1973), *Building an Austrian Nation. The Political Integration of the Western State*, New Haven.

Fischer, H. (ed.) (1982), *Das politische System Österreichs*, Vienna (third edition).

Gerlich, P. and Ucakar, K. (1981), *Staatsbürger und Volksvertretung. Das Alltagsverständnis von Parlament und Demokratie in Österreich*, Salzburg.
Lehmbruch, G. (1967), *Proporzdemokratie. Politisches System und politische Kultur in der Schweiz und in Österreich*, Tübingen.
Nick, R. and Pelinka, A. (1983), *Bürgerkrieg-Sozialpartnerschaft. Das politische System Österreichs 1. und 2. Republik. Ein Vergleich*, Vienna.
Nick, R. and Pelinka, A. (1984), *Parlamentarismus in Österreich*, Vienna.
Plasser, F. and Ulram, P. A. (1982), *Unbehagen im Parteienstaat. Jugend und Politik in Österreich*, Vienna.
Steininger, R. (1975), *Polarisierung und Integration. Eine vergleichende Untersuchung der strukturellen Versäulung der Gesellschaft in den Niederlanden und in Österreich*, Meisenheim.
Sully, M. A. (1981), *Political Parties and Elections in Austria*, London.
Widder, H. (1979), *Parlamentarische Strukturen im politischen System. Zu Grundlagen und Grundfragen des österreichischen Regierungsystems*, Berlin.

Chapter 5

Berchtold, K. (1967), *Österreichische Parteiprogramme 1868–1966*, Vienna.
Göhring, W. (1985), *Zur Entwicklung der Sozialistischen Partei Österreichs 1945–1985*, Vienna.
Kaufmann, F. (1978), *Sozialdemokratie in Österreich*, Vienna.
Nick, R. and Pelinka, A. (1983), *Bürgerkrieg-Sozialpartnerschaft. Das politische System Österreichs 1. und 2. Republik. Ein Vergleich*, Vienna.
Nowotny, E. and Tieber H. (eds.) (1985), *Perspektiven 90*, Vienna.
Pollak, W. (1979), *Sozialismus in Österreich*, Vienna.
Rabinbach, A. (1983), *The Crisis of Austrian Socialism*, Chicago.
Sully, M. A. (1982), *Continuity and Change in Austrian Socialism*, New York.

Chapter 6

Berchtold, K. (1967), *Österreichische Parteiprogramme 1868–1966*, Vienna.
Boyer, J. W. (1981), *Political Radicalism in late Imperial Vienna–Origins of the Christian Social Movement 1848–1897*, Chicago.
Diamant, A. (1960), *Die österreichischen Katholiken und die Erste Republik-Demokratie, Kapitalismus und soziale Ordnung 1918–1934*, Vienna.

Edmundson, E. (1978), *The Heimwehr and Austrian Politics 1918–1936*, Athens.

Reichhold, L. (1975), *Geschichte der ÖVP*, Vienna.

Weinzierl, E. and Skalnik, K. (eds.) (1983), *Österreich 1918–1938: Geschichte der Ersten Republik, Vol. I*, Vienna.

Chapter 7

Berchtold, K. (1967), *Österreichische Parteiprogramme 1868–1966*, Vienna.

Piringer, K. (1982), *Die Geschichte der Freiheitlichen*, Vienna.

Reimann, V. (1980), *Die Dritte Kraft in Österreich*, Vienna.

Reiter, E. (1982), *Programm und Programmentwicklung der FPÖ*, Vienna.

Chapter 8

Berchtold, K. (1967), *Österreichische Parteiprogramme 1868–1966*, Vienna.

Gartner, H. (1979), *Zwischen Moskau und Österreich–Analyse einer sowjetisch unabhängigen Kommunistische Partei*, Vienna.

Gulick, C. A. (1948), *Österreich von Habsburg zu Hitler, Vol. 1*, Vienna.

Kulemann, P. (1979), *Am Beispiel des Austromarxismus*, Hamburg.

Leser, N. (1968), *Zwischen Reformismus und Bolschewismus*, Vienna.

Pelinka, A. (1979), *KPÖ–Kleinpartei in der Isolierung*, Vienna.

Spira, L. (1979), *Ein gescheiterter Versuch des Eurokommunismus*, Vienna.

Chapter 9

Beckmann, M. (1979), *Theorie der sozialen Bewertung*, Munich.

Busek, E. (1969), *Demokratiekritik, Demokratiereform*, Vienna.

Giller, J. (1984), *Soziale Bewegung und Wertwandel in Österreich*, Vienna.

Schulmeister, O. (ed.) (1980), *Spectrum Austriae*, Vienna.

Stock, W. (ed.), (1986), *Ziviler Ungehorsam in Österreich*, Vienna.

Chapter 10

Abele, H., Nowotny, E., Schleicher, S. and Winckler, G. (eds) (1984), *Handbuch der österreichischen Wirtschaftspolitik*, Vienna.

Arndt, S. W. (ed.) (1982), *The Political Economy of Austria*, Washington D. C.

Butschek, F. (1985), *Die österreichische Wirtschaft im 20. Jahrhundert*, Vienna.

Kitzmantel, E. (1979), *Steuern-Wer sie zahlt, wer sie trägt*, Vienna.

Kramer, H. and Butschek F. (eds), (1985), *Vom Nachzügler zum Vorbild–Österreichische Wirtschaft 1945–1985*, Vienna.
Nowotny, E. (1985), 'Beschäftigungsorientierte Wirtschaftspolitik und Strukturwandel–der Weg Österreichs', in J. Langkau and C. Köhler (eds), *Wirtschaftspolitik und wirtschaftliche Entwicklung*, Bonn.
Suppanz, H. and Wagner, M. (eds) (1981), *Einkommensverteilung in Österreich*, Vienna.

Chapter 11

Beyer, E. (1974), *125 Jahre Wiener Handelskammer*, Vienna.
Brusatti, A. (1970) 'Österreichs Wirtschaft in der zweiten Republik', in K. Gutkas, A. Brusatti, and E. Weinzierl (eds), *Österreich 1945–1970*, Vienna.
Geissler, F. (1949), 'Die Entstehung und der Entwicklungsgang der Handelskammern', in Mayer, H. (ed.), *Hundert Jahre österreichischer Wirtschaftsentwicklung 1848–1948*, Vienna.
Geissler, F. (1977), *Österreichs Handelskammerorganisation in der Zwischenkriegszeit*, Vienna.
Mitic, M. and Klose, A. (1966), 'Die Handelskammerorganisation in Österreich', in T. Pütz (ed.), *Verbände und Wirtschaftpolitik in Österreich*, Berlin.
Wenger, K. and Seidel, H. (1966), 'Freie Verbände in der gewerblichen Wirtschaft', in T. Pütz (ed.), *Verbände und Wirtschaftspolitik in Österreich*, Berlin.

Chapter 12

Deutsch, J. (1929, 1932), *Geschichte der österreichischen Arbeiterbewegung* (2 vols), Vienna.
Gulick, C. A. (1948), *Österreich von Habsburg zu Hitler, Vol. 1*, Vienna.
Klenner, F. (1959), *The Austrian Trade Union Movement*, Brussels.
Klenner, F. (1951, 1953, 1979), *Die österreichischen Gewerkschaften* (3 vols), Vienna.
Traxler, F. (1982), *Evolution gewerkschaftlicher Interessenvertretung*, Vienna.
Weidenholzer, J. (1985), *Der sorgende Staat*, Vienna.

Chapter 13

Wenger, K. and Seidel, H. (1966), 'Freie Verbände in der gewerblichen Wirtschaft', in T. Pütz (ed.), *Verbände und Wirtschaftspolitik in Österreich*, Berlin.

Chapter 14

Klenner, F. (1951, 1953, 1979), *Die österreichischen Gewerkschaften* (3 vols), Vienna.

März, E. and Weissel, E. (1966), 'Die Kammer für Arbeiter und Angestellte', in T. Pütz (ed.), *Verbände und Wirtschaftspolitik in Österreich*, Berlin.

Weidenholzer, J. (1980), 'Arbeiterkammern und Sozialpolitik', in J. Czerny, O. Martinek and J. Weidenholzer (eds), *Arbeitswelt und Sozialstaat*, Vienna.

Chapter 15

Greil, L. (1959), *50 Jahre Präsidentenkonferenz landwirtschaftlicher Hauptkörperschaften in Österreich*, Vienna.

Chapter 16

Albrecht, G. (1965), *Die soziale Funktion des Genossenschaftswesens* Berlin.

Rauter, A. E. (ed.) (1976), *Verbraucherpolitik und Wirtschaftsentwicklung*, Vienna.

Seibert, F. (1978), *Die Konsumgenossenschaften in Österreich. Geschichte und Funktion*, Vienna.

Chapter 17

Ruppe, H. G. (1970), *Das Genossenschaftswesen in Österreich*, Franfurt/Main.

Weber, W. et al. (1972), *Wirtschaft in Politik und Recht am österreichischen Beispiel 1945–1970*, Vienna.

Chapter 18

Gerlich, P., Grande, E. and Müller, W. C. (eds) (1985), *Sozialpartnerschaft in der Krise*, Vienna.

Klose, A. (1970), *Ein Weg zur Sozialpartnerschaft: Das österreichische Modell*, Vienna.

Marin, B. (1979), *Wachstumskrisen in Österreich?* (2 vols), Vienna.

Marin, B. (1982), *Die Parititätische Kommission — Andgewandter Technokorporatismus in Österreich*, Vienna.

Rainer, N. and Pelinka, A. (1983), *Bürgerkrieg — Sozialpartnerschaft*, Vienna.

Weidenholzer, J. (1985), *Der Sorgende Staat*, Vienna.

Chapter 19

Bundesministerium für Soziale Verwaltung (1982), *Soziale Struktur Österreichs*, Vienna.

Bundesministerium für Soziale Verwaltung (1979), *Kampf gegen die Armut in Österreich*, Vienna.

Lederer, M. (1932), *Grundriss des österreichischen Sozialrechts*, Vienna.

Legat, E. and Grabner, S. (1963), *Sozialversicherungsrecht*, Graz.

Talos, E. (1981), *Staatliche Sozialpolitik in Österreich:* Rekonstruktion und Analyse, Vienna.

Tomandl, T. (ed.) (1978), *System des österreichischen Sozialversicherungsrechts*, Vienna.

Chapter 20

Botz, K. (ed.) (1975), *Ist eine gerechte Einkommensverteilung möglich?* Munich.

Frisch, H. (ed.) (1967), *Beiträge zur Theorie der Einkommensverteilung* Berlin.

Kalecki, M. (1954), *Theory of Economic Dynamics*, London.

Lagler, E. and Messner, J. (eds) (1952), *Wirtschaftliche Entwicklung und soziale Ordnung*, Vienna.

Preiser, E. (1961), *Wachstum und Einkommensverteilung*, Heidelberg.

Schuster, E. (1926), *Das Einkommen. Eine kritische Untersuchung*, Tübingen.

Chapter 21

Achs, O. (1974), *Drillschule–Lernschule–Arbeitsschule*, Vienna.

Filla, W., Leichtenmüller, E. and Pfniss, A. (1985), *Bildung für Alle*, Vienna.

Fischer, M. and Strasser, H. (1973), *Selbstbestimmung und Fremdbestimmung der österreichischen Universität*, Vienna.

Fischl, H. (undated), *Schulreform, Demokratie und Österreich 1918–1950*, Vienna.

Hörburger, F. (1967), *Geschichte der Erziehung und des Unterrichtes*, Vienna.

Neugebauer, M. (1972), 'Schulwesen', in E. Weinzierl, and K. Skalnik, (eds), *Die Zweite Republik*, Graz.

Universität Wien (1965), *Aufgaben der Universität Wien in Gegenwart und Zukunft*, Vienna.

Weinhäupl, W. (1981), *Pädagogik vom Kinde aus*, Vienna.

Chapter 22

Bluhm, W. T. (1973), *Building an Austrian Nation. The Political Integration of a Western State*, New Haven.

Kreisky, B. (1986), *Zwischen den Zeiten. Errinerungen aus fünf Jahrzehnten*, Vienna.

Leser, N. (1982), *Grenzgänger. Österreichische Geistergeschichte in Totenbeschwörungen*, Vienna.

Weiss, W. (1975), 'Literatur', in E. Weinzierl and K. Skalnik (eds), *Das neue Österreich. Geschichte der neuen Republik*, Vienna.

Chapter 23

Fabris, H. H. (1982), 'Das österreichische Mediensystem', in H. Fischer (ed.) *Das politische System Österreichs* (3rd ed.), Vienna.

Fabris, H. H. *et al.* (1984), *Auswirkungen der Einführung neuer Medien in Österreich*, Vienna.

Fritz, W. (1981, 1984), *Kino in Österreich* (2 vols), Vienna.

Institut für Publizistik und Kommunikationswissenschaft der Universität Salzburg (ed.) (1983), *Massenmedien in Österreich*, Vienna.

Ivan, F., Lang, H. and Pürer, H. (eds) (1983), *200 Jahre Tagezeitung in Österreich*, Vienna.

Pürer, H. (ed.) (1984), *Praktischer Journalismus in Zeitung, Radio und Fernsehen*, Salzburg.

Chapter 24

Fischer, H. (ed.) (1982), *Das politische System Österreichs* (3rd ed.), Vienna.

Katz, E. and Lazersfeld, P. T. (1962), *Persönlicher Einfluss und Meinungsbildung*, Vienna.

Klosterman, F. *et al.* (1967), *Kirche in Österreich 1918–1965*, Vienna.

Vaskovics, L. A. (1970), *Familie und religiöse Sozialisation*, Vienna.

Zulehner, P. M. (1967), *Kirche und Austro marxismus*, Vienna.

Zulehner, P. M. (1969), *Religion ohne Kirche?: Das religiöse Verhalten von Industriearbeitern*, Vienna.

Zulehner, P. M. (1973), *Religion und Kirche in Österreich*, Vienna.

Chapter 25

Arbeitskreis für ökonomische und soziologische Studien (1973), *Gastarbeiter: Wirtschaftsfaktor und soziale Herausforderung*, Vienna.

Bauer, O. (1924), *Die Nationalitätenfrage und die Sozialdemokratie*, Vienna.

Drabek, A. et al. *Das österreichische Judentum*, Vienna.

Federal Chancellery, (1977), *The Legal Status of Ethnic Groups in Austria*, Vienna.

Renner, K. (1899), *Staat und Nation*, Vienna.

Renner, K. (1902), *Der Kampf der österreichischen Nationen um den Staat*, Vienna.

Chapter 26

Annerstedt, J. (1979), *A Study of World Research and Development Efforts*, Roskilde.

Briefs, U. (1984), *Informationstechnologien und Zukunft der Arbeit. Ein politisches Handbuch zu Mikroelektronik und Computertechnik*, Cologne.

Freeman, C. (1974), *The Economics of Industrial Innovation*, London.

Friedrichs, J. and Schaff, A. (eds) (1982), *Auf Gedeih und Verderb–Mikroelektronik und Gesellschaft*, Vienna.

Hirsch, S. (1967), *Location of Industry and International Competitiveness*, Oxford.

Ihlau, T. and Rall, L. (1970), *Die Messung des technischen Fortschritts*, Tübingen.

Kosta, H. G., Krammer, H. and Sláma J. (1971), *Der technologische Fortschritt in Österreich und in der Tschechoslowakei*, Vienna.

OECD (1977), *Interfutures*, Paris.

Sauer, W. (1984), *Der dressierte Arbeiter*, Munich.

Schaff, A. (1985), *Wohin führt der Weg?* Vienna.

Seidl, H. (1979), *Die österreichische Wirtschaft. Entwicklung, Erfolge und Probleme*, Vienna.

Selected bibliography

This bibliography consists of a selection of books covering the broad themes of the Reader and complements the specific references for further reading under each chapter.

Aldcroft, D. (1978), *The European Economy, 1914–1970*, London.

Bauer, O. (1920), *Bolschewismus oder Sozialdemokratie?* Vienna.

Bauer, O. (1936), *Zwischen zwei Weltkriegen?* Bratislava.

Bauer, R. (1970), *Österreich*, Berlin.

Breuss, F. (1975), *Komparative Vorteile im österreichischen Aussenhandel*, Vienna.

Brusatti, A. (1965), *Österreichische Wirtschaftspolitik vom Josephinismus zum Ständestaat*, Vienna.

Butschek, F. (1981), *Vollbeschäftigung in der Krise: Die österreichische Erfahrung 1974 bis 1979*, Vienna.

Charmatz, R. (1947), *Vom Kaiserreich zur Republik*, Vienna.

Deiser, R. and Winkler, N. (1982), *Das politische Handeln der Österreicher*, Vienna.

Gulick, C. A. (1948), *Österreich von Habsburg zu Hitler*, (3 vols), Vienna. (Also in English as: *Austria from Habsburg to Hitler* (2 vols), Berkeley 1948.)

Kann, R. A. (1974), *A History of the Habsburg Empire 1526–1918*, Berkeley.

Kleindel, W. (1978), *Österreich: Daten zur Geschichte und Kultur*, Vienna.

Knopf, R. (1981), *Österreichische Industrie 1873–1938*, (3 vols), Vienna.

Komlos, J. (ed.) (1983), *Economic Development in the Habsburg Monarchy*, New York.

Konrad, H. (ed.) (1978), *Sozialdemokratie und Anschluss*, Vienna.

Konrad, H. and Neugebauer, W. (1983), *Arbeiterbewegung, Faschismus, Nationalbewusstsein*, Vienna.

Leser, N. (1968), *Zwischen Reformismus und Bolschewismus*, Vienna.

Leser, N. (1986), *Genius Austriacus*, Vienna.

Leser, N. (ed.) (1986), *Die Wiener Schule der Nationalökonomie*, Vienna.

Litschauer, G. F. and Jambor, W. (1970), *Österreichische Geschichte*, Vienna.

Macartney, C. A. (1978), *The House of Austria*, Edinburgh.

Mantl, W. and Zsifkovits, V. (eds) (1980), *Katholischer Soziallexikon*, Vienna.

März, E. (1965), *Österreichs Wirtschaft zwischen Ost und West*, Vienna.

Portisch, H. and Riff. S. (1985), *Österreich II*, Vienna.

Powell, B. (1970), *Social Fragmentation and Political Hostility, An Austrian Case Study*, Stanford.

Renner, K. (1916), *Österreichs Erneuerung* (3 vols), Vienna.

Renner, K. (1953), *Österreich von der Ersten zur Zweiten Republik*, Vienna.

Rothschild, K. (1950), *The Austria Economy Since 1945*, London.

Rudolph, R. (1976), *Banking and Industry in Austria-Hungary*, Cambridge.

Seidel, H. and Kramer, H. (eds) (1973), *Wirtschaftsforschung in Österreich*, Vienna.

Siegler, H. (1969), *Austria. Problems and Achievements since 1945*, Vienna.

Stadler, K. R. (1971), *Austria*, London.

Steiner, H. (1968), *Gestorben für Österreich*, Vienna.

Steiner, K. (1972), *Politics in Austria, Boston.*

Steiner, K. (ed.) (1981), *Modern Austria*, Paole Alto.

Stourzh, G (1980), *Geschichte des Staatsvertrages 1945–1955*, Vienna.

Verdross, A. (1978), *The Permanent Neutrality of Austria*, Vienna.

Vodopivec, A. (1962), *Wer regiert in Österreich?* Vienna.

Vodopivec, A. (1976), *Die Dritte Republik*, Vienna.

Wailand, G. (1983), *Wer regiert Österreich?* Hamburg.

Weber, W. (ed.) (1961), *Österreichische Wirtschaftsstruktur gestern–heute–morgen*, Vienna.

Weissel, E. (1976), *Die Ohnmacht des Sieges*, Vienna.

Index